With Om & Love,

Raju Chidambaram

12.12.12

Law of Love & The Mathematics of Spirituality

Raju Sitaram Chidambaram, Ph.D.

CENTER FOR ADVANCEMENT OF SCIENTIFIC STUDIES IN SPIRITUALITY
Alexandria, VA

authorHOUSE®

AuthorHouse™
1663 Liberty Drive
Bloomington, IN 47403
www.authorhouse.com
Phone: 1-800-839-8640

Cover design by Vinod Ajmani, Alexandria, VA.

First published by AuthorHouse 11/16/2011

ISBN: 978-1-4567-9500-9 (sc)
ISBN: 978-1-4567-9499-6 (hc)
ISBN: 978-1-4567-9498-9 (e)

Library of Congress Control Number: 2011915102

Printed in the United States of America

This book is printed on acid-free paper.

Keywords: Spirituality- Mathematical Models- Vedanta Philosophy- Relativity & Quantum Physics- Concept of Time- Free Will- Uncertainty- Evolution- Intelligent Design - Meaning of Life- Problem of Evil- Liberation from Suffering- Love and Altruism- Economics.

DEDICATED

AT HIS FEET

yat karoṣi yat aśnāsi
yat juhoṣi dadāsi yat
yat tapasyasi kaunteya
tat kuruṣva madarpaṇaṁ
(Gītā, IX, 27)

Swami Tejomayananda

Chinmaya Mission West
Krishnalaya
P.O. Box 129
Piercy, CA 95587
707-247-3488
fax: 707-347-3422

ॐ

FOREWORD

The title of this book, *Law of Love and the Mathematics of Spirituality*, is unique in that it creates interest and curiosity in the minds of both, spiritual and rational people. Generally, spirituality is considered as the field of intuition and revelation, and material science as one of reasoning and logic. However, in this book, Dr. Raju Chidambaram has beautifully and successfully shown that both these disciplines need not be contrary to each other. The introduction itself gives the gist of the thought development to unfold in the entire book.

I congratulate Dr. Chidambaram for such a thought-provoking work, written after years of dedicated and devoted study.

With best wishes,

Tejomayananda
July 20, 2010
Pittsburgh

Swami Tejomayananda

Head, Chinmaya Mission Worldwide

Acknowledgement

The author acknowledges with gratitude his indebtedness to Brahmaleen

Gurudev Sw. Chinmayananda, Guruji Sw. Tejomayananda, Sw. Dheerananda and several other teachers and friends of the Chinmaya Mission from whom he learnt *Advaita Vedānta*. To Guruji Swami Tejomayananda, I am doubly indebted for writing a Foreword to the book. I thank Mr. Benjamin Root of Alexandria, VA for countless hours of invigorating discussions held in our home during the early stages of this work. It helped me fine tune many of the concepts used in the book. My special thanks are also due to Mr. Vinod Ajmani of Fairfax, VA for the strikingly beautiful cover design, and to Swami Siddhananda of Chinmaya Mission Publications, Philadelphia, PA for the photograph used in the dedication page. The other photographs and images of the scientists, teachers and philosophers found in this book were taken from public INTERNET websites such as Wikipedia.

Special mention must be made of Prof. S.N. Bhavsar of University of Pune, who reviewed and commented extensively on the manuscript. He took the time to do this in spite of the heavy commitments he had to own projects. His genuine words of appreciation for my effort are highly valued.

This book would not have been possible except for the encouragement received from many quarters. My heartfelt thanks to Mr. R.P. Jain of Motilal Banarassidas, New Delhi, who helped bring the book to a completion and ready for publication; to Mr. Chib Roth of Authorhouse Publishing for assistance with the graphics; to Prof. Bal Ram Singh,

Director of Indic Studies at University of Massachusetts, Dartmouth and Dr. Pramod Pathak of World Association for Vedic Studies for encouraging me to present and publish my papers in the WAVES Conferences; and to my wife Shobha Chidambaram, M.D., for being instrumental in introducing me to Chinmaya Mission and Vedanta. The author also gratefully notes the benefit he had from exchanges with several Vedāntins, including Dr. Ram Chandran and Prof. V. Krishnamoorthy, in the early days of this work through the on-line discussion group advaitin@yahoogroups.com.

Preface

The future of mankind, as far as we can see it today, is at once promising and perilous. Man's intellectual capacity, evidenced by his impressive ability to control the external world of matter and energy, promises to make his material life progressively more comfortable. But his inability to control the internal world of mind and thoughts imperil that future as violence fanned by political, economic and religious feelings flare up into ever more destructive confrontations. When Swami Chinmayananda caricatured modern man as someone with a huge head and a tiny heart, he was only pointing out to this tragic state where man's intelligence has far outpaced his wisdom.

Spirituality, and the wisdom it bestows, is sorely needed today if mankind is to avert a calamitous end to its dreams. The spiritual wisdom is readily available but its acceptance and dissemination is thwarted by some unfortunate circumstances, including the historic association of spirituality with religion. In-fighting between religions, as well as the controversies it has had with science, have by and large hurt the credibility of religions in the eyes of many thinking people. By association, it has hurt the credibility of spirituality also. Secular societies find it difficult to encourage spiritual education in fear of violating the principles of separation of state and religion. Youth trained in science often choose to avoid spirituality together with the religions they mistrust. Result is that humanity is turning a blind eye today to the prospect of peace and harmony that can be achieved by spiritual education.

This is indeed tragic considering that the association of spirituality with religion, while a historical fact, is not a logical necessity. In fact, in advancing a mathematical theory of spirituality, this book presumes that spirituality can be pursued as a science in its own right and that it can be studied and taught as any other science, without reference to any religion. Vedāntic philosophy is used in the book as the foundation for the mathematical theory since it has the necessary logical rigor to make the effort successful. The essential facts about spirituality that Vedānta teaches apply to all people regardless of their religious background.

The use of mathematics has allowed modern science to gain precise insight into the workings of the material world. It has excelled time and again in bringing out the common principles that often underlie different branches of science. In the same vein, mathematics applied to spirituality can be expected to facilitate a better, more precise understanding of our spiritual nature and reveal any similarity it may have with other branches of knowledge. I believe this expectation has been realized to a degree by the ideas presented in this book. It is possible now to represent key ideas of spirituality- such as detachment, suffering, spiritual evolution, suffering and liberation- using graphs and mathematical expressions. This opens up a new approach to discuss, understand, and teach abstract spiritual concepts clearly and effectively using graphical and other mathematical representations. The theory presented here also brings out clearly a number of mathematical similarities between the spiritual realm, as seen in Vedānta, and the material world as seen through Relativity theory and Quantum Mechanics. For example, the Law of Love, which is one of the first and basic results of the theory of spirituality in this book, appears as a mathematical twin of the space-time relationship in Relativity theory. Nevertheless, matter is not spirit; therefore the similarities noted are not an indication of the identity of the two.

The work which has culminated as this book began about ten years ago when I sought to understand in terms of modern decision theory the effect of our innate tendencies (*vāsanas*) on our thoughts and actions. The resulting ideas formed the basis for the Prakṛti-Īśvara Paradigm used in this book and were published in an article in the December 2000 issue of *Chinmaya Management Review*. The mathematical theory which took shape over the next five years or so was presented in various WAVES (World Association of Vedic Studies) conferences held during 2004-2008.

What is presented in this book is not offered as the final definitive theory of spirituality, but as the outline of a promising new field which will be hopefully enriched by contributions from more Vedāntins, philosophers, mathematicians and spiritual scientists. The outcome of such a joint effort will be to firmly establish spirituality as a science that transcends all religions and which can be taught as a course in science in schools and colleges everywhere.

"*What the world needs now, is Love, sweet Love*" is how a popular song of yesteryear expresses the yearning for freedom from the tyranny of materialism. Spiritual knowledge alone can sow that Love in the hearts and minds of all people.

Alexandria, VA
April 14, 2011

- Raju Chidambaram

Guide to Pronunciation of Sanskrit Words

The use of Sanskrit terms from Vedanta as well as quotations from Sanskrit texts such as Bhagavad Gita and Upanishads are unavoidable in a book such as this. In transliterating Sanskrit words, the book follows the IAST system shown below.

Transliteration Convention (IAST System)

Letter	***to be pronounced as in***
	A. Vowels
a	hut or son
ā	audit or mom
i	inn or it
ī	east or feel
u	foot or full
ū	moot
e	effort
ai	item
o	obey or toe
au	mouse
ṛ	rhythm or rig
ṁ	(Nasalization of preceding vowel)
ḥ	(Aspiration of preceding vowel)
	B. Consonants
k	custom
kh	khaki, Kate, or blockhead
g	goat or gate
gh	ghost or gawk

ṅ	ring
c	charm
ch	Mitchell or match
j	Java
jh	hedgehog
ñ	injury or inch
ṭ	gate
ṭh	time, also anthill (approximate)
ḍ	duck
ḍh	dumb
ṇ	money
t	think
th	thumb (approximate), pithy
d	then
dh	No equivalent
n	Nancy or numb
p	spin
ph	loophole
b	ball or bun
bh	abhor
m	Mary
y	yellow
r	perimeter, also drama
l	luck
v	vile, also wile
ś	stand or pistachio
ṣ	shop
s	so
h	hall

C. Special Combination Characters

jñ	Gnosis (approximate)
kṣ	perfection
ñc	inch

Table of Contents

Introduction....xix

Part I: Of God, by God, for God - The Vedāntic Vision of Creation

Chapter 1: Vedānta, the Science of Spirituality....1
Chapter 2: Basics of Vedānta....15
Chapter 3: The Prakṛti-Īśvara Paradigm....45
Chapter 4: The Logic of Vedānta....61

Part II: Mathematical Representation

List of Mathematical Symbols....77

Chapter 5: The Experiencer and the Experienced....79
Chapter 6: Universal Love and the Fundamental Law of Spirituality....115
Chapter 7: Sri Ramana's Principle of Personal Will....145
Chapter 8: A Theory of Vāsanas....157
Chapter 9: The Mystery of Time....201

Part III: Vedānta's Answers to Life's Persistent Questions

Chapter 10: Riddles of Life....219
Chapter 11: The Love That Cures All Ills....235
Chapter 12: The Path Ahead- Research and Education in Spirituality....247

Appendices....255
References....259
Glossary of Sanskrit Terms (Alphabetically Listed)....267

Introduction

You will find in this book a rather unfamiliar mix of spirituality, Vedānta and mathematics. As such the reader's first reaction may be to question what Vedānta has to do with Mathematics or how mathematical analysis can help a discussion on spirituality. While the long answer to this question is in the pages of this book itself, I would like to address these questions now as a way of introducing the subject matter of the book.

Deep within all human beings there is a longing for truth, love, beauty and peace. This dimension of our existence is separate from the physical comforts we seek from the world and is a manifestation of our spiritual nature. The spiritual needs of human beings are as real as their physical needs. Being real, it should be possible to investigate this spirituality with the same objectivity found in the sciences dealing with the physical world. Scientific methods, including mathematical analysis, that have so well succeeded in furthering our understanding of the universe of matter and energy should also help in studying spirituality. This is the rationale for my views; the inspiration for this view has come to me from two great thinkers and teachers of our time, Dr. S. Radhakrishnan and Swami Chinmayananda.

In the summer of 1961, I and my fellow graduate students in the Indian Statistical Institute, Calcutta, were sent to New Delhi to learn about the ways the various departments of the Government in India collected and utilized statistics in their work. A small group among us took the opportunity of our month long presence in the capital city to seek audience

Dr. S. Radhakrishnan

with the then Prime Minister Jawaharlal Nehru and separately with Vice-President Dr. Radhakrishnan. Our requests were promptly granted, partly based no doubt on the reputation our institution and its director Prof. Mahalanobis had with Mr. Nehru and others. While our encounter with the Prime Minister was polite but brief, the one with the Vice-President at his official residence was more engaging. Seated cross-legged in an overstuffed chair and without his customary turban, the eminent philosopher appeared quite relaxed and willing to talk. He opened his remarks tauntingly with the cliché *"Ah, Statistics and lies!"* meant clearly as a bait, but then quickly moved to soften the blow by adding another well worn phrase *"Figures do not lie, but liars do figure."* To our relief, however, the discussion turned away soon from statistics and more towards philosophy.

What I recall most about that evening was his response to a question I asked him: What did he have to say about the historic stand-off between Science and Religion? I expected a long answer to a difficult question, but what I got instead was a stern put-down followed by a memorable one-liner.

"Don't tell me tall stories!" said Dr. Radhakrishnan, as though my question was presumptuous. Then, after a brief pause, he added:

"A little bit of science takes you away from religion—but a little bit more of it will bring you right back to it!"

I do not remember much else the Vice President said in answer to my question, but probably that is because everything else that followed was somewhat redundant. The sharp insight behind his short answer was indeed impressive. Guruji Swami Tejomayananda, the current Head of the global Chinmaya Mission, who we had the honor of hosting once at our home, thought well enough of Dr. Radhakrishnan's statement to quote it in his fascinating book *Hindu Culture* [1].

Dr. Radhakrishnan was a scholar renowned for his understanding of world religions, but his ideas were particularly well rooted in the Gītā and Upaniṣads. To me his answer revealed his conviction that modern science and the Vedānta taught in the Gīta and Upaniṣads are not in conflict and that in fact they have edged closer to each other in recent times. In making his statement, Dr. Radhakrishnan was very likely referring to the revolutionary ideas in the 20th century science, especially in Physics.

One of the most effective teachers and practitioners of Vedānta in the 20th century was Swami Chinmayananda, the founder of the world-wide Chinmaya Mission. The author is fortunate to have had the opportunity to listen to his talks on Vedānta and also to be closely associated with the Mission for over two decades. Gurudev, as he is known to many in the Mission, usually referred to Vedānta as the "subjective science" where the object of scientific enquiry is one's own self or "the seer". He emphasized that in its rigor of reasoning and analysis, Vedānta was no less scientific than the "material sciences" where the object of enquiry is the outside world or "the seen". Vedānta's theoretical constructs are logically sound and its practical inferences verifiable by experience. Swami Chinmayananda brought this out clearly by what he taught as well as by the way he lived among us.

Vedānta and Mathematics

"*Nyāya śāstra*" is a venerated system of logic used by Vedānta and other Hindu schools of philosophy as a sure guide to correct reasoning. It is appropriate to note the impact this system of logic has had on the development of modern mathematics itself. Mary Everest Boole, wife of the nineteenth century mathematician George Boole and herself a mathematician, has observed how the *Nyāya śāstra* influenced her husband's work in developing what is now known as Boolean Logic, fundamental to many branches of mathematics and computer science [2].

With its basis in logic, Vedānta's approach to spiritual questions has a distinctively modern-day scientific air to it. It is this logical basis that makes it feasible to apply mathematical tools to understand spirituality as taught in Vedānta.

Mathematics and the Power of Disciplined Thinking: Science, with the countless blessings it has brought to the material world, has demonstrated the apparently limitless potential of the human intellect to provide answers to profound questions through disciplined thinking. This success of modern science is in no small measure due to mathematics which verily embodies the art and power of disciplined thinking. The tremendous progress in mathematical techniques (and computer technology) has made it possible for researchers in all disciplines to use mathematical models to develop a deeper understanding of the phenomena of interest to them. There are several attributes that give mathematics its power and beauty. Parsimony and precision are two such attributes. A mathematical approach demands precision in the definition and use of concepts. It encourages the use of as few concepts as necessary to model a problem, highlighting what is important as opposed to what is redundant or even irrelevant. In contrast, operational meaning of concepts used in verbal reasoning can be ambiguous and more easily misunderstood; this could lead to conclusions which are not robust, or are vague or incomplete. A second virtue of using mathematical analysis is that it forces into open all assumptions underlying an argument so that the conclusions drawn from an analysis can be understood in their proper context with all necessary caveats.

Mathematical reasoning has been made rigorous by centuries of painstakingly meticulous work by many brilliant minds. Compared to verbal reasoning, the logical rigor of mathematical analysis is clearly superior and nearly infallible. Communicating abstract ideas and arguments to others also becomes more reliable with the use of mathematical analysis. A great help in this respect is no doubt the visual appeal of graphical representation that often becomes possible with the use of mathematics. The reader himself or herself will have an opportunity to assess this benefit from the graphs and charts used throughout the book.

Perhaps the greatest advantage of using mathematics is because of its status as the "Law of Laws". Once a problem or phenomenon has been satisfactorily modeled using mathematical concepts in geometry, calculus, probability, etc, further analysis can proceed with the aid of the vast array of results already available to us in those fields. This is because mathematical laws are the same whether the context of study is physics or biology or economics, or, for that matter, spirituality.

Mathematics itself is abstract in the concepts and methods it uses and there is nothing worldly or material about it to suggest that it is suitable only for the material sciences. On the contrary, many eminent mathematicians have been inclined to view mathematics in wholly spiritual terms. To Srinivasan Ramanujan every proven mathematical equation was the voice of God. Thus there is no *a priori* reason to conclude that mathematics is appropriate only for material sciences;

on the contrary, it may be even more appropriate for a spiritual science such as Vedānta.

An Overview Of The Contents

I do believe that the claims regarding the benefits of mathematical analysis have been vindicated in the case of spirituality through the theory and results presented in this book. The book, arranged in three parts, is meant to be as self-contained as possible so that readers not familiar with the Vedāntic philosophy can also profit from it. Part I, with four chapters, provides the necessary footing in the Vedāntic concepts required later. Chapter 1 discusses basic questions relating to science, religion, and spirituality. The purpose is to draw the necessary distinctions between religion and spirituality and to show that any conflict between science and religion does not extend to spirituality. On the contrary, spirituality, as systematized in Vedānta, is a science in its own right. It is the science of knowledge as opposed to the science of matter and energy. Chapter 2 introduces the concepts of Vedānta and shows how they explain an ever changing cosmos that is actively experienced by sentient beings. The basic view regarding the experiencer, experienced, and experiences is developed leading to ideas of suffering, detachment and liberation. Knowledge acquired through life's experiences is the essence of spiritual progress. Chapter 3 develops the important *Prakṛti- Īśvara* paradigm in order to explain the nature of uncertainty found throughout creation, its function, and its implications regarding free will. The basic idea is that while the world that an individual meets is as willed by God, how it meets that world is up to the individual's free will to decide. The final Chapter of Part I presents the emerging views of neuro-cognitive sciences and how they square with the Vedāntic concepts of consciousness and cognition. It is clear that science is yet to fully grasp the nature of consciousness and that Vedāntic views continue to maintain their logical validity in the face of the evidence from neurosciences.

Part II consisting of five chapters develops the mathematical framework reflecting the Vedāntic views described in the earlier chapters. The theory is built in a fairly straight forward manner using a few key concepts such as *Mahat* (cosmic mind), *vāsanas* (innate tendencies), *vairāgya* (spiritual detachment), *puruṣārtha* (will power or self-effort), suffering, and Realization. These concepts are given a mathematical expression, and the inter-relationship among them is studied using relatively simple mathematical methods. The results of analysis conform to the conclusions of Vedāntins, thus providing an important validation of the model. While the results are not new, the methods used in arriving at the results are new and provide a greater and clearer understanding of the basic processes involved in spiritual evolution. The relationship between spiritual detachment and *vāsana*s is one example of the added insight gained by mathematical analysis. The graphic representation made possible by the model can be valuable in visualizing and communicating some of the abstract concepts in spirituality.

A welcome surprise of the mathematical exploration has been the sharp focus into which it has brought the many similarities shared by Vedānta and modern physics. Substitute the words "Self" for "space" and "Knowledge" for "light" and we transform results in relativity physics into teachings of Vedānta. Many physicists and philosophers have speculated for a longtime on the similarities between eastern philosophies and modern science, as the quote from Dr. Radhakrishnan suggests. We see this clearly demonstrated in Chapter 6 where several basic features of the time-space continuum and the cosmic mind space (*Mahat*) are described using identical mathematics. The similar views that science and Vedānta have regarding Free Will are also remarkable.

The concept of time turns out to be as important in a theory of spirituality as it is in Physics. In Chapter 9 we present ideas from physics, neurosciences and Vedānta all of which point strongly to a universe which itself is timeless. How sentient creatures can experience time in a timeless universe is therefore an enigma. Resolution of this mystery requires a drastic revision of our commonly held beliefs about reality and leads to a viewpoint which may appear to be stranger than fiction, yet is in full accordance with the teachings of Vedānta.

One may mistakenly conclude from the nature of the discourse in Parts I and II of the book that Vedānta is just a set of abstract concepts and theory fit only for academic discussion. Part III of the book is devoted to show that, quite to the contrary, Vedānta is very relevant to individual and social life. Spirituality taught by Vedānta can root out ignorance and bring joy to daily life. Much of our suffering is due to misunderstandings we have about life, the world, and ourselves. Vedānta removes these misunderstandings with convincing logic as shown in Chapter 10. Swami Chinmayananda's own personal life exemplified the transformative power of Vedāntic knowledge. His energy and enthusiasm were phenomenal in spite of pressures of work and health problems. The aura of joy that surrounded him all the time was infectious. He demonstrated that the hallmark of a spiritually evolved soul is the love and joy that spreads from it to brighten the world around. Spiritual knowledge is a requirement for individual happiness; it is also the cure for the many economic and social problems facing society as a whole. We discuss in Chapter 11 the power of selfless love and altruism to transform societies. All this is possible, of course, only if spiritual instruction is available to all people and is actively encouraged. The need for scientific education in spirituality is emphasized in the final chapter of the book, where we also look at some of the areas for further research in spirituality.

Highlights of the Mathematical Theory of Spirituality

A main contribution of the book is the mathematical theory of spirituality it advances. It may be helpful to list some of the highlights of that theory as an introduction to the book.

1) The mathematical model is based overall on a view best expressed in modern times by Sri Ramana: While the world that a jīva, or "individual soul", encounters moment after moment is totally under the controlling Will of *Īśvara*, the manner in which it faces that world is up to the jīva to decide. The jīva may meet the world in *bhoga* attached to the Non-Self or in *yoga*, established in Self. As a *bhogī*, the jīva suffers; as a *yogī*, it takes one step further towards Perfection. This choice is available to the jīva every moment.
2) "*Mahat*", the Cosmic Mind space is the space in which the "*tripuṭi*" of all possible worlds experienced, all experiencing jīvas, and all conceivable experiences exist. This space is described mathematically in polar coordinates (t,θ) where t denotes the experienced world at time t, and θ denotes a jīva with detachment theta. (t,θ) together denote the jīva's experience

at time *t*. An interesting feature of this representation is that only one-quarter of the *Mahat* space (namely the first quadrant) is required to denote all possible worlds and experiences; the other three quadrants remain undefined, beyond anything objectively experienced. This is curiously reminiscent of the famous first few verses of the hymn well known as *Puruṣa Sūktaṁ*.

3) The analysis reveals an unexpected and unexplained similarity between the *Mahat* space and the four dimensional time-space continuum of Relativity Theory. Past, present, and future co-exist in the time-space continuum, according to Einstein. *Mahat* also is beyond time. That is, time is in Cosmic Mind, but Cosmic Mind is not in time. Further, in parallel with the well known relationship between (ordinary) space and time in special relativity theory, there is a mathematically identical relationship between a jīva's state of spiritual evolution and its worldly suffering. This relationship can be stated in words thus: *"As a jīva gains more and more in Universal, Unconditional Love and Understanding, it suffers less and less in the world".* This statement is a first and immediate result of the model and hence it may qualify as the "fundamental result of mathematical spirituality", especially since Love is acknowledged as a supreme, necessary virtue in all major religions.

4) $\theta = 0$ characterizes a jīva fully attached to the world. Increasing value of θ denotes spiritual progress. God-Realization occurs when θ reaches the maximum possible value, namely $\pi/2$. A result that is likely to be gratifying to mathematicians is the relevance of the Euler's equation, namely $e^{i.\pi} + 1 = 0$, to the model in describing Realization. This equation - acknowledged by many as the most famous and beautiful of all equations in higher mathematics- has held a mystical significance for mathematicians since its discovery nearly 250 years ago.

5) The jīva can choose to identify with the Self or to identify with the Non-Self at any time, according to Sri Ramana. A probabilistic equivalent of the model is derived to reflect this freedom which gives a new interpretation for the variable $\theta(t)$, the spiritual detachment at time *t*. The *a priori* probability that the jīva will identify with the Self is $\sin^2\theta(t)$, implying higher

probability of identifying with Self with higher detachment $\theta(t)$. Upon Realization, the probability of identifying with Self becomes 1, as one would expect. Jīvas with low detachment are more likely to identify with the Non-Self if left to their usual nature. But even such a worldly jīva can identify at any time with the Self provided its will power is strong enough to overcome the pull of its lowly vāsanas.

6) A theory of vāsanas has been proposed which integrates well with the overall mathematical model of detachment and spiritual evolution. Vāsanas of a jīva at time *t* are represented as a function V(x,t) indicating the energy with which the jīva's mind responds to vāsana stimulus x. The variable x ranges from 0 to 1 with value 0 corresponding to lowest *tamas*ic vāsanas (e.g. survival instincts) and the values of x close to 1 corresponding to the highest *sāttvic* vāsanas (i.e. search for Truth and Realization). Based on this representation, the mathematical relationship between spiritual detachment $\theta(t)$ and the vāsana function V(x,t) has been derived. In essence, it relates $\theta(t)$ to the mean value of V(x,t). More *sāttvic* the mind, higher is its detachment.
7) Mathematically speaking, *sādhana* or spiritual practice, involves the re-shaping of the vāsana function V(x,t) so that its mean value gets increasingly closer to 1. From this perspective, questions such as limits to spiritual evolution and the nature of Realization are discussed leading to observations consistent with Vedāntic teachings.
8) The model permits incorporation of the Advaitic views on how jīvas derive happiness (or its opposite) by contact with objects of the world. This leads to a final result showing how the "suffering" of jīva at any time can be expressed as the product of three factors: i) the level of alertness of the jīva's mind, ii) the degree to which the jīva accepts good and bad outcomes with equanimity, and iii) its spiritual detachment. The *karma, bhakti, and Jñāna Yoga* recipes for reducing suffering are reflected in this result.

The above theory is *a* mathematical representation of the Vedāntic theory of spirituality. I am careful not to claim that it is the only such representation possible; other mathematicians and Vedāntins may well propose better models after reviewing the book.

The reliability of the conclusions drawn from a mathematical model is largely determined by the "goodness of fit" or how well the model fits the phenomenon studied. In physical science, one can validate a theory by comparing its predictions with the observed results in the laboratory. This technique however may not be feasible for a theory of spirituality. The best one can probably do in this case is to stay consciously consistent with the spiritual insights gleaned from teachers, scriptures, and the morals of mythological stories. In other words, we should judge a mathematical theory of spirituality by how consistent it is with the teachings already available in spiritual literature. There should be no expectation that mathematics will lead to discovery of new spiritual truths hitherto unknown in Vedānta. Vedānta is a complete theory of spirituality backed by the thoughts and experiences of seers over many centuries and it is doubtful there are any new spiritual truths unknown to them.

A book of this nature cannot avoid using Sanskrit terms for the many Vedāntic concepts. I have tried to explain each such term wherever they occur first. The Glossary at the end of the book lists these terms alphabetically and can serve as a useful reference for those not familiar with these terms. Sanskrit terms are usually, but not always, in italics; well known terms such as yoga as well as oft-repeated terms such as Brahman, Ātman, Īśvara, Prakṛti, and Jīva are not always italicized.

The mathematics needed to follow discussions in Part II is roughly at the high school AP or college entrance level with a basic knowledge of calculus and probabilities. Parts I and III of the book do not require any mathematics whatsoever; readers may find these chapters useful for the understanding they provide about the spiritual science of Vedānta.

PART I

Of God, by God, for God - The Vedāntic Vision of Creation

CHAPTER 1

Vedānta, the Science of Spirituality

This book approaches spirituality using mathematical methods similar to those which one will find in science to explain the material world. The credibility of this approach can be questioned if spirituality is viewed as irrevocably wedded to religions which are faith based and not altogether scientific. Association of spirituality with religion is however a historical fact and raises many important questions about the true nature of spirituality: Is spirituality based on faith or can it, like science, be "evidence-based"? Should spirituality necessarily remain distinct from science or do the two have anything in common? Is spiritual progress possible only by the faithful performance of vaguely understood religious rituals or is there a more substantive, objective basis to it? Is its validity totally dependent on the legends and personalities sacred to religions? Do religions have exclusive ownership of spirituality or is it conceivable that science one day may also contribute to its advancement? Can the benefits of spirituality be actually experienced in this life by all who practice it, or, is the reward some unnamed heaven to be experienced by a chosen few after their death only?

In short, can spirituality be intelligently pursued, rationally understood and actually experienced here and now? Vedānta, the philosophical system on which much of this book is based, says "Yes". Spiritual and material realms are part of the one and the same creation. As such, logically speaking, science and spirituality cannot stand in opposition. We will explore in this chapter the mutual relationship between science, spirituality, and religion and show how each can contribute to the welfare of individuals and society without running afoul of one another. The present chapter will also serve as a brief introduction to Vedānta before we get into a more detailed discussion of this philosophy in the subsequent chapters.

Science vs. Religion

Much has been said and written about the constrained relationship between our scientific and religious institutions. Both are great, vital institutions that have served mankind well, though it is not difficult to find numerous instances where both have also been a source of suffering. Science has been generally a constructive force bringing with it many blessings to the modern man. But it has also been misused quite frequently as a destructive power. Similarly, there is no doubt that the great religions of the world have succeeded in providing peace and comfort to their faithful followers from the stress and strain of worldly life; but they have also been misused to incite intense animosities between groups of people resulting in much suffering. These are well documented facts of history.

Well documented too are the many instances where science and religion have clashed. No doubt, both science and religion seek to be on the side of truth. Confrontation occurs when what religion holds as true is not acceptable to science, or *vice versa*. The approach taken by science to seek and assert truth is quite different from that used by religions. Science accepts as truth only that which can be verified by any observer at anytime by appropriate objective observations. Consistent with this view, science generally preoccupies itself with questions that can be verified through human observation. Religions, on the other hand, deal with many questions which, by their very nature, are beyond the capability of direct observation. They rely on scriptural authority to assert their views on these questions. To the extent the issues of respective interest to science and religion are not overlapping, confrontation between the two can be avoided.

There is some overlap, however, and clashes do occur. For example, religions do have views on origin of the universe and the genesis of human beings which also happen to be areas of great interest to modern science. Here the traditional religious views tend to be at odds with the results of scientific observations. Similarly, some personal and social customs mandated by religions (dietary restrictions, for example) may be contraindicated by scientific principles. Religious dogmatism is often blamed by scientists for the continuation of the controversy in the face of what they consider as objective evidence. But science itself has been blamed as being dogmatic for its view that basic questions of concern to religion, such as God or life after death, are not worthy of discussion since anything we say regarding these cannot be verified by direct observation.

One may rightly despair whether this stand-off between Science and Religion can ever get resolved. A resolution is possible provided we have a right understanding of science and religion and of the mediating role of spirituality. Vedānta, this author believes, provides us with this necessary understanding [3].

What is Vedānta?

Vedānta is a highly developed system of philosophy that finds its first expressions in the scriptures of ancient India known as Upaniṣads. This philosophy has been further developed in other scriptures such as Bhagavad Gītā and *Brahma sūtra* and interpreted in the elaborate commentaries of generations of subsequent philosophers. Vedānta contains the highest truths in spirituality; many consider it as the *science* of spirituality because of the rigorous logic employed in analyzing and discriminating truth. It is a science also because of its emphasis on suggesting practical techniques for spiritual development whose promised goals can be personally experienced by the practitioners in their present life. This after all is what a good science is supposed to be- its theories logically sound and predictions personally verifiable.

It is no accident then that the teachings of Vedānta strike a responsive chord in the hearts of many who sincerely study it. For centuries, great philosophers and scientists around the world have found in it a source of profound wisdom and inspiration. At the same time the real life examples of modern day sages such as Sri Ramana, Nisargadatta Maharaj and Sri Ramakrishna demonstrate the glorious perfection to which any human being can aspire by practicing its teachings. When the German philosopher Schopenhauer exclaims *"In the whole world there is no religion or philosophy so sublime and elevating as Vedānta… this Vedānta has been the solace of my life; it will be the solace of my death"* it has to be the result of understanding the logic of this science as well as personally experiencing its benefits. Erwin Schrödinger, whose mathematical formulations laid the foundations for Quantum Mechanics, found in the Vedāntic identity of Brahman and Ātman "*the quintessence of deepest insight into the happenings of the world*" [4]. Coming from a scientist with a keen understanding of the behavior of matter and energy in their most subtle form, this comment is indeed a powerful endorsement of Vedānta.

Erwin Schrödinger

Vedāntic View of Spirituality

The terms spirit and matter are widely used in Western philosophies. The two terms can be best understood by the "seer- seen distinction" central to Vedānta: spirit is concerned with the "seer" whereas matter is everything "seen". The seer itself cannot be seen, asserts Vedānta. The spiritual life of an individual is then something distinct from its worldly life. The worldly life of an individual consists of transactions at the physical level performed with the aid of its sense organs and organs of action, as well as reactions at the mental level, such as thoughts and emotions. The goal of these worldly transactions is to sustain own life, ensure survival of the species, and more generally to satisfy the emotional and physical needs through appropriate interaction with the world outside. The individual finds worldly happiness to the extent it can satisfy these needs.

The spiritual life of a jīva, on the other hand, has the primary goal of knowing the truth about own self, the world, and the Ultimate Reality (Brahman) underlying both the self and the world. It is not enough to know the truth, but one must live that truth by transforming one's life accordingly. Spiritual progress demands changing one's relationship to oneself, to the world around, and to God. The individual realizes peace to the extent it has correct knowledge, and lives established in that knowledge steadfastly.

The happiness in worldly life is obtained through finite actions which can produce only finite results. Therefore worldly happiness is never permanent or complete (i.e. never without some sort of limitation). In contrast, the peace sought after in spiritual life is obtained through knowledge, and not action, and is both total and permanent. It is in this sense that spiritual life is said to lead to Perfection, or salvation, from the limitations of worldly existence. Vedānta teaches the knowledge of own self, the world, and Brahman for our understanding at the intellectual level, and it also prescribes the various practical means by which to realize or live this knowledge so as to attain the promised peace. We need not dwell on this further here since the subsequent chapters of the book are meant to do just that.

Spirituality vs. Religion

Spirituality does not conflict with religion; on the other hand, as mentioned earlier, it is often considered inseparable from religion. This does not mean that the two are the same. For a religion to be effective, it must recognize certain core spiritual truths. This is because the spiritual nature and spiritual development are same in all human beings regardless of time, space, gender, race, nationality etc. Therefore, the various religions that have come into vogue at different epochs in different cultures, even though looking very different, necessarily incorporate many similar, if not identical, basic beliefs about spirituality. Thus, all major religions

1) Place emphasis on controlling the tumultuous mind and living a disciplined, virtuous life,
2) Believe in the existence of a higher power whose Will dictate the events of the world and experiences of the individuals,
3) Preach love and self-less service and require surrender of personal will to the higher Will,
4) Discount the importance of the perishable body in deference to the imperishable indwelling "soul" within each individual,
5) Hold that spiritual practices bring peace and happiness to daily life, and
6) Recognize the potential of all souls to reach Perfection, though some religions suggest that this potential is realized only by own believers.

But religions do not stop with just acknowledging and promoting these spiritual truths. They have found it necessary and useful to surround the core truths with several layers of additional theories and practices. The relevance of these additional layers is not universal since they are the product of the particular time, space, and culture in which they are created. As such they do not have the same absolute validity that the core spiritual truths do.

The anatomy of a religion can be visualized as rings surrounding the central core of spiritual truths (Fig 1.1)

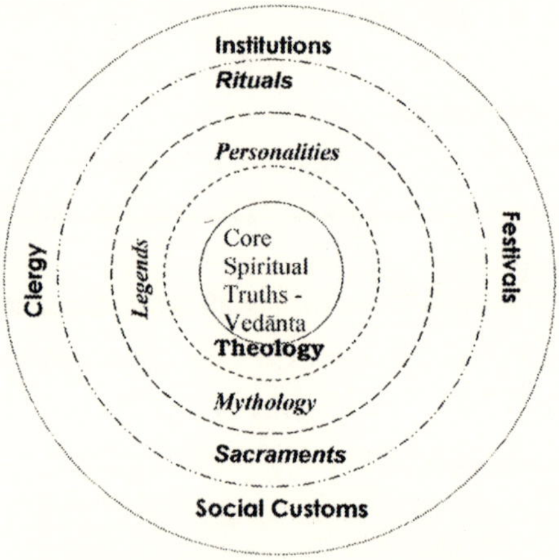

Fig 1.1 **ANATOMY OF A RELIGION**

The outmost ring consists of the institutions, the temples and churches, the clergy officiating in various positions, the social customs, dress and dietary habits, religious festivals etc. This is the external face the religion presents to the world. The next layer inside represents the various rituals and sacraments that the followers are expected to observe. Usually, this facet of a religion is not open to everyone, but only to its adherents. The third layer is perhaps the most significant of all. It includes the legends and mythologies associated with the various prophets, saints, and deities of the religion. The personalities, ideals and beliefs introduced in this layer often are the factors determining the character of the religion. The next inner layer immediately surrounding the core is Theology dealing with beliefs regarding God, origin of the world, soul, death, life after death etc. Typically, theology involves abstract concepts and theories which the average follower may not totally relate to, but is expected to accept on faith. Vedānta has been identified in Fig 1.1 with the central core because it is the core spiritual truths that are of primary concern to Vedānta. Paul Hourihan put it very effectively when he said *"Vedānta is the essence of religion, the truth embedded in the heart of every religion. Vedānta is the Godhead that makes every religion Divine"* [5]. This Vedānta, as taught in the Upaniṣads and lived by the Hindu sages, is remarkably simple, honest, and devoid of any worldly embellishments. It recognizes no institutions, no rituals, stipulates no personality other than own Self, as absolutely necessary for salvation[1].

As mentioned earlier, the outer layers that distinguish one religion from others are very much the product of the cultural milieu in which that religion was founded. But the spiritual truths at the core of every religion are invariant over time and space and have no cultural or historic connotations. In this respect they are similar to scientific truths which also must be invariant over time, space and culture.

Much of the difficulty science has with religions has to do with the theology, mythology, personalities and rituals found in the outer layers and less so with the core spiritual truths. We will soon return to discuss this important point at length later.

Religion vs. Religion

Conflict among religions is an unfortunate fact of history, a fact that has repeated itself far too many times. What is the source of this conflict? At some risk of over simplification, we may say it is just plain "competition".

Religions do subscribe to essentially the same core truths but frame them in the context of the theology, personalities, institutions, etc that set them apart from other competing religions. In this process, the universal nature of the core truths is often significantly de-emphasized. What is common and unifying is sacrificed in the interest of promoting the brand image of own religion. Some religions are more aggressive than others in pursuing this competitive path.

In this respect, religions may be likened to competing pharmaceutical companies packaging the same generic drug but using different formulations and delivery systems. The formulation can include several ingredients other than the key active agent. The method of delivering the

---

1 There are other spiritual traditions and philosophical systems around the world which are close to Vedānta. Jainism, Buddhism, Sikhism, Sufism, Taoism, and Christian Mysticism offer parallel systems of thought.

drug could also differ: it could be administered orally, intra-muscularly, by a patch worn on the skin etc. The basic efficacy of the treatment depends, of course, on the pharmacology of the drug and not on its packaging. But when marketing their product, the companies would like to emphasize the benefits of their superior formulation. This is done in order to maximize their market share. No doubt each formulation and delivery method often has its individual advantages and disadvantages in terms of side effects, cost etc. A patient may therefore have a good reason to prefer one brand over others. But it is also true that no single formulation can be considered the best for all patients. A similar situation prevails in the religious scene. One religion does not answer the spiritual needs of all human beings. The true genius of Hinduism lies in recognizing this very important fact. Hinduism respects all religions as potentially equally efficient. But more importantly, it itself offers not one, but a wide range of options for its believers to choose from, all paths having the Vedāntic wisdom as the basis.

There can be no denial of the comfort and support religion provides in one's day to day life. It is something to which many believers in every religion can bear testimony based on direct personal experience. Social scientists and psychologists also agree on the succor religion provides in facing the problems of life. The positive effect of religion and spirituality on health, and on ability to cope with life, has been documented in scientific studies in recent years [6,7]. However, as far as this author knows, there has been no "head-to-head" unbiased, scientific study in the literature whose results could support a claim of uniform superior efficacy of any one religion over another. As long as the "key active ingredient" in all major religions is the same set of spiritual truths, such evidence is not likely to emerge from future studies either. The conclusion to be drawn here is that the scientifically demonstrable successes of religion are attributable to their common spiritual content and not to the differences in packaging.

Science vs. Spirituality

It can be surmised from what has been said so far that science should have fewer problems with spirituality than with religion. A good deal of spirituality is concerned with practices to ensure happiness here and now in this world rather than in some distant heaven after death.

Yoga and meditation, to name two of these practices, have gained acceptance by scientists as having demonstrable salutary benefits on the physical and mental well being of the practitioners. Of the six core spiritual truths listed earlier, the first, third, and fifth have to do with our mental or "inner" life. Scientists do not refute the existence of mind or the importance of inner happiness, even if they do not have a consensus among themselves as to what mind really is. As such, they will not have much to dispute with these three points.

The second, fourth, and sixth points in the list of core truths do refer to concepts of "higher Will" and "imperishable soul" which are not observable entities. Scientists can raise objections as to their validity but close examination will show that these objections themselves are not totally scientific. Thus, we note that modern science has come to accept uncertainty as an inescapable and insurmountable feature of the universe, affecting the very fundamental particles of which matter and energy are constituted. Uncertainty is also inherent in human decisions and affects our daily lives even more directly and profoundly. It can be argued that acknowledging this basic uncertainty is tantamount to postulating a higher Will dictating the actual course of events in the universe. Science may not talk overtly of God, but it does accept that there is a "something else" that affects the manifested affairs of things and beings of the universe. This "something else", scientists will agree, is beyond any deterministic laws or cause-effect relations they can postulate.

Similarly, while science does not talk of "soul", there are many scientists who believe that not everything about a human being can be explained in terms of its material body. Of particular relevance to this discussion are the advances being made in neurosciences and artificial intelligence. It is true that modern brain imaging techniques are revolutionizing our understanding of the structure and processes of the brain and how they relate to our mental and physical functions. However, science is not anywhere close to answering a fundamental question: A human being experiences the world and is aware of its experiences. *How do all the neuronal activities and processes inside the brain add up to a knowledge and vivid experience of a world outside?* Neuroscientists have no answer.

Computer scientists making great strides in artificial intelligence have also no insight to offer regarding this question. Computers play games and music, predict weather, and solve mathematical problems with great speed and versatility. But when playing chess, does the computer *know* it is playing chess? When solving a mathematical problem does it know *what* problem it is solving or its significance? It does not. No computer scientist can categorically assert that computers "know" or experience anything they are doing. Robots built by future computer scientists may look and behave so very much like human beings that it may be difficult to tell them apart. But even then, the hardware and software of which robots are made, cannot vest them with the quality of knowing and experiencing. This is because *knowing and experiencing are not attributes of physical matter, but of "something else".*

As Adi Sankara, the great Advaita Vedānta philosopher of the 8th Century AD, says [8]:

> *"asti kaścit svayaṁ nityaṁ ahaṁ pratyayalaṁbanaḥ,*
> *avasthā traya sākṣī san pañca kośa vilakṣaṇaḥ"*

Something there is, which is the Absolute Entity, the Eternal Substratum for the very awareness of the Ego. It is the Witness of the three states and it is distinct from all the five sheaths.

The three states refer to the awake, dream and sleep states; the five sheaths to the physical, physiological, mental, intellectual, and sub-conscious components of the personality. That "eternal something", asserts Sankara, is the knower of all three states yet not part of any of the five sheaths. If so, where is this witnessing knower?

According to Vedānta, it is the *conscious* mind which knows and experiences the world and that Consciousness is an entity distinct from the brain or any other part of the physical or mental body. This experiencer, called jīva, dwells in the body but does not die when the physical body dies. It is the jīva which can possess knowledge and not the physical body.

The Spiritual Journey: From Ignorance to Perfect Knowledge through Worldly Experiences

This brings us to a key distinction we can make between Science and Spirituality. The basic "natural sciences", such as Physics, Chemistry and Biology, deal with matter and energy and they seek to explain all natural phenomena in terms of the known laws affecting matter and energy[2]. But matter and energy is not all there is to this universe. There is also knowledge. Vedānta postulates that the world of mind and matter is a manifestation of the three *guṇa*s or qualities of *Prakṛti* or Nature, namely *tamas, rajas*, and *sattva*. Matter and energy correspond to *tamas*, and *rajas* respectively, while knowledge is an entirely different *guṇa* corresponding to the *sattva* attribute of *Prakṛti*. For example, Science, which is a body of verified knowledge, is one manifestation of the *sattva* attribute. *Therefore, existence of science itself disproves the materialist's claim that everything in creation is matter and energy.*

If science is focused on matter and energy, spirituality is concerned with Knowledge. One may rightly ask "Knowledge of *what*?" The spiritual aspirant does gain knowledge of how mind interacts with the world to produce experiences and how that mind could be disciplined and made pure enough to acquire the most sublime knowledge. Vedānta makes one of the highest statements in metaphysics when it says that the spiritual aspirant finally seeks not knowledge *of* anything, but Knowledge itself. That is, spirituality is ultimately concerned with knowing the "knower" and "experiencer", the source of all Knowledge.

One of the sobering facts about science is that, while it acknowledges the world and its myriad of experiences, it cannot comprehend the purpose behind any of these. One must turn to spirituality to find the purpose of life. It is by learning the intelligent way to meet all worldly experiences that an individual gradually gains knowledge about self, just as it is by observation that scientists slowly build the edifice of science. To repeat what was stated earlier, the knowledge of importance in spirituality is not any worldly knowledge relating to matter and energy, but the knowledge of the Knower that possesses all knowledge- in other words, Knowledge of the Self. Attainment of this "Supreme Knowledge" is what is called in spiritual traditions variously as "Salvation" or "*Nirvāṇa*" or "Enlightenment". Echoing this spiritual principle, all religions give less importance to *what* we experience in life, pointing out that *how* we meet those experiences is the key to a successful spiritual life leading to salvation. The journey to Knowledge and spiritual perfection is through the world of experiences.

2 Disciplines such as Psychology, Economics, Management, and Sociology must also take into account subtle mind and may be classified as "behavioral sciences".

The purpose of our worldly life is to give us the experiences necessary to advance towards Perfection.

Spirituality as a Science

Science and spirituality, as discussed above, deal with two different aspects of reality and therefore there is no room for conflict between the two. What is more to the point is that spirituality is itself a science. The same techniques used in science, including controlled experiments and mathematical analysis, can be and have been used in understanding spirituality also[3]. We need not delve deeper into this topic here, since a bulk of this book is devoted to such a study of spirituality. When spirituality is approached thus, it takes on a definitely science-like look, capable of providing insights into our spiritual nature. Based on the work so far, there is evidence to support the view that spirituality can be studied as a distinct scientific discipline. Looking further down the road, it may become possible to teach spirituality as a science to young adults regardless of their cultural or religious background. This may be one way to cure the woes that beset the modern world due to a general lack of understanding of the true nature of spirituality and religion among both the young and older generations today.

Religion: Spiritual Food Cooked to Cultural Taste

If it is the core spiritual truths that make religions effective, is there then any real value added by the outer layers of theology and rituals? That is, do religions have any value to offer over and above what spirituality already does?

The answer is "Yes". Religions do have a very practical value. Spirituality without religion can be too abstract and intellectual for many of us. The Upaniṣadic approach of contemplation on the Unmanifest Brahman may not be a practical choice for many since it is a hard path to follow. We have the authority of Bhagavad Gītā to back this view where the Lord explains it thus [10]:

---

3 The Maharishi University of Fairfield, Iowa has been among those in the forefront of this effort to explore and develop the scientific basis of spirituality. For a very comprehensive account of its work, the reader is referred to a recent book by Dr. Robert Boyer [9].

"kleśo adhikatarasteṣāṁ avyaktāsaktacetasāṁ; avyaktā hi gatir dukhaṁ dehavadbhir avāpyate"

Greater is their troubles whose minds are set on the Unmanifested; for the goal, the Unmanifested, is very hard for the embodied to reach.

Spiritual advancement through contemplation of the Unmanifest is certainly possible for those who have learnt not to identify themselves with their own body and mind. But for the rest of us, who are "embodied", it is hard to even conceptualize an Unmanifest Reality, let alone meditate on It. The Lord therefore goes on to suggest that, for most of us, devotion to a concrete representation of that Reality is the easier path to follow. This in fact is what religions do. The rich symbolism behind the personalities, legends and mythologies introduced by religions- the third layer in our Fig. 1.1- makes the abstract more understandable and the spiritual practices more enjoyable to everyone.

Religion, in this respect, is not unlike the food we eat. To stay healthy one must take in the necessary nutrients, the proteins, carbohydrate, vitamins etc. Now, it is certainly possible to provide these nutrients through a daily regimen of raw vegetables, grains, fruits and nuts, etc and supplemented by a handful of vitamin pills. Indeed a few well-disciplined souls may actually stick to such a Spartan diet and manage to stay healthy and happy. Future space travelers may also learn to survive on pre-packaged food designed to provide just the right amount of nutrients, but offering little by way of variety and taste. But it is far easier for most of us if the nutrients are made available in the form of an appetizing meal. That is what good cooking does. It adds flavor and appeal to the food while preserving the nutrients the body needs. Good cooks are careful not to lose nutritional value by overcooking or by adding too much fat and sugar just to make the food taste better.

In much the same way each religion has its own style of adding sugar and spices and serving spiritual truths in an appetizing way to satisfy the spiritual hunger that is in all of us. Just as many different culinary styles have evolved around the world, each capable of providing the nutrition necessary for the human body, so too many religions have developed to cater to the nutrition our spiritual body needs. The choice of food we eat is a matter of personal preference, largely determined by what we are accustomed to since childhood. As long as the method of cooking does not diminish the nutritional value of the ingredients, one cuisine is as good as another for nourishing the body. Similarly, as long as religions preserve the core spiritual values while dressing them up with the outer layers of theology, rituals etc, they will be equally efficient in providing the necessary spiritual nourishment[4]. Religion, like food, is therefore also a matter of choice largely determined by the culture in which we grow up.

In the modern "global village", especially in cities, we see young people enjoying "ethnic" food from different parts of the world. It is dinner in a Chinese restaurant one day, lunch from an Italian carry-out stand the next day and snacking on falafel at a Middle East café yet another day. Their bodies tolerate all food equally well and are nourished equally well too. How wonderful it will be if our understanding and tolerance of religions grow to the extent that we can attend service in a church one day, pray in a mosque on the next, and worship at a temple on the following day! Indeed, the Indian mystic, Sri Ramakrishna, proved that this can be done with all due sincerity and respect towards all religions. The distinctions made today between religions are mostly superficial and not meaningful from a spiritual point of view. Like the infamous Berlin Wall, the barriers that exist between religions are artificial and unjustly divide people from people. Spirituality, on the contrary, unites us all.

In conclusion, the Vedāntic vision of spirit and matter makes it possible to more clearly understand the nature of science, spirituality and religion. We come to appreciate that each has a positive contribution to make in our lives and that they are not mutually incompatible. The material sciences, with their focus on matter and energy, bless us by making our worldly life more comfortable. Spirituality, the science of life and knowledge, blesses us individually with inner happiness and collectively with communal harmony. Religions, when practiced at their best, can serve the mankind by rendering spirituality more readily comprehensible and accessible to the average person.

---

4 Religions at times do tend to focus entirely on the symbolic aspects of their outer layers and lose sight of the core metaphysical spiritual truths. When this happens, it becomes a serious detriment to the credibility and effectiveness of that religion. In a now classic work, Alan Watts has very eloquently elaborated on this point in the context of the catholic Christian religion [11].

CHAPTER 2

Basics of Vedānta

"He who, like a juggler or a great Yogī, unrolls this universe just out of His own free will - the universe, which before creation remained unmanifest like the future tree in a seed, and has later on projected Himself out to be the world of endless variety, due to the delusory play of time and space, both products of Māyā- to Him, the Divine Teacher, Sri Dakshinamoorthy, is this prostration.

"Before its creation this entire field of experience (Jagat) was without any distinction such as we now experience in the play of the subject, object and their relationship. The distinction between the experiencer, the experienced, and the experiencing were not there in the One Infinite Homogeneous Truth which alone was before creation."

Swami Chinmayananda [12].

Whether it is science or Vedānta, its world-view must account for four fundamental, overarching, facts:

1) *A world (of gross matter and subtle mind stuff) exists.*
2) *That world is in constant change.*
3) *The changes are unpredictable.*
4) *There is knowledge of the above facts.*

Vedānta addresses all four facts whereas science, as it stands today, is nearly totally focused on the second fact. Science must be given due credit for discovering a great deal about the cause- effect chains underlying the changes we see in the world and for utilizing this knowledge to bring about changes that help human beings. But science has not fully accounted for the other three facts and faces significant challenges in trying to do so. This chapter is a quick summary of the Vedāntic world-view, introducing the basic Vedāntic terms and their definition. The concepts used in this book follow by and large the teachings of mainstream Vedānta, especially Advaita Vedānta. While not meant to be an exhaustive exposition on Vedānta, the overview will hopefully give sufficient grounding on the philosophy to enable readers to follow the discussions in the rest of the book. It should also help in another important respect: Some Vedāntic terms have multiple interpretations and it is useful to clarify at the very outset the particular interpretation followed in the book in order to avoid any misunderstanding[5]. Readers desiring a more in-depth understanding of Vedānta have a vast array of resources to choose from, such as books by Swami Chinmayananda [13]. People brought up in the West may find a good introduction to the science in the book *"Children of Immortal Bliss"* by Paul Hourihan [14].

The World-View Of Vedānta

The phenomenal world can be explained in terms of three Vedāntic concepts: the unmanifest Brahman and its manifestation as *Īśvara* and *Prakṛti*. We shall begin by examining each of these concepts in detail and their place in cosmos as well as in the life of individual creatures. The reader should find the Figures 2.1, 2.2, and 2.3 useful in visualizing and following the discussions.

Brahman: The concept most basic to Advaita Vedānta is that there always has been one, and only one, Reality, the Brahman. As the venerable Taittirīya Upaniṣad says [15]:

yato vā imāni bhūtāni jāyante, yena jātāni jīvanti
yatprayantyabhisamviśanti, tad vijijñāsasva, tat brahmeti.

"Whence indeed these beings are born; whereby, when born, they

5 For example, the terms māyā and *Prakṛti* are often used interchangeably. The terms *Mahat* and *Hiraṇyagarbha* are also considered synonymous by some. In this book, however, all these terms have been given a distinct meaning.

live; wherein, when departing, they enter; That seek thou to know. That is Brahman".

The many things that seemingly exist are only an appearance projected on this Reality. A common example given to illustrate this idea is that of a rope mistaken in bad light for a snake. The appearance of snake is projected on what really is a rope due to lack of adequate light or a defect in sight. Similarly, Brahman is mistaken for the world due to *Avidyā*, lack of correct knowledge of Truth. Brahman being the only Reality at all times, all things and beings that appear to exist are nothing but Brahman. This is represented in Fig 2.1 by enclosing all of macrocosm within the box labeled Brahman.

This Brahman, being the ground of all things including senses, intellect, and mind, is beyond the capability of senses to perceive or the ability of mind and intellect to fully comprehend. Therefore Brahman itself remains unmanifest. Since it is that which appears as all things that exist and as all sentient beings capable of knowledge, Brahman is of the nature of *Sat* (Existence) and *Cit* (Knowledge). Further, since everything that ever can be is in Brahman, there is nothing wanting, or lacking, in Brahman. Therefore it is also of the nature *ānanda* or Bliss. Thus, in short, Brahman is *sat-cit-ānanda*.

Māyā: The creative power because of which the *jagat* (world of things and beings) is superimposed on Brahman is called *Māyā*. This power is dependent on Brahman. Therefore *Māyā*, and the *jagat* projected with this power, does not exist independent of Brahman. *Māyā* is said to be "*triguṇātmikā*"; i.e. possessing of three qualities: *sattva, rajas,* and *tamas.* As a result, all things and beings of this universe also manifest these three qualities in their nature and behavior. At the most general level, the three qualities correspond to matter (*tamas*), energy (*rajas*) and knowledge (*sattva*). *Māyā* itself is unknowable, and is known only from its projective and delusory effects. We will see shortly what these effects are.

Īśvara: Brahman associated with the creative power of *Māyā*, is Īśvara, the "Creator" and "Controller". Īśvara creates or "projects" the world with Māyā's projective power and also exercises its Free will to control all things and beings of the world. Īśvara does not depend on any external matter, equipment, or intelligence to create the world. Thus Īśvara is simultaneously the material, efficient, and intelligent cause of creation. The analogy often used to illustrate this point is that of a dreamer projecting a dream world of people and things in own mind. Similarly, Īśvara is said to project the universe on the *Mahat*, the Cosmic Mind. But unlike a dream of an ordinary being, this Cosmic Dream is fully under the conscious control of Īśvara. Īśvara is never under the spell of *Māyā* or caught in the web of own cosmic dream[6].

Dream objects and dream activities are only apparently real and not absolutely real. They appear real during the time of dream itself, but on waking up are recognized as false. Similarly, as projections on the Cosmic Mind, the world is only apparently real [16]. They appear real to the individual beings which are under the spell of *Māyā*. When a jīva is "liberated" out of the hold of *Māyā* it "realizes" the false nature of the world and own true nature as Brahman. The *sat-cit-ānanda* nature of Brahman is also the essential nature of Īśvara. Besides, as the Creator and Controller, Īśvara is endowed with omniscience and omnipotence. Whereas Brahman itself is nirguṇa (without any attributes), Īśvara is considered as the abode of Infinite Knowledge and Infinite Virtue, attributes required for efficient and just administration of the creation. In this sense, Īśvara is Brahman with attributes (*saguṇa brahman*).

Mahābhūta (The Five Great Elements): First to be created are the five "Great Elements": Space, Air, Fire, Water, and Earth in that order. The elements are to begin with in "subtle form", implying that they cannot be seen, heard, touched, smelled, or tasted. However, the same elements can also become "gross" by undergoing a process of mutual combination and re-combination known as "*pañcīkaraṇaṁ*". In this gross state, elements do become perceptible. It can be noted that the last four of the great elements (namely, earth, water, air and fire) represent the four different modes in which we commonly encounter matter; namely the solid, liquid, gas, and plasma states. Space of course is that which accommodates matter in all these states.

All things and beings in creation evolve from these *mahābhūta*s. Subtle aspects of creation, such as mind and intellect, are created from the subtle form of the elements, while all physical objects seen in the universe arise from the five elements in their gross state. A detailed

6 Īśvara does "incarnate" in the world to play a role in world affairs from time to time. In these "*avatār*s", or incarnations, the role played is that of a fully realized being beyond māyā, here to teach jīvas the eternal Truth.

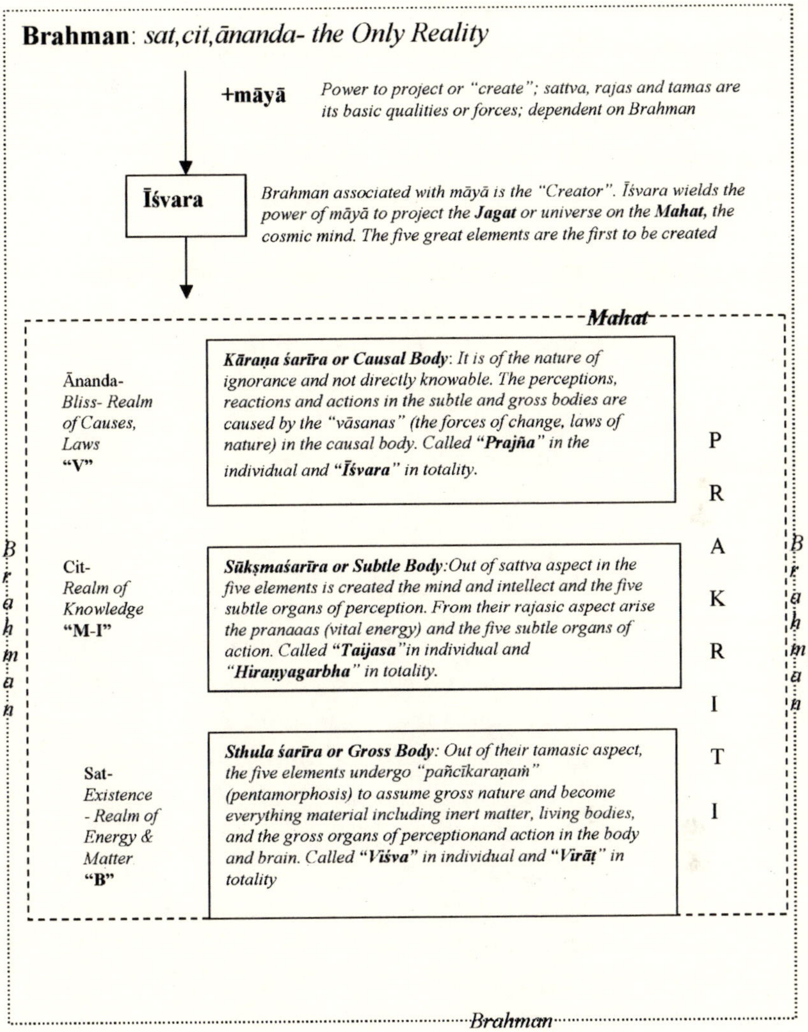

Brahman: sat,cit,ānanda- the Only Reality
+māyā
Power to project or "create"; sattva, rajas and tamas are its basic qualities or forces; dependent on Brahman
Īśvara
Brahman associated with māyā is the "Creator". Īśvara wields the power of māyā to project the Jagat or universe on the Mahat, the cosmic mind. The five great elements are the first to be created
Mahat
Ānanda- Bliss- Realm of Causes, Laws "V"
Kāraṇa śarīra or Causal Body: It is of the nature of ignorance and not directly knowable. The perceptions, reactions and actions in the subtle and gross bodies are caused by the "vāsanas" (the forces of change, laws of nature) in the causal body. Called "Prajña" in the individual and "Īśvara" in totality.
Cit- Realm of Knowledge "M-I"
Sūkṣmaśarīra or Subtle Body: Out of sattva aspect in the five elements is created the mind and intellect and the five subtle organs of perception. From their rajasic aspect arise the pranaaas (vital energy) and the five subtle organs of action. Called "Taijasa" in individual and "Hiraṇyagarbha" in totality.
Sat- Existence - Realm of Energy & Matter "B"
Sthula śarīra or Gross Body: Out of their tamasic aspect, the five elements undergo "pañcīkaraṇaṁ" (pentamorphosis) to assume gross nature and become everything material including inert matter, living bodies, and the gross organs of perceptionand action in the body and brain. Called "Viśva" in individual and "Virāṭ" in totality
PRAKRITI
Brahman
Brahman
Brahman

FIG 2.1: THE MACROCOSM

description of the process of this evolution is given in treatises such as *Tattvabodha* and is summarized below [17].

Prakṛti (Nature): The term *Prakṛti* as used in this text denotes all things and beings of the world as well as the laws governing their behavior. It roughly corresponds to the commonly used concept of "Nature" by which one means both the objects of nature and the natural laws they are subject to. The objects of Prakṛti can be "things" which have only a material "body" or they could be a "being" ("jīva") which have a sentient "mind-intellect" besides possibly a physical body. Whereas Brahman and Īśvara are unitary entities admitting no division or parts, Prakṛti incorporates a multiplicity of things and beings within herself. She hosts the world of plurality that appears to arise from the Non-Dual Brahman. Fig 2.1 shows the three macrocosmic aspects of Prakṛti, called the gross, subtle, and causal bodies, which broadly correspond to the *sat-cit-ānanda* nature of Brahman and Īśvara. Following a notation popularized by Gurudev Swami Chinmayananda we denote these three components by the symbols B, M-I, and V for reasons that will become clear soon.

"B" –The Total Body- Realm of Gross Matter : The totality of the realm of gross matter is called "*Virāṭ*" or the cosmic body. It includes the stars, the galaxies, the earth with all its life forms and in short everything perceived and perceivable. *Virāṭ* is, as it were, the manifest "body" of the Creator itself. The physical body (*sthūla śarīra*) of every individual being, including all its gross organs of action and perception, is part of this totality.

This physical world, as pointed out earlier, has evolved out of the great elements in their gross state and therefore constitutes the entire perceptible universe of matter and energy. The "*sat*", or existence, aspect of Brahman is reflected in the physical universe.

"M-I" –The Total Mind- Realm of Subtle Matter: *Tattvabodha* teaches us that the instruments of knowledge, namely the mind-intellect complex of all sentient beings, have evolved out of the "*sattva*" aspect of the five great elements. Since this evolution occurs with the elements in their subtle state (i.e. without undergoing *pañcīkaraṇaṁ*), the mind-intellect complex is called "subtle body" or *sūkṣma śarīra*. The subtle body in a sentient individual consists of the *manas* or mind that mulls and questions, the *buddhi* or intellect that analyzes and determines, the *ahaṁkāra* or ego giving rise to the notion of individuality, and *citta* or memory. Further it also includes the five *jñānendriya*s or subtle sensory organs, namely the "inner" faculties of seeing, hearing, tasting, smelling, and touching.

The subtle body additionally includes the "*prāṇa maya kośa*"or the vital energy sheath and the five *karmendriya*s or subtle organs of action evolving out of the "*rajas*" aspect of the five great elements. Befitting their "*raja*sic" origin, these faculties of the subtle body are externally manifested in the autonomous physiological functions such as breathing, circulation etc as well as the functions of the five gross organs of action, namely hands, legs, mouth, genitals and anus.

A question might arise at this point regarding the precise function of the subtle organs of action and perception vis-à-vis their gross counterparts. Even though Vedāntic text books do not seem to explicitly address this question, the very fact of postulating the "subtle vs. gross" division carries with it a suggestion: It is these subtle organs that mediate between gross physical brain and the subtle mind. More specifically, the subtle sense organs translate the gross electrochemical activities of the brain into subtle "experiencable" sensory perceptions. For example, the stimuli received through the physical eyes activate the neurons in a part of the brain responsible for vision. These electrochemical activities are interpreted by the "subtle eyes" as a visual image and it is this interpreted or "computed" image that the subtle mind can see. Thus, the subtle sense organs make the brain-to-mind transition possible. The subtle organs of action achieve the reverse mind-to-brain transition. They code the intentions (*saṁkalpa*) of the mind into physical commands for the brain to execute through the gross organs of action.

The totality of subtle bodies is called *Hiraṇyagarbha*, sometimes translated as the "Golden Egg" or the "Golden Womb". The mind of an individual is the repository of all potential *saṁkalpas* (intentions) that the individual can entertain, some of which turn into actual intentions and then into actions. This, we might call, is the process of creation at an individual level. In the same way *Hiraṇyagarbha*, or the total mind-intellect, is the womb which holds all potential *saṁkalpas* at the macrocosmic level. Some of these *saṁkalpas* get actually expressed as the divine will to set the course for the creation as a whole.

Mahat, the cosmic mind and *Hiraṇyagarbha* the total mind-intellect, as defined above are distinct, though not all Vedānta texts may agree. Some texts identify *Hiraṇyagarbha* with the cosmic mind. However it is useful to draw a distinction between the two. The *Mahat* was earlier compared to the mind of a dreamer, the dreamer here being Īśvara. The dream itself can contain individuals each with own mind. The totality of these individual dream minds is the *Hiraṇyagarbha*. It no doubt has no existence independent of the *Mahat*, the dreamers mind, yet it is not quite the same as *Mahat*. As shown in Fig 2.1, *Mahat* includes *Hiraṇyagarbha* as well as the *Virāṭ* and Īśvara aspects of Totality.

The "*cit*", or knowledge, aspect of Brahman is predominant in the Subtle Body, since it is the conscious Mind-Intellect of the individual that knows.

"V" –The Total Vāsanas- The Realm of Causal Laws: Both the gross matter and subtle mind are subject to incessant change. Science has investigated competently and comprehensively the changes affecting gross matter and has discovered many natural laws that explain the same. But success of science in understanding mind has been relatively limited. Vedānta on the other hand has focused more on mind than on matter. It posits that the forces behind the activities of mind are the "*vāsanas*" or tendencies deep within the individual being. The vāsanas are in the inner most core of the individual personality called the Causal Body or *Kāraṇa śarīra*. It is called the "causal body" since it is the cause of activities of both the subtle and gross bodies.

In Swami Chinmayanandaji's notation, the causal body is denoted by the letter "V", standing for *vāsanas*. Vāsanas are uncountable and numerous, but each is an admixture of the three primary "*guṇas*", or qualities, found throughout Prakṛti, namely *sattva, rajas,* and *tamas*. As we will see in later chapters, vāsanas play a very basic role in spirituality. The goal of spiritual effort (*sādhanas*) is the eventual elimination of all vāsanas. The seekers are advised to initially reduce predominantly *tamasic* and *rajasic* vāsanas and replacing them with more *sāttvic* ones.

There is no conceptual reason why we cannot consider the natural laws such as gravity and nuclear forces affecting gross bodies also as vāsanas. With this understanding vāsanas are seen as the cause behind the evolution of both the subtle and gross realms. The causal realm which includes the vāsanas is also often called the "bliss sheath", *ānandamaya kośa* and represents the "*ānanda*", or the Bliss, aspect of Brahman. For Īśvara, creation is an act arising out of Bliss (as opposed to ordinary jīvas which toil for happiness). Therefore, *ānanda* can be regarded as the primordial vāsana that launches the cosmos[7]. Divine Creation is an ongoing process and the same *ānanda* continues to operate at all times in creation in the guise of all vāsanas. This raises an interesting question.

Why do the things and beings of Prakṛti seem to meekly follow vāsanas and the so-called "laws of nature"?

---

7 This statement only implies that the two concepts, ānanda and vāsana, are related. It is not implied that *ānanda* is a vāsana. Īśvara, of the nature of Infinite Bliss, has no vāsanas to be satisfied through creation. The chapter on Vāsanas will elaborate on this point.

Carrots or Sticks?

We can take either the "carrot view" or the "stick view" in answering the above question. Taking the "stick" view, we may say that objects of Prakṛti are *forced* by something to follow the vāsanas. The term "*forces* of nature" that is frequently used in this context carries this stick implication. But who wields the stick? Is it Īśvara? Do creatures follow the laws out of fear of the Creator? True, some religions and even Vedānta does use this imagery at times. However, it puts Īśvara, known more for compassion, in an unsavory light.

The "carrot" view is more appealing: We say that things and beings follow "natural laws" because the laws only codify what is their *svabhāva* or own nature and because there is an element of "*ānanda*" or happiness in following what is in one's nature. The truth of this view is more evident in the case of sentient beings which do act seeking happiness. When following the vāsanas, jīvas are in fact "satisfying the vāsanas" which leads to *ānanda* or happiness by temporarily reducing the vāsana pressure. This process has been explained by Acharya Vidyaranya Swami in his well known Advaita Vedānta text *Pañcadaśi* [18]. Where inert matter is concerned, it is of course difficult to assert that they seek happiness by following natural laws. However we note that some basic principles of physics- such as "principle of least action" in dynamics or the universal tendency in systems to seek a state of equilibrium where all "forces" (vāsanas) mutually cancel out- suggest that inert systems can also be viewed as acting in such a way as to reduce their vāsana pressures.

The "carrot view" is also more consistent with the term "*ānandamaya kośa*" (sheath of bliss) used for the causal body. We will generally adhere to the "carrot interpretation" in this book.

Inter-Connectedness at the Causal Level

There are two significant features to note about the Causal Realm. The first of these is that the scriptures identify the total Causal Realm with Īśvara itself. Bhagavad Gītā says that Īśvara, seated in "heart" (*hṛt*) of all beings, controls them, heart here signifying, as it does throughout Vedānta, the psychic center of our being [19]. On the other hand, the text *Māṇḍukya Kārika* identifies the location of *Prājña* as the "heart-space" in the individual. Taken together, these two statements suggest that Īśvara resides in each jīva as *Prājña*. What our scriptures have to say about *Prājña* and heart-space is very revealing. The *Māṇḍukya* extols *Prājña* thus:

"This is the Lord of all; this is the inner controller; this is the source of all. And, this is that from which all things originate and in which they finally dissolve themselves. [20]"

This is indeed remarkable. *Prājña,* the individual, is being praised here in this venerable Upaniṣad in terms one would reserve for *Īśvara,* the Totality, itself. This, if we are not mistaken, speaks to an awesome truth: At the deepest innermost level of each being, there is no separate individuality, but only totality. Unlike the gross and subtle realms, the causal body is one undivided whole, and not a collection of disparate bodies. That is, all things and beings are inter-connected at the causal level. Other schools of thought have also arrived at similar observations. In his work titled "*The Archetypes and the Collective Unconscious*", the noted psychologist C. Jung states that "the deeper 'layers' of the psyche lose their individual uniqueness as they retreat farther and farther into darkness" [21]. Quantum physicists will tend to agree with this conjecture too. One startling implication of their theory is what Einstein dubbed as "spooky action at a distance". This is a phenomenon wherein a pair of elementary particles co-ordinate their (otherwise unpredictable) behavior and act in perfect unison even when they are galaxies apart. It is as though the two particles can read each other's mind instantaneously! Bizarre as it sounds, this phenomenon has been experimentally confirmed.

Laws are necessarily universal and not individual; to that extent, it makes sense to suggest that the causal body is one whole. However, we recognize that the manner in which a law affects an individual does depend on the characteristics of that individual- e.g. gravitational law is universal, but its effect on an object depends on the mass of the object. In the same way, the laws of vāsana are universal but their effect on an individual depends on the "vāsana make-up" of the individual. These ideas will be elaborated in Chapter 8 where a mathematical theory of vāsanas is developed.

A second important characteristic of the causal body noted by Vedānta is that it is, at the individual level, of the nature of ignorance. The causal body is enveloped in darkness in the sense that it is beyond jīva's perception. A jīva can, and usually is, aware of the state of its gross and subtle bodies, but not that of its causal body. The causal body is, to borrow a term from psychology, "sub-conscious". Prakṛti's vāsanas and Īśvara together control the individual from the causal body, a realm not accessible to the individual's awareness. The implications of this Īśvara-Prakṛti Paradigm will be the subject of the next chapter.

Jīvas And The Microcosm

So far we have used the terms "beings" and "jīvas" to indicate the individual sentient entities in Prakṛti, namely entities like you and me which act consciously. The word "soul" is sometimes used as an approximate translation of "jīva", but this is not totally satisfactory and hence we will use the Sanskrit term itself. At this point, we need to spell out more clearly what a jīva is, its origin, its structural make-up, and how it differs from insentient things, or objects, of the world.

Insentient objects have gross body and associated vāsanas, but do not have a subtle body. For example, individual 2 in Fig. 2.2 refers to an object. A jīva, on the other hand, is a microcosmic replica of the macrocosm shown in Fig 2.1. The jīva too possesses three bodies: a gross body consisting of the physical body, external sense organs and organs of action; a subtle body consisting of the mind, intellect, ego, memory, the subtle sense organs and the subtle organs of action; and a causal body consisting of the vāsanas (Fig. 2.3). But there is something in this microcosm that is not a feature of

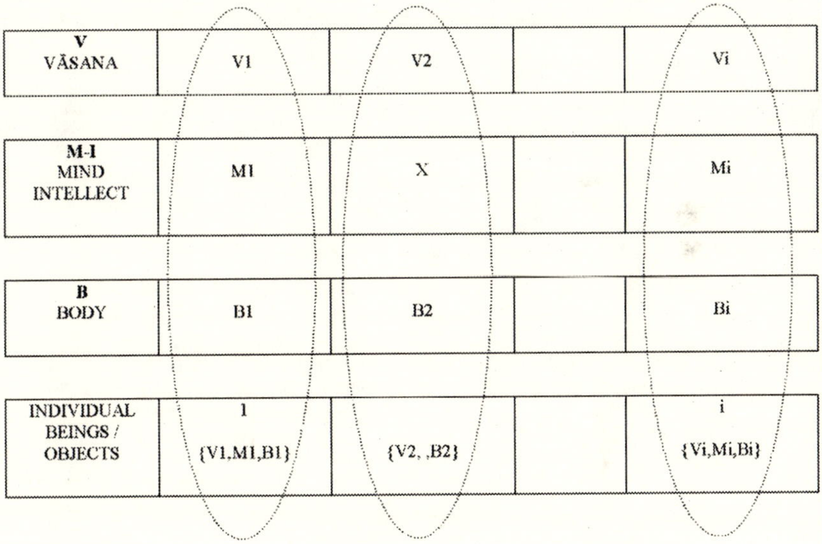

INDIVIDUAL 1: {V1, M1, B1}-*This is a sentient jīva with mind-intellect M1*
INDIVIDUAL 2: {V2, , B2}- *M and I being absent this is an insentient object.*
INDIVIDUAL i: {Vi, Mi, Bi} *Another jīva*

Insentient objects have gross bodies, but no subtle body.
Jīvas are sentient beings with subtle body and usually gross body. Both jīvas and objects have associated vāsanas (causal body) that define their behavior.

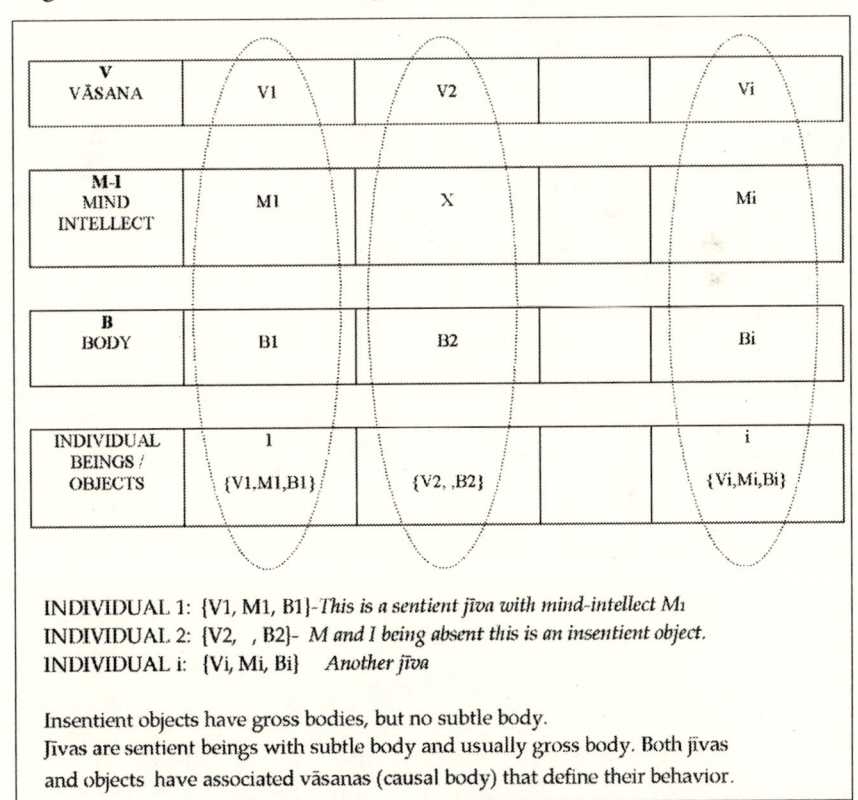

Fig. 2.2: Prakrti Consisting of Individual Things and Beings

the macrocosmic totality. We are referring to the very basic problems of life lived as a jīva, complete with its many joys and grief. Practical spirituality is all about providing a measure of relief to the suffering jīva. Jīvas therefore rightfully occupy the central stage in any discussion on spirituality. The problem of suffering does not exist at the macrocosmic level. Salvation or liberation that religious traditions hold out as their supreme promise applies to the jīvas and not to their Creator.

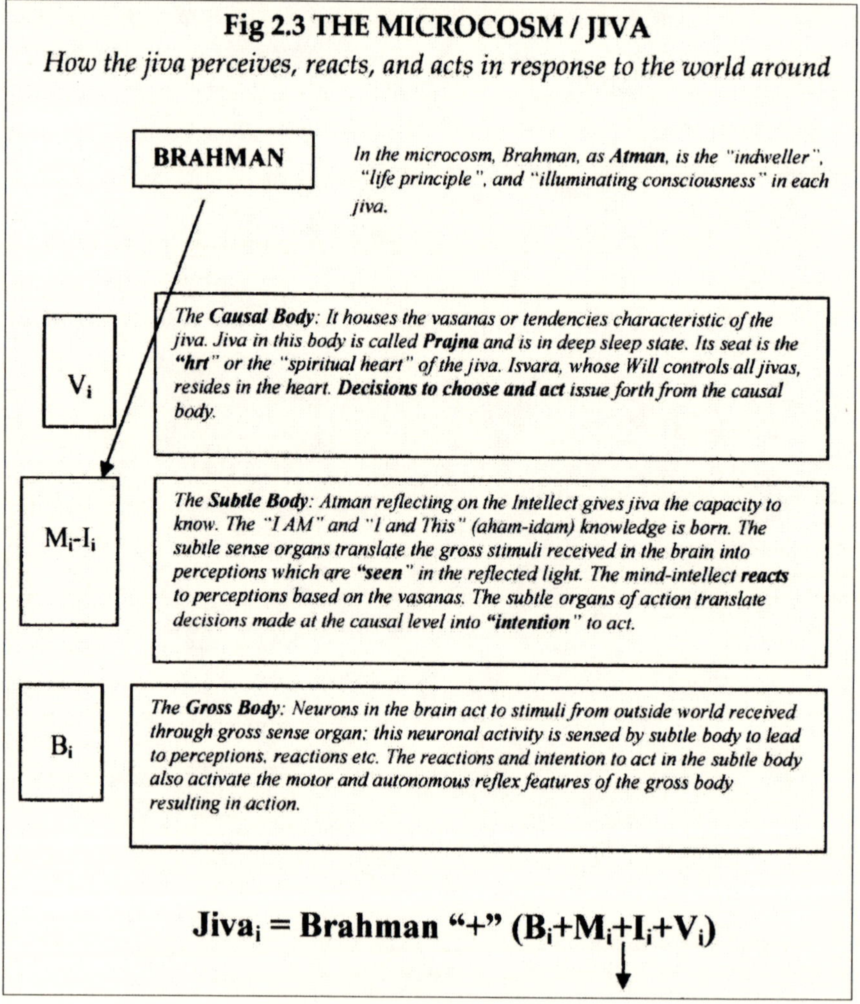
Fig 2.3 THE MICROCOSM / JIVA
How the jiva perceives, reacts, and acts in response to the world around
BRAHMAN
In the microcosm, Brahman, as Atman, is the "indweller", "life principle", and "illuminating consciousness" in each jiva.
V$_i$
The Causal Body: It houses the vasanas or tendencies characteristic of the jiva. Jiva in this body is called Prajna and is in deep sleep state. Its seat is the "hrt" or the "spiritual heart" of the jiva. Isvara, whose Will controls all jivas, resides in the heart. Decisions to choose and act issue forth from the causal body.
M$_i$-I$_i$
The Subtle Body: Atman reflecting on the Intellect gives jiva the capacity to know. The "I AM" and "I and This" (aham-idam) knowledge is born. The subtle sense organs translate the gross stimuli received in the brain into perceptions which are "seen" in the reflected light. The mind-intellect reacts to perceptions based on the vasanas. The subtle organs of action translate decisions made at the causal level into "intention" to act.
B$_i$
The Gross Body: Neurons in the brain act to stimuli from outside world received through gross sense organ: this neuronal activity is sensed by subtle body to lead to perceptions, reactions etc. The reactions and intention to act in the subtle body also activate the motor and autonomous reflex features of the gross body resulting in action.
Jiva$_i$ = Brahman "+" (B$_i$+M$_i$+I$_i$+V$_i$)

Fig. 2.3 The Microcosm / Jīva

What is this jīva? How does it get its sentiency and its ability to know and experience the world? What, and why, is its suffering?

The gross, subtle, and causal bodies of a jīva are part of Prakṛti, as indicated in Fig 2.2. Yet in one important respect a jīva is beyond Prakṛti also. The jīva is sentient and this sentiency is not attributable to Prakṛti. As per Vedānta, Brahman is the one and only Conscious Principle and jīvas owe their sentiency to that Principle. Vedāntic texts describe the process by which jīvas beget their sentiency thus: The Brahman (or specifically the Consciousness aspect of Brahman), gets enchanted, as it were, by the objects of Its own creation in Prakṛti. It then "enters" them thus giving rise to sentient jīva*s*. This delusion, because of which the Consciousness identifies with the otherwise insentient creations in Prakṛti, is the origin of individual jīvas. This is somewhat like a child playing with her dolls. In a make-believe game, the child engages in a lively conversation with the doll. She does this of course by lending her own voice to the doll. In the language of Vedānta, the child has thus "entered" the insentient doll to give it life and voice. The Vedāntic texts *Kapila Gītā* and *Yoga Vasiṣṭa* describe the process thus:

guṇairvicitrā sṛjatīm sarūpāḥ prakṛtiṁ prajāḥ
Vilokya mumuhe sadyaḥ sa iha jñāna gūhayā

"Prakṛti with its qualities creates a variety of beings similar to itself. The Lord/Self having seen the creation got (as it were) completely deluded through veiling of knowledge" [22].

sa tathā bhūta evātmā svayam anya ivollasan
jīvatāṁ upayātīva mananāt sthūlatāṁ gataḥ

"Through the process of thinking, that very Self, as though becoming gross and appearing different from itself, attains to the state of the individual soul by itself." [23]

The above truth applies to all jīvas. It is our true birth story! Each of us is that Self which has presently identified with our respective body-mind-intellect because of delusion. The same Self is the real thing (*sat vastu*) in each of us, our B-M-I being a mere changing projection in the Cosmic Mind. Release from the jīvahood is possible only when the delusion ends and we realize our real nature.

The delusion Vedānta talks about is not unlike what happens in a jīva's dream. The objects and people seen in the dream are projections in the mind of the dreaming jīva. But the jīva is ignorant of the fact that these are only dream objects and people, and hence takes them all to be real. Because of this mistake, the people seen in a dream act as if they are sentient, when in fact their sentiency is that of the dreamer only.

Pratibiṁba Vāda- The Theory of Reflected Consciousness

Other Vedāntic texts explain that it is the *reflection* of the Pure Consciousness on the intellect that makes a being sentient [24]. In other words, Pure Consciousness endows the intellect with capacity to cognize, without being directly involved in this process.

This process of cognition is often explained by Gurudev Sw. Chinmayananda and other teachers, using the analogy of sunlight reflected off a bucket of water (Fig 2.4.) Imagine a room totally dark except for a narrow pencil of sunlight streaming through a chink in one of the walls. This light falls on a bucket of water kept on the floor, making the water surface luminous. Light reflects off the shimmering water sending out a diffuse beam of light revealing the objects in the otherwise dark room. This simple picture serves as an apt analogy for the process of cognition. The bright sun shining outside represents the Brahman. Sun is self-shining and thus is an appropriate symbol for the self-luminous Brahman. The bucket of water inside the room represents the individual jīva. The bucket is the gross body of the jīva while the water is its subtle body or M-I. The bucket itself has no reflective capacity, but the water inside it does.

Reflecting the light of Consciousness, the mind-intellect complex sends out through the opening in the gross body (namely eyes, ears and other gross sensory organs) the "beam of awareness" in which the objects of the world are revealed to it.

The reflection of Consciousness on the M-I is referred to as *cidābhāsa*. In the above analogy, the sun is not directly illuminating the objects inside the room, but it is the reflected beam off the water which does so. Similarly, Consciousness does not directly cognize anything other than itself. It is in the reflected light of Consciousness that the jīva's intellect cognizes other objects and beings of the Prakṛti. The "seer-seen" duality of "I" (*ahaṁ*), and "the world" (*idaṁ*), and the "I AM" notion are born as a result of this cognition. This is at the root of a jīva's individuality.

This is verily the origin of the jīva, and the beginning of its worldly life of suffering known as *saṁsāra*.

The Complex Jīva

The above characterization shows that a jīva is part Prakṛti and part Brahman. Its three bodies (causal, subtle and gross) are part of Prakṛti, but the sentiency because of which it qualifies as a jīva is in reality Brahman only. Now, it is true that even the Prakṛti and the jīva's bodies

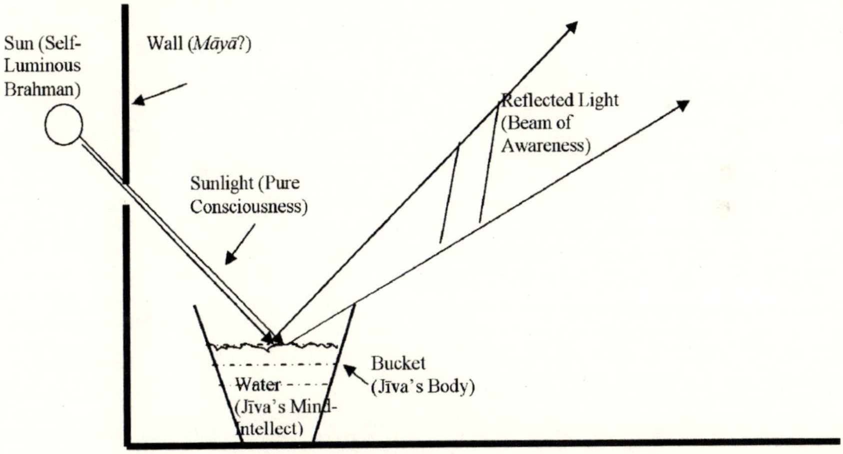

Fig. 2.4: Reflected Consciousness

are Brahman. The difference is that Prakṛti, being the product of *Māyā*'s projective power, is only apparently real. On the other hand, that knowing principle in the jīva, namely Brahman, because of which it is sentient and has the knowledge "I AM", is absolutely real. One may represent this hybrid "part Prakṛti and part Brahman" nature of a jīva symbolically as

$$\text{Jīva}_i = \text{Brahman} + \text{Prakṛti}_i$$

where the "+" sign denotes identification of Brahman with the "i-th" being in Prakṛti[8]. Brahman, in this aspect of its association with the

8 Alternatively, the "+" sign indicates superimposition (*adhyāropa*) of Prakrti_i on Brahman. The bulk of the body of spiritual teachings in Vedānta, and to a degree in all religions, has to do with the reverse process of how a jīva may realize Brahman by gaining release from B-M-I identification:

$$\text{jīva}_i - \text{Prakrti}_i = \text{Brahman}$$

where the symbol "–" signifies the process of jīva's dissociation from B-M-I through spiritual practices.

jīva is generally addressed as the Self, or Ātman. Every jīva is thus a complex entity that has the same real part (Brahman or Ātman) and an imaginary (i.e. apparently real) part, namely, the individual Body-Mind-Intellect which is part of the overall Prakṛti.

The B-M-I Notation

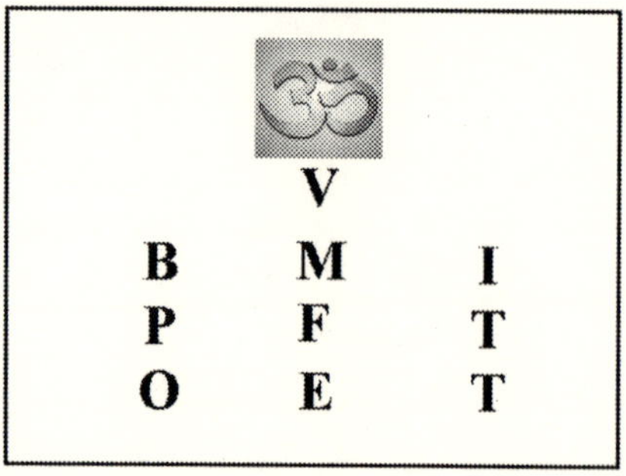

The "B-M-I Chart" shown to the left was developed by Gurudev Swami Chinmayananda as an aid to communicate these Vedāntic concepts efficiently. It portrays the jīva, its gross, subtle, and causal bodies, the world and the Brahman, all in one simple chart. The "OM" symbol at the top stands for Brahman, which is the real nature of the jīva. The letter **V** stands for **vāsana**s and the causal body. **B,M,I** in the next row stand for **B**ody, **M**ind, **I**ntellect and thus incorporate both the gross body (**B**) and the subtle body (**M-I**). The jīva is represented in the next row by **P,F,T** standing respectively for **P**erceiver, **F**eeler, and **T**hinker. The last row of letters stands for **O**bjects, **E**motions, and **T**houghts. Taken together O-E-T represents the physical and mental world.

The chart conveys simply the many ideas discussed so far. OM, the Self, enlivening the B-M-I gives them the sentiency to perceive objects of the world and perform actions, feel emotions, and think thoughts. Self identifying itself with the actions, perceptions, feelings and thoughts generates the notion of Perceiver-Feeler-Thinker, which is the jīva. The actions and reactions of the jīva vary depending on the individual vāsanas V. We shall frequently use this B-M-I notation throughout the book.

Experience And Experiencing

The *cit* or consciousness aspect of Brahman "reflecting" on M - I of a jīva gives rise to the illusion of a sentient, knowing, individual "enjoying" (i.e. experiencing) the world. As the Gītā says it

"puruṣaḥ prakṛtistho hi bhuṅkte prakṛtijān guṇān" [25]

meaning, *"Puruṣaḥ, seated in Prakṛti, enjoys the world."*

Life is a continuous stream of experiences; in fact Swami Chinmayananda sees it appropriate to expand the very word "life" to mean "Limitless, Incessant, Flow of Experiences". To be alive is to be experiencing. The terms "experience" and "experiencing" are to be frequently encountered in our discussions and it is necessary that we explore their meaning a bit more deeply.

The word "experience" in English is both a noun and a verb. As online dictionary.com defines it, as a noun the word experience means *"the totality of the cognitions given by perception; all that is perceived, understood, and remembered"*. As a verb it means *"to have experience of; meet with; undergo; feel"* and "Experiencing" is its present continuous form. Experiencing is always in the present moment. The act of experiencing may leave an impression in the M-I of the jīva as a "memory" of that experience. Being in the M-I, this memory is an object of O-E-T (albeit a "mental" object) and hence itself can be recalled and experienced at a later time.

The Experiencer, experienced, and experiencing are collectively called in Vedānta as the *"tripuṭi"* or basic triad. Experiencing is the result of an experiencer making contact with an object in O-E-T, the realm of the experienced. The "beam of awareness" shown in Fig. 2.4 makes the contact possible. What ensues following such a contact is a set of complex interactions among the causal, subtle, and gross bodies of the jīva. The interactions are best understood with the help of the schematic in Fig. 2.5.

Perception, Reaction, and Action

Perception, reaction, and action are the three phases of each experience a jīva undergoes as a result of its contacts with the world. On each contact with the world we first "see" the world, then react to what we see with pleasure or pain, and finally take actions deemed necessary to avoid pain or realize pleasure. We perceive the world through the sensory organs of eyes, ears etc and react to what we perceive depending on our likes and dislikes. Fig. 2.5 shows in detail how these two phases involve our gross sense organs, subtle sense organs, brain, causal body, vāsanas, and the subtle body. Similarly, our actions in response to contacts with the world involve the gross and subtle organs of action, subtle body, vāsanas, brain, and the gross body.

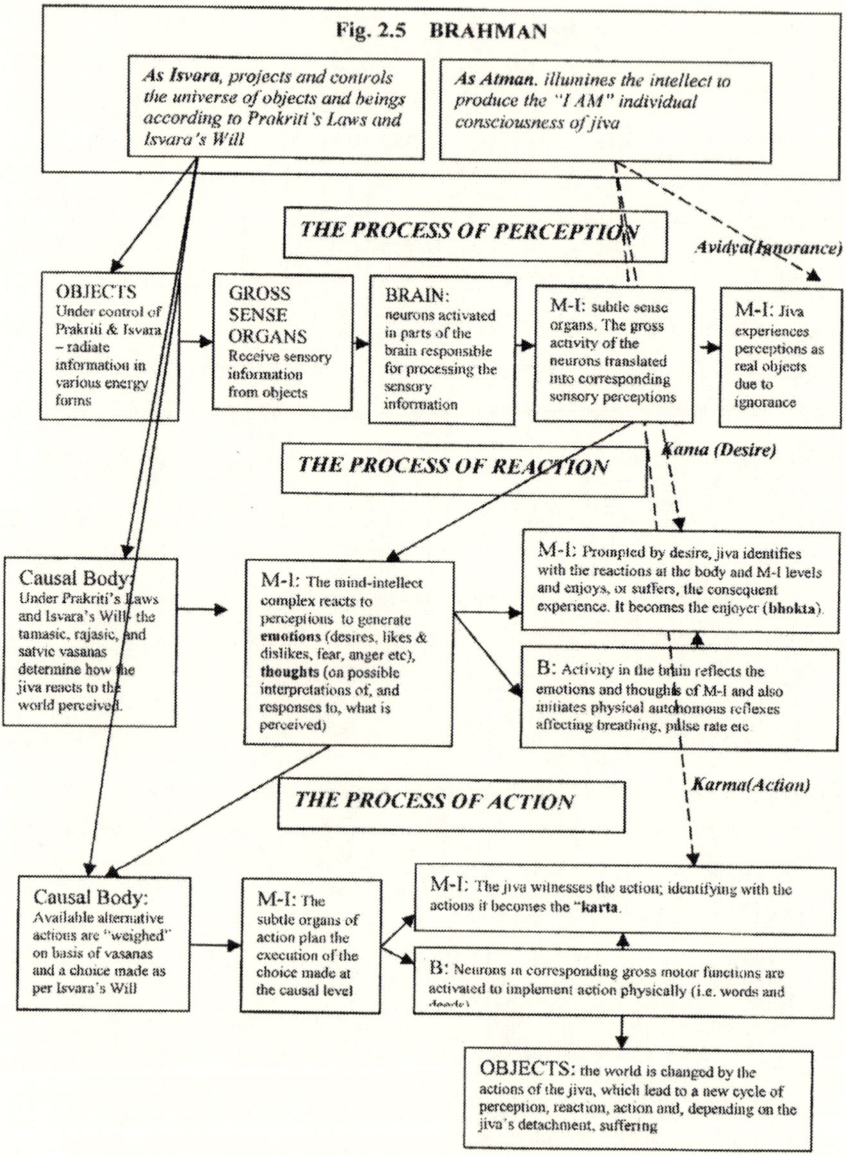
Fig. 2.5 BRAHMAN
As Isvara, projects and controls the universe of objects and beings according to Prakriti's Laws and Isvara's Will
As Atman, illumines the intellect to produce the "I AM" individual consciousness of jiva
THE PROCESS OF PERCEPTION
Avidya(Ignorance)
OBJECTS Under control of Prakriti & Isvara – radiate information in various energy forms
GROSS SENSE ORGANS Receive sensory information from objects
BRAIN: neurons activated in parts of the brain responsible for processing the sensory information
M-I: subtle sense organs. The gross activity of the neurons translated into corresponding sensory perceptions
M-I: Jiva experiences perceptions as real objects due to ignorance
THE PROCESS OF REACTION
Kama (Desire)
Causal Body: Under Prakriti's Laws and Isvara's Will the tamasic, rajasic, and satvic vasanas determine how the jiva reacts to the world perceived.
M-I: The mind-intellect complex reacts to perceptions to generate emotions (desires, likes & dislikes, fear, anger etc), thoughts (on possible interpretations of, and responses to, what is perceived)
M-I: Prompted by desire, jiva identifies with the reactions at the body and M-I levels and enjoys, or suffers, the consequent experience. It becomes the enjoyer (bhokta).
B: Activity in the brain reflects the emotions and thoughts of M-I and also initiates physical autonomous reflexes affecting breathing, pulse rate etc.
THE PROCESS OF ACTION
Karma(Action)
Causal Body: Available alternative actions are "weighed" on basis of vasanas and a choice made as per Isvara's Will
M-I: The subtle organs of action plan the execution of the choice made at the causal level
M-I: The jiva witnesses the action; identifying with the actions it becomes the "karta.
B: Neurons in corresponding gross motor functions are activated to implement action physically (i.e. words and deeds)
OBJECTS: the world is changed by the actions of the jiva, which lead to a new cycle of perception, reaction, action and, depending on the jiva's detachment, suffering

Fig. 2.5: Process of Perception, Reaction and Action

Robots can also interact with the world and perform actions in response to inputs received from the world. They could be programmed to simulate "likes and dislikes" for objects around them. Thus, many of the processes shown in Fig. 2.5 could also apply to an automaton. What is special to jīvas in Fig. 2.5 is the Ātman because of which they are aware of, and witness to, own perceptions, reactions, and actions. A jīva's life is what it is precisely because of this awareness. Robots do not have this faculty and therefore they cannot be said to experience anything.

The Three Knots of Māyā

The sentiency we have is no doubt a divine blessing, but indirectly can be also a cause of problems in ordinary jīvas. As a general rule, the sentient jīva is not merely a witness to the three internal processes described above; unfortunately it also gets identified with them. This is unfortunate because it is the cause of the jīva's bondage and suffering. In Fig. 2.5 we show the three fetters binding the Ātman to the world by the lines marked "*Avidyā*" (ignorance), "*Kāma*" (desire), and "*Karma*" (actions). In Vedānta, these three ties of *Māyā* are called as "*granṭhis*" (knots). They tie by a knot, as it were, the Ātman, to what the jīva sees, reacts, and acts. Not recognizing the one Brahman that appears both as the seen and the seer, the jīva experiences the duality of "I, the seer" (*ahaṁ*), and "this, the seen" (*idaṁ*). From this is borne reaction to the seen. Identifying with the pleasant and unpleasant reactions, the jīva eats the sweet and bitter fruits of its experiences and has the notion of "I enjoy" or "I suffer". Similarly, identifying with the actions performed it has the notion of "I do".

The effects of the three knots may be explained with the "rope-and-snake" example. A person encountering a length of rope may mistake it for a snake in bad light or any other condition causing poor vision. The perception of snake in this case is due to ignorance (*avidyā)* of the fact that it is only a rope. Reacting to the sight of the snake, the person feels fear and aversion. This reaction arises from the person's desire (*kāma*) for survival or protection of own life. The person thereupon acts to minimize potential harm to himself, by running away from the snake or by beating the snake. The action (*karma*) taken depend again on the jīva's vāsanas. In this example, the jīva, bound by the three knots of *māyā*, goes through vivid experiences of seeing a snake, being fearful, and running for dear life.

This is what happens in general in all our encounters with the world. A jīva is aware of what it sees and, by this alone, no real harm is done. But because of ignorance, we forget that whatever is perceived is unreal and only a superposition on the Brahman, just as the snake is falsely superimposed on the rope. Taking the seen to be real, we fall victim to its attraction or repulsion, as the case may be. What follows are actions either to acquire and enjoy what is liked or run away from what is disliked. *Avidyā* (ignorance) is thus at the root of *kāma* and *karma*.

This teaching is brought out beautifully in the following two verses from Kapila Gītā as commented on and translated by Swami Tejomayananda [26]:

Evaṁ parābhidhyānena kartṛtvaṁ prakrteḥ pumān
karmasu kriyamāṇeṣu guṇairātmani manyate
tadasya samsṛtir bandhaḥ pāratantryaṁ ca tatkṛtaṁ
bhavatyakartur īśasya sākṣino nirvṛtātmanaḥ

"Thus, by brooding over the other (Prakṛti), man assumes doer ship of actions that are actually done by qualities of Prakṛti.

That doership causes bondage of saṁsāra and enslaves this non-doer, witness, and peaceful Self, the Lord."

Eating (Bhoga) vs. Witnessing (Yoga)

The basic technique for alleviating suffering therefore consists in snipping these three ties off, as indicated in Fig. 2.5 by the scissors. *Karma yoga* (the path of action) teaches us how to act while reducing desires and desire-driven actions, and thus overcome the effects of *kāma* and *karma* bondages. But one must also finally destroy the root cause of *avidyā* itself through Knowledge (*Jñāna*) and Goodness or Love (*Bhakti*). Casting these ties off, and having firmly understood that all the perceptive, reactive, and active processes of the gross and subtle bodies are powered by the laws of Prakṛti and the Will of Īśvara, the jīva no more entertains egoistic notions of "I do" or "I enjoy". Instead, it merely witnesses the world within and without, while remaining established in the peaceful Self.

The jīva has thus two basic options available to it every time it makes contact with the world: to "eat" the experience resulting from the contact or to merely "witness" the experience: the "*bhoga*" vs. "*yoga*" choice. In the former case, the jīva is attached to the perceptive, reactive, and active processes through the three ties of *avidyā, kāma*, and *karma*. Consequently it "eats" whatever joy or sorrow that experience offers. In the second case, the jīva, by its will power, overcomes the vāsana pressures and stays as a detached witness to that experience.

This choice to be a "*bhogī*" or a "*yogī*" is available to a jīva at all times it confronts the world. How it makes this choice moment after moment determines its spiritual evolution. The mathematical model of spiritual evolution proposed in this book is a straight forward adaptation of this Vedāntic principle.

Spiritual Evolution of the Jīva and Liberation

The process of perception, reaction, and action, arising out of a jīva's contact with objects in O-E-T, goes on continuously during the life of a jīva, with the exception of periods of deep sleep. As a result, the jīva experiences the world in numerous ways. Eating, sleeping, partying, romancing, talking, traveling, sightseeing, meditating, exercising...... there is truly no end to the variety of experiences a jīva can have. But are they all really different or is there something common to them all?

Bhagavad Gītā as usual has a simple answer which is summed up thus [27]:

mātrā sparśāstu kaunteya śītoṣṇa sukhadukhadāḥ
āgamāpāyinonityāstāṁstitikṣasva bhārata"

Contact of the senses with sense objects produces, says Gītā, "heat and cold, joy and grief". The bottom line of every experience is one of these "*dvandas*", or pairs of opposites, indicated by the words such as "heat and cold" and "joy and grief". We either like our experience or dislike it based on our "vāsana makeup". Every experience of life ultimately boils down to a state somewhere between extreme joy and extreme grief. A jīva lives thus continuously tossed between these opposite states. This is *saṁsāra*, a life of "suffering". Experiencing joy and grief through contact with sense objects is termed in Vedānta as "suffering"; the concept of suffering also forms the bedrock of Buddhist philosophy. The choice of this term is not to deny the existence of moments of happiness in worldly life, but to point out that such moments are sure to be followed by moments of unhappiness sooner or later in a world where nothing is permanent. Even while enjoying the sunshine of good times, the uncertainty surrounding the future can cast its long shadow of anxiety.

World and its experiences no doubt cause suffering if the jīva "eats" its experiences rather than witness it in *yoga*. But that very world of joy and grief also serves as the field where the jīvas evolve spiritually. The lessons jīvas learn from their worldly experience is a very important part of spiritual evolution. The suffering jīva yearns for relief and if possible for a permanent end to suffering. Gradually, over many life times, it learns that the way to achieve this is by purifying its reactive mind. This involves getting rid of the *tamasic* and *rajasic* parts of its "vāsana makeup" and acquiring more *sāttvic* vāsanas in their place. The learning often takes place from contact with a Guru (teacher) who instructs the jīva on the Truth in scriptures and the paths to achieve that Truth. As its mind becomes increasingly more pure, the jīva becomes more virtuous in its conduct, and gains more in spiritual knowledge. The physical energy spent by the jīva in gathering worldly experience thus gradually increases its spiritual knowledge over many life times. Spiritual knowledge is the long-term effect of experiencing life and arguably the very purpose of material life.

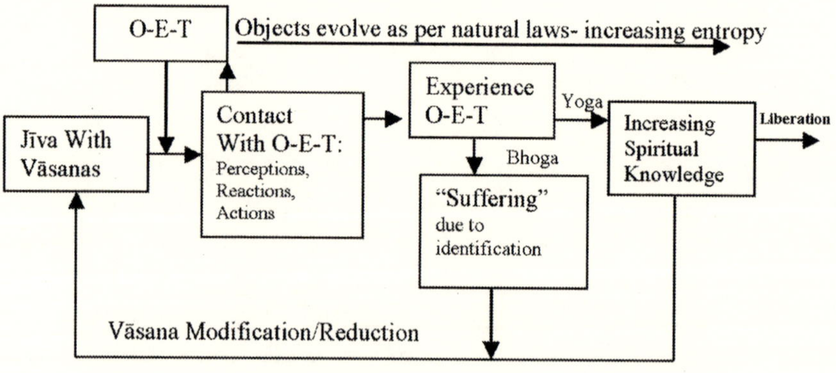

Fig. 2.6 The Life of a Jiva Until Liberation - A Grand View

Fig 2.6 shows schematically the choice available to a jīva as it proceeds from contact to contact with the O-E-T in its worldly life.

Each contact produces an experience which the jīva has the choice of either suffering "in bhoga" or merely witnessing "in yoga". The former leads to tightening the fetters of bondage to the world, and the latter to reducing the ignorance and increasing spiritual knowledge. Liberation from *samsār* is attained upon perfection of knowledge when all ignorance is destroyed. Vedānta promises this liberation to all jīvas, though each jīva progresses to this goal at its own pace. Thus, as Vedānta sees it, Īśvara has a "no-jīva-left behind" policy in which every jīva sooner or later must reach its true home, or source, the Self. Every jīva is guaranteed salvation in due course of time.

But what about the material world?

Long Term Fate of the Material World

It is remarkable that neither modern science nor most of the religious doctrines promise a bright eternal future for the material world. The world as we see it now will end one way or the other. Some say it will be a fiery end, while others suggest it will be a watery one, but in any case the end will not be pretty.

The Vedāntic term for the end of the universe is "*pralaya*" (dissolution) when the names and forms of Prakṛti, which originally issued forth out of the Unmanifest by the power of *Māyā*, is withdrawn back into the same Unmanifest. The currently manifest universe simply dissolves back into the source it came from. This is an endless cyclical process in as much as that another universe will be born again from the Unmanifest. As Lord Krishna explains it to Arjuna [28]:

sarvabhūtāni kaunteya prakṛtiṁ yānti māmikām;
kalpa-kṣaye punastāni kalpādau visṛjāmyahaṁ

"O son of Kunti, at the end of the millennium every material manifestation enters into My nature, and at the beginning of another millennium, by My potency I again create."

In science, the second law of thermodynamics has something to say about the fate of the universe. It postulates that the entropy (which is a measure of disorder) of the universe increases with time. High disorder is associated with low information content. All biological organisms depend for their life on a certain degree of order in nature. The universe that we see today is highly ordered as clearly seen from formations of huge galaxies, planets and vibrant life. But there will be fewer such recognizable "names and forms" in the less ordered material universe of the future. This is a state which well describes the term "*pralaya*" in which things and beings of Prakṛti "dissolve" back into the very source from which it was created earlier by Īśvara. As per the Hindu scriptures the *pralaya* for our universe will occur at the end of the life of the present Brahma in about 150 trillion years. It is interesting to note that some modern cosmologists also predict that our present universe, which is expanding at ever increasing rate, will thin out to become just a huge void in 100 trillion years [29].

There are other competing views among cosmologists (known by such colorful names as "Big Crunch", "Big Bounce" and "Big Freeze") about the fate of the universe but none promise a fairy tale end to the world where we may all "live happily ever after". After all, such permanent happiness is not to be sought in the material world, but only in spiritual perfection.

A Law of Conservation of Information?

The picture that emerges is that of a material world becoming increasingly disorderly as entropy increases with corresponding loss in information. This happens even as jīvas gain in spiritual knowledge over time, as shown in Fig. 2.6. It is as though there is a kind of balancing process in effect with information loss in the material world offset by the gain in knowledge in the spiritual realm. Given the meager understanding we have today of the relationship between the material and the spiritual, this is quite speculative but some further discussion of this question can be found in Appendix 1 at the end of the book.

Heaven, Earth, and Hell

Karma refers to a jīva's actions. The doctrine of *karma* maintains that a jīva must reap the rewards of its good and bad *karma*s sooner or later. The "bad *karmas*" of unintelligent living eventually bring suffering to the jīva and this suffering will motivate the jīva to seek ways to avoid them in future. The search must lead to spiritual knowledge which alone can confer durable happiness. In taking this view, Vedānta strikes a distinctively optimistic note compared to other traditions which see eternal hell as a possibility for some souls. Given the Vedāntic view that the real nature of every jīva is the Blissful Self, it is logically inconsistent to suggest eternal damnation for any jīva. A finite time of suffering in "hell" (-which could as well be right here on earth-) is what a jīva may get based on its bad actions. Suffering ends when the jīva learns the folly of its ways. Heaven, which the jīva gets to enjoy for its good actions, is not a permanent paradise either but one from which the jīva must eventually return [30]:

te tam bhuktvā svargalokaṁ viśālaṁ, kṣīṇe puṇye martya lokaṁ viśanti

"They, having enjoyed the vast heaven-world, when their merits are exhausted enter the world of mortals."

Adi Sankara

In Vedānta, the only thing eternal is Brahman; everything else is bound up in the realm of time, subject to change, and necessarily impermanent. While good *karma*s do take one to an impermanent heaven, permanent happiness is to be attained by gaining the Supreme Knowledge of the Self, not by any action. Adi Sankara reiterates this Vedāntic teaching thus:

avirodhitayā karma nāvidyāṁ vinivartayet,
vidyāvidyāṁ nihantyeva tejastimirasaṁghavat

"Action cannot destroy ignorance, for it is not in conflict with or opposed to ignorance. Knowledge does verily destroy ignorance as light destroys deep darkness." [31]

Knowledge and Goodness

In the discussions above Knowledge is characterized as the spiritual means and also as the spiritual goal. Terms such as "Knowledge of the Knower" and "Knowledge of the Self" are used to distinguish this Knowledge from the ordinary knowledge of the objective world. But such distinctions may be inadequate to convey what this Knowledge really is. Its true nature becomes clearer on noting that Vedānta equates Knowledge with Goodness and Virtue. Knowledge and Goodness are not two distinct spiritual characteristics, but one and the same. In the thirteenth chapter of the Bhagavad Gītā, the Lord lists a string of twenty one virtues such as humility, non-violence, straightforwardedness, truthfulness, and dispassion and then declares

"etat jñānaṁ iti proktaṁ, ajñānaṁ yadatonyatha"

meaning, these (virtues) constitute Knowledge, and ignorance is contrary to these [32].

One need not have any virtues (other than a keen intellect and will power) to become knowledgeable about the world. All such worldly knowledge is "lower knowledge", according to *Muṇḍaka Upaniṣad* [33]. Even scholarly knowledge of the scriptures is only lower knowledge, avers the Upaniṣad. Lower knowledge does not bestow permanent happiness. The Knowledge of the Self is the only "higher knowledge" since it alone can lead to the permanent, unlimited Bliss associated with Brahman. Knowledge of the Self is indistinguishable from Goodness; that Goodness manifests in a realized jīva as Universal, Unconditional Love.

Universal Unconditional Love – the Acme of Goodness

If there is one virtue that subsumes all other virtues, it is selfless, unconditional Love towards all beings. The Upaniṣads and Bhagavad Gītā repeatedly stress that the hallmark character of a Realized jīva is that it sees own Self in all beings. Says the Lord

Sarvabhūtasthamātmānaṁ sarvabhūtāni cātmani;
īkṣate yogayuktātmā sarvatra samadarśanaḥ

With the mind harmonized by Yoga he sees the Self abiding in all beings, and all beings in the Self; he sees the same everywhere [34].

We may at times be unhappy with what we are or how we behave. Yet, in spite of all personal failings, everybody, deep in the heart, has only love for oneself. That is to say, one's love for oneself is unconditional. A mother's love for her baby is also unconditional since she sees an extension of her own self in the infant. She serves the baby's needs happily without expecting anything in return. Mother's happiness is simultaneous with her love for the child; that is, the unconditional love she has for the child expresses itself as joy inside. This is one example of the general truth that unconditional love coincides with joy. The converse is also true. When we are joyful we tend to see the world with love and compassion. Love and Joy are the two faces of the same coin.

As the Gītā verse quoted above shows, the Knowledge of the Self sought by a Yogī consists in the realization of the one Self everywhere. Seeing own Self in everything, the Yogī bears a mother's unconditional love towards every being. This love is universal and unconditional, without any attachment. There can be nothing but Bliss for one who has attained this state.

Love vs. Attachment

The term "unconditional" used above to qualify love is significant. If unconditional love brings joy, its opposite, namely conditional love, often brings only misery. A mother no doubt loves her child even when the child has grown up to be a teenager, but the love often is no longer unconditional. The mother has so many expectations now from the teenager. Unconditional love is replaced by attachment to the expectations she has from her child. When these expectations are not met, there is disappointment. In many instances, what is called love is not true love, but only attachment to a goal or an object.

Knowing Goodness, Experiencing Goodness, and Being Goodness

The progress towards Knowledge and Goodness occurs in three phases. The first phase consists of knowing Goodness. By this is meant the intellectual efforts of the seeker to learn the truth about spirituality from teachers, books and self-reflection. In Vedāntic terms, this corresponds to the listening (*śravaṇaṁ*) and reflection (*mananaṁ*) phases of a seeker's efforts. In the second phase the seeker performs spiritual practices (*sādhanas*) such as various yogas, to increasingly control and purify the mind. During this phase, sometimes called as meditation (*nidhidhyāsaṁ*), the student enjoys Goodness in the form of peace and equipoise of mind. But this is not the end point of the spiritual journey. In his text "*Aparokṣānubhūti*", Adi Sankara cautions us against stopping short of the ultimate goal, lulled by the peaceful mind that obtains during meditation [35]. There is no victory until the mind itself is transcended.

Long and assiduous *nidhidhyāsaṁ* leads to the final state of *samādhi* or *nirvāṇa*, when the seeker attains to the status of being Goodness itself. This is Enlightenment or the attainment of Supreme Knowledge.

The Supreme Knowledge That Ends All Knowledge

The spiritual knowledge gained by a jīva during its evolution is indirect in the sense that it is acquired from teachers, scriptures, and association with other seekers. If correctly learnt it opens a grand new vision of own self and the world around. The jīva begins to appreciate the full implication of the basic truth: That there is but One Reality, manifesting in diverse forms; all that is happening around -including one's own actions- is at the Will of the creator Īśvara; that there is no "mine" and "others", and all suffering is unnecessary as they are due to ignorance of the Truth.

With this understanding the jīva is able to tune its being more and more with that supreme, sublime, benign reality pervading all existence. Some Vedāntins say that self-effort can take a seeker not to the final Truth, but up to *Brahmalok* (the world of *Brahma*), the last stage in evolution before full realization. Passage from *Brahmalok* to full realization is not by self-effort, but only by Divine Grace. The direct knowledge of the Truth is revealed as if in a flash as the jīva experiences the Truth of its identity with Brahman. As the experiencer experiences itself, the experiencer becomes the experienced, and all seen-seer-seeing distinctions (*tripuṭi)* disappear. This is the Knowledge that ends all quests for further knowledge, there remaining nothing else to know. This is Liberation, having obtained which the jīva no longer suffers, and crosses the "ocean of *saṁsāra*", never to return.

Death, Re-Birth, And The Doctrine Of Karma

Jīvas do not generally reach the exalted state of Liberation in one life time. As we see it, many spend a whole life time devoted to worldly pursuits and die while still attached psychologically to family, fame, and material possessions. What happens on death? Death is the separation of the subtle and causal bodies of the jīva from its present gross body. Without the M-I (which, reflecting Consciousness, gives sentiency to the jīva) and the vital energy (*prāṇa*) of the subtle body, the gross body that is left behind on death has neither sentiency, nor physical vitality.

The departed jīva, on the other hand, leads for a while a disembodied life, but still carrying within its causal body the vāsanas it had at the time of death. As long as there are residual unsatisfied vāsanas, a jīva must take birth again. That is, it takes another gross body suitable for satisfying the residual vāsanas. This is the logical imperative behind reincarnation.

Agama, Sañcita and Prārabdha Karma

The term *sañcita karma* is used to denote the ensemble of all residual vāsanas accumulated (*sañcita*) over past lives of a jīva. Only some, and not all, of these vāsanas can be expressed or satisfied in a single lifetime. The term *prārabdha karma* applies to those vāsanas which the jīva is destined to express in its present life. The word *prārabdha* means that which has commenced. If the jīva acts wisely in its present life, it can reduce these *prārabdha karma*s significantly before moving on to its next life as a spiritually more evolved person. On the other hand, if it is spiritually ignorant, it may actually accumulate even more vāsanas due to its actions in present life. The additional vāsana burden acquired during present life is called "*āgāmi karma*". As one may logically expect, it is added to the *sañcita karma* of the jīva awaiting to be expended in some future life.

Scriptures make it clear that a jīva need not work through to exhaust all its *sañcita karma*s before attaining Realization. This is because all *sañcita karma*s and *āgāmi karma*s are instantly burned-off upon Realization. The Realized jīva continues its present bodily existence until the *prārabdha karma*s, for which the present birth was taken, are also exhausted. Even these *prārabdha karma*s, though active, do not bind or cause suffering to the Realized jīva. Such a jīva is called a "*jīvanmukta*" or one liberated while bodily alive.

The Vedāntic Vision of Oneness

The Vedāntic vision of creation described in this chapter can be summarized thus: The Creation is "Of God, by God, and for God". The creation exists and evolves as per *Prakṛti*'s laws and *Īśvara*'s Will. Jīvas experience the creation. But the One God, or Reality, behind Īśvara, Prakṛti, and Jīva is Brahman. Therefore we say that the world of things and beings is made *of* God (namely, *Prakṛti*), and is controlled *by* God (namely, *Īśvara*), *for* the experience of God (namely, jīvas, or Brahman identifying with the individual beings of Prakṛti).

Brahman, the *sat-cit-ānanda*, permeates the creation. The universe is manifested for no reason other than the joy, *ānanda*, which the Brahman is. The *sat* or existence aspect of Brahman lends material existence to things and beings, and the *cit* aspect manifests as knowledge and experience of the world. The agents of change, or forces, in *Prakṛti* are the vāsanas, which act on things and beings of the world, causing them to move constantly from one state to another. Īśvara, the Lord, has command over Prakṛti and over the happenings of this world.

This in a nutshell is how Vedānta explains the existence of the world, the forces that change it, and knowledge there is of the world. There remains, however, one of the four basic facts we cited at the beginning of this chapter yet to be elaborated on, namely, the prevalence of Uncertainty. We take up this question in the next chapter where we will also examine how Īśvara's Will and Prakṛti's Laws work together without conflict in the affairs of the world.

CHAPTER 3

The Prakṛti-Īśvara Paradigm

We begin with a short story.

A man and his wife, following their annual *Dīpāvali*[9] tradition, enter a fashionable saree shop to buy a silk saree for the wife. This couple is a rarity in that husband is wise and sensitive to every wish of his wife while the wife accepts her husband's judgment without reservation. (So you may rightly suspect that this story cannot be all that real.) At the saree shop, the sales assistant spreads before them dozens of dazzling sarees that are the rage of the year. Husband listens attentively to his wife as she examines each saree and comments variously:

"I really like this green one. It is gorgeous and it feels so nice to touch. Too bad, because I already have too many in green".

"This blue looks great too, especially the border. May be I should get this. Price is not bad either. What do you think?"

"Wait! Look at this one! Wonderful design. And the red color is so pretty. I bet nobody else I know will have one like this. But the price!"

After about half an hour and two rounds of complimentary soft drinks, the husband knows the time has arrived when his wife turns to him holding several sarees in her hand and asks:

"Well, what do you suggest? I can't make up my mind. Which one should I buy? The red, blue or green?"

The husband, having in the meantime judged her inclinations well, makes the choice for his wife. She is relieved that a decision is made

9 Dīpāvali, the Festival of Light celebrated by Hindus to signify the victory of Good over Evil.

and is also happy at the prospect of wearing her new saree. Satisfied, husband and wife return home from the happy shopping trip.

True, as a story, the above narrative is not very sensational. Its purpose however is to suggest a paradigm within the structure of Vedānta to explain one of the mysteries of life: Uncertainty, because of which it is not possible to predict what this world will be like at the next moment.

Uncertainty's reach is all encompassing; behavior of both matter and mind are unpredictable. Theory and experiments of modern physics confirm the fundamentally unpredictable nature of matter and energy because of which they behave in very strange, incomprehensible ways. For example, an elementary particle can apparently be at multiple locations at the same time. However, when one attempts to observe it, it is found in just one of the many locations it can possibly be in. It is as if, in the absence of a witnessing observer, matter exists merely as an ethereal, abstract cloud of all possible states. When brought under conscious observation, the cloud condenses to one definite state. The state into which it will condense cannot be predicted in advance; one can at best only compute the probability it will be found in each of the different states.

This "Quantum Mechanical" behavior is very real at the level of elementary particles, such as photons and electrons, of which all matter and energy is composed. However, when the particles aggregate to form larger objects (such as a molecule, or a tennis ball or a chair), the degree of uncertainty, while still present, is quantitatively negligible. In other words, the behavior of larger objects is more accurately predictable. This fact is of enormous practical importance: Activities of daily life would be well nigh impossible if macro objects were subject to same relative levels of uncertainty as elementary particles are.[10]

However there is another source of uncertainty that has a large impact on our daily lives. The reference here is to human decision making. The small and big decisions we make in life affect our personal lives

10 Significant levels of uncertainty can and do exist at the level of large structures for other very different reasons. Incomplete information, inaccurate knowledge of the system dynamics, non-linearity, etc make it very difficult to predict the behavior of many phenomena which affect human life. Long-term prediction of weather is one of many examples of this type of uncertainty.

very significantly and intimately. That there is uncertainty surrounding human decisions should be obvious. Logically speaking, a decision, to qualify as a decision, must not be a foregone conclusion. There should be some unpredictability as to what that decision may be. Were it possible to predict a decision ahead of time with certainty, then in truth there is no real decision to be made in that case. Decision making requires free will and free will implies uncertainty.

Uncertainty thus affects the behavior of everything from elementary particles to human mind. Science does not attempt to give meaning to uncertainty, except to acknowledge grudgingly that it is here, it is unavoidable, a nuisance, and a mystery. However, it is possible to discuss this question intelligently within the framework of Vedānta and the Īśvara- Prakṛti Paradigm [36].

Decision Making by Human Beings

A key to this framework is to recognize vāsanas, the agents of change in *Prakṛti*, as "tendencies" or "propensities". A tendency does not force the entity it acts on to behave in a particular way, but only makes it more *likely* that it will behave that way. For example, someone who likes coffee need not accept coffee every time it is offered. True, the likelihood of drinking coffee will be higher if the desire is stronger. To make things more complicated, at any given time, not one but several vāsanas act simultaneously on a jīva with each vāsana pulling the jīva in different directions. Arjuna's dejection and confusion in the battlefield is an all too common human condition. As a result of the play of multiple vāsanas, it is difficult to predict which way a jīva may lean or act. The probability of various behavior modes will depend on the relative strengths of the different vāsanas.

Let us illustrate this by reverting to our lead story. There, the wife has several vāsanas affecting her mind that day: her liking for green color; the need to economize on spending; bragging right that comes from possessing something her friends do not have etc, etc. Each saree she can potentially choose "exhausts" (i.e. satisfies) each of these vāsanas to different degrees. It is difficult to reconcile readily the pull of the different vāsanas and hence her mind is in a mixed-up state. It is not possible to predict accurately which saree she might settle on. The best we can hope to do is to state how probable she is to choose the red saree over the green and blue, or the blue over the green and red etc. The probabilities will depend on how strong each vāsanas is, and how well each potential choice satisfies her needs. For example, if the need for wearing something stunning is more dominant than her concern for price, she is more likely, let us say 50% likely, to choose the red saree. Similarly we may be able to estimate that likelihood of choosing green and blue sarees are 30% and 20% respectively. Until the choice is made, all anyone can possibly know about the impending decision are these probabilities. Even the lady herself cannot tell what her choice will be until that choice is made. We may say that her mind is in a mixed state of Red, Green and Blue sarees, or - to borrow a term from quantum mechanics- in a state of "superposition of sarees" (Fig 3.1). This is when in our story she looks to her husband for advice. Upon making the selection based on his advice, the superposed state of her mind ends, or "collapses", into one definite choice of saree.

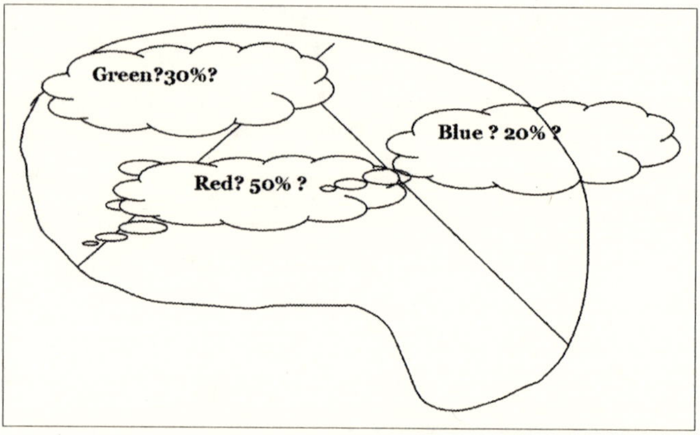

Fig 3.1: Faced With Choices, Mind is in a Mixed-State

There appear to be several similarities between the quantum mechanical uncertainty enveloping matter and the process of decision making by humans as shown in the table below, reproduced from [37].

Quantum Behavior of Elementary Particle	Decision Making by Human Beings
Particle in "superposition" is in multiple states (before observation)	Decision Maker's (DM) mind is in a mixed state of various choices (before decision is made)
"Wave Function" gives the probability of different states	(Subjective) Probabilities can be assigned to each choice open to the DM
When physically observed, particle is found in just one state ("Collapse of the Wave Function")	When decision is made just one of these options is selected
Outcome of observation is unpredictable (Uncertainty Principle)	Outcome of decision is not predictable (Implication of Free Will)
Process of "Collapse of Wave Function" is not understood	Process by which decision is made in human brain/mind is unknown to science
Von Neumann's Conjecture: "Collapse occurs in observer's mind."	Common Assumption: Decision is made in the "mind-intellect" complex of DM.

Table 3.1: Elementary Particle Like Behavior of Decision Maker's Mind

Many Possibilities, One Actuality

The key point of the above discussions is that, whether it is gross matter or subtle mind, Nature and its forces can tell us only the probability of various possible future states for the world. They, by themselves, do not determine which of the many possibilities will actually happen.

Of the many possibilities one, and only one, becomes actuality[11]. The process by which one of the many possibilities is selected to become the actuality is indeed the central mystery of Uncertainty. Science has no understanding of this process; indeed it even seems to suggest that the process must necessarily remain beyond human understanding. On the other hand, Vedānta asserts in no uncertain terms that Īśvara is the supreme controller of everything and every being. This means that the choice of one actuality out of the many possibilities is made at the Will

11 Some physicists hypothesize that all possibilities are in fact realized, but in different copies of the universe. Since a jīva experiences only one of these universes, this is not of concern to us.

of the Supreme Lord, Īśvara, who thereby exercises control over the entire creation, from the minutest of inert matter to the subtle mind of the most evolved being. Natural laws prescribe the probabilities, Īśvara dictates the actual choice. Thus, Īśvara's free will directs the universe while still remaining within the bounds of the natural laws. There is, under this paradigm, no conflict between *Prakṛti* and *Īśvara*. They could be the ideal couple in the saree shop with the wife expressing her many priorities and the husband making the choice after reading her mind well. Only, the world that *Prakṛti* and *Īśvara* together create is anything but unexciting!

Her Wish, His Will*Prakṛti* and *Īśvara* are thus the vital cooperating partners in the affairs of this creation. Without *Īśvara*'s will to make the choice, *Prakṛti* is in limbo. The world does not emerge, remaining a mere possibility. On the other hand, without *Prakṛti*, *Īśvara* has nothing to choose from, and again there is no possibility or need of creation. This is the core of the *Īśvara- Prakṛti* Paradigm that explains the role and meaning of uncertainty in the universe. *Prakṛti* proposes various choices and makes known her preferences for these choices; *Īśvara* makes the choice with due deference to Prakṛti's preferences, but in a probabilistic sense. Thus the world moves as per Her Wish and His Will.

The *Īśvara-Prakṛti* theme is amply echoed in Hindu traditions including its theology, mythology, and iconology. For example, it is the principle behind the symbolism of *śiva* and *śakti* portrayed as the dancing divine couple in the figure on the right. Creator being one, it has to be both the male and female principle of creation. This is also suggested by Śiva's hermaphrodite form (half male, half female form of *Ardha nārīśvara*). Every jīva incorporates within itself this macrocosmic Īśvara-Prakṛti principle since it both wishes and wills.

The Divine Duo: The World Dances to Her Wish and His Will

A question might be asked at this juncture: Does not the need to conform to Prakṛti's preferences imply some sort of a limitation on Īśvara's Will? If it does, then Īśvara cannot be said to have free will, which in turn will contradict what Vedānta and most religions teach us. The answer is provided by the fact that nature's preferences are expressed only as probabilities and not as certainties. A full philosophical discussion on the nature of probabilities and randomness is very complex and beyond the scope of this book. They are also rather elusive concepts. The mathematician-philosopher Bertrand Russell is said to have remarked that while everybody uses probabilities, nobody understands it. Randomness is also hard to define. We tend to label an event as "random", "by chance" or "accidental" when it leaves us in puzzlement and cannot attribute any cause to it. True randomness, like God, points to a "causeless cause", to something fundamentally unpredictable. Also, it will be noted that under probabilistic laws -as opposed to deterministic laws- almost anything is permitted to occur, and will occur sooner or later. In terms of the example we just used, the husband can choose any of the three sarees without really contradicting the wish expressed by the 50%-30%-20% probabilities. That is just the nature of probabilities. Under the Prakṛti- Īśvara Paradigm there is room, therefore, for Īśvara to exercise freely His compassion and justice without explicitly violating Prakṛti's laws.

There is an analogy here that may be interesting to those familiar with computer simulation of stochastic systems (i.e. systems subject to many uncertain factors). The processes to be simulated are represented by probabilistic laws in the computer code. The various possible behavior patterns of the system are then simulated using a random number generator to make choices from the probability laws. The point to note here is that the random number generator has to have absolute freedom to choose from its domain of numbers, otherwise it is not random. By analogy, Īśvara's freedom of choice is also totally unconstrained. Īśvara is often called as the "causeless cause" referring to the concept that God is the original cause of all and itself not caused by anything else. Randomness also shares a similar feature in that no causal law can underlie a truly random sequence. Absent such a causal law, a random sequence cannot be consistently predicted. Nor can anyone second guess Īśvara's Will, unless that jīva be already Realized and become One with God.

There is a different empirical ("Bayesian") approach one can take in answering the question regarding Īśvara's Will vis-à-vis Prakṛti's Laws. Our knowledge of the nature's laws, a scientist will agree, is based on the observed behavior of gross and subtle matter. The observed behavior, in turn, is commanded by Īśvara and hence already reflects Īśvara's Will. Therefore, it is not that Īśvara conforms to Prakṛti's laws, but in fact Prakṛti's laws – as we understand and enunciate them- are based on Īśvara's Will.

Whichever way we choose to answer the question, we see that there is no ground for conflict between Prakṛti's laws and Īśvara's Will.

Theory of Evolution and the Creativity of Īśvara

Charles Darwin's theory of evolution of species and natural selection ranks among the major milestones in scientific advance. The theory suggests that living organisms evolve into different species as they adapt to survive in a changing environment. Nature's mechanism for adaptation involves random mutations of the genetic material. It gives rise to many variant life forms of which the best variant survives by reproducing more abundantly in the changed environment. This theory has been verified and backed up by extensive scientific evidence over the last 150 years. The simple, elegant logic behind the evolutionary mechanism is so compelling that computer scientists now use it in so called "genetic algorithms" to generate intelligent solutions to many practical problems.

Darwin's theory has had its opponents among some religious groups which see in it a disavowal of God as the true creator of all beings. They argue that evolution through random mutations is clearly contradicted by the "intelligent design" seen in creation which is not possible without an intelligent creator behind it. However it is this author's view that there is in fact no conflict between the scientifically proven theory of evolution and belief in God's supremacy. Uncertainty and randomness, as we have seen, characterize the behavior of every bit of matter and mind and is consistent with the vision of an omnipresent Īśvara who pervades and controls all things and beings. The idea that evolution of life forms is also subject to randomness is therefore not upsetting to one who will see in this randomness the very handprint of the ultimate "causeless-cause", Īśvara.

The objection that natural selection through random mutations is contradictory to intelligent design is also not valid. As a case in point, we may note the success engineers have had with the aforementioned genetic algorithms in designing electronic circuits. These algorithms have come up with hitherto unknown, intelligent, and even patentable designs with practical applications [38]. The truth is that intelligent creative activity is aided, and not obstructed, by the capacity to experiment with a large variety of "random" ideas and concepts. Creativity in an Einstein or Shakespeare necessarily involves working with several possible competing theories and plots out of which emerges the most survivable science and theater. The different possible theories and plots arising in the mind of a creative genius may appear random and unpredictable. Wisdom lies in seeing the God behind that randomness.

That said, creative process is not, and cannot be, totally random, but ought to have some order and structure to go with it. In music, the composer has to have the freedom to be creative so that the composition is original, but if she uses that freedom to choose notes totally randomly, what results is noise, not music. The notes chosen must follow the laws and logic of music. Similarly this creation is colorful and abundantly rich in variety, because it is within the laws of Prakṛti and at the same time subject to Īśvara's Free Will.

Personal Free Will

In the Īśvara- Prakṛti paradigm, *Īśvara*'s Will and Prakṛti's laws determine how every material particle acts and every jīva's mind reacts. If this is the case, what is left for any jīva to do? Does it not negate the personal free will of individual beings? It does indeed, with an important exception which we will go into only later. The verdict of scientists and sages alike seem to support the view that free will of jīvas is at best a false notion born of a deluded ego. Our personal experience is also consistent with this view. It is not uncommon for us to sometimes surprise ourselves by what we do. Our act may be contrary to what we generally believe in and we may never quite understand why we did what we did. There are also situations where we have to make a decision quickly without having any time to think it through and we make the choice mechanically.

This shows that our decisions are not necessarily dependent on our conscious will. But it will be a shock to us to be told that our decisions even in other cases are not ours. No doubt denial of personal free will is very unpalatable to our usual way of thinking, yet our scriptures, logic, science, and seers all seem to proclaim this as the truth.

Sages: Mother Sri Amritanandamayi Devi says *"Human beings have the arrogance to claim that by simply pressing a button, they could burn the world to ashes. But to press that button, one's hand must move. We don't think about the Power behind that movement…… Suppose someone gets angry with you for no reason. As a spiritual aspirant, you should respond with an attitude of humility towards that person, realizing that what is happening is a play of God, enacted in order to test you."* [39]. Sri Ramakrishna Paramahamsa, Sri Ramana and other realized sages have commented on several occasions affirming the same view [12]. Realized masters are said to live as mere instruments of the Lord, acting as dictated by His will. It cannot be that, on attaining realization, the Masters give up some real personal will-power they once had. Realization is not supposed to diminish one's power; it is supposed to bless one with even more powers. Therefore, it is more likely that, on realization, it just becomes clear to the sage that there is no, nor there ever was, such a thing as personal free will.

Scriptures: "Akartāhaṁ" ("I am not the doer") is a phrase heard again and again in Vedānta. In Bhagavad Gītā, the Lord calls those who consider themselves as the doers of their actions as "deluded by ego", reminding us that all actions are in fact accomplished by the forces of Prakṛti [41].

"prakṛteḥ kṛiyamāṇāni guṇaiḥ karmāṇi sarvaśaḥ,
ahaṁkāra vimūṭātmā kartāhaṁ iti manyate"

Elsewhere in the Gītā, as we noted earlier, it is said that Īśvara, seated in the "heart" of all things and beings, controls them using His *māyā*:

---

12 Thus, Sri Ramakrishna says *"A man becomes liberated even in this life when he knows that God is the doer of all things… Not even a leaf moves except by God's Will. Therefore I say "O, Mother, I am the machine and Thou art the Operator; I am the chariot and Thou art the Driver. I move as Thou movest me; I do as Thou makest me do"."* [40]

"Īśvaraḥ sarvabhūtānāṁ hṛddeśerjuna tiṣṭati,
bhrāmayan sarva bhūtāni yantrārūṭāni māyayā"

Thus, the notion we have that what we do is a result of our individual will, ignores the truth that all actions issue out of the forces of Prakṛti and Will of Īśvara.

Logic: There is a logical fallacy in the presumption of personal will. This is highlighted by Einstein when he pointedly asks "*Do we will to will?*" The implication of the question is that willing is not a conscious action. Any conscious action requires a conscious decision to perform the action, otherwise it is a spontaneous, unconscious or reflexive action. Therefore, if willing were a conscious action, we should have consciously willed to will. If we willed to will, the same logic suggests that we should have "willed to will to will" and so forth, *ad infinitum*. But this process cannot go endlessly and should end somewhere in a spontaneous "unwilled" decision. Willing, we therefore conclude, involves an "unconscious" decision arising somewhere deep inside us. In other words, *willing is not really something we do, but something done to us*. This place "deep inside us" is indicated as the "heart" in the Upaniṣads and in the above quotation from the Gītā.

Neuroscience: How the human brain wills or decides is largely unknown to neuroscientists today, according to a noted scientist surveying the state of the science at the beginning of this century [42]. Experiments done in 1977 by Dr. Libet, of University of California, demonstrated that choices made by subjects were registered by the brain half-a-second before the subjects were aware that they have made a choice [43]. Similar experiments, repeated more recently using state-of-the-art fMRI techniques, have produced evidence of even longer delays before subjects become aware of their choices. These results are consistent with the notion that we are not the real authors of our decisions. All actions, and the decisions behind these actions, are the product of Prakṛti's forces (vāsanas) and Īśvara's Will.

The Spiritual Heart

Īśvara must be all pervasive in order to affect every inert thing and sentient being of the creation. That Īśvara, as mentioned earlier, is said to be in the "heart" of each jīva. It is here in the "heart" that decisions are made for the jīva. It is not, as often assumed, in the intellect. Surely, intellect helps us with assembling and analyzing facts useful in decision making, but it is not where decisions are made. The intellect in this respect is like a young MBA who analyzes various management options for the C.E.O of a company. The decision is made by the Chief Executive and not the MBA, but the MBA's analysis, if done right, improves the chance that the CEO will make a good decision. So too, while the intellect does not make the choice, it can, if properly employed, improve the chance that the right decision is made. To use the language of Quantum Mechanics, we may say that intellectual analysis alters the "wave function" - the probability of choosing the various alternatives- but does not "collapse" it. The seat of free will where the collapse occurs lies, if science and scriptures are to be believed, much deeper in our personality, beyond the realm of conscious mind and intellect.

The "heart" is not of course the physical heart, but where is it? As explained in Chapter 2, Īśvara is the macrocosmic counterpart of *Prājña*, the indweller of the causal body (*ānanda maya kośa)* in the individual. It was also mentioned there that the locus of the *Prājña* is identified in scriptures with the spiritual heart of a jīva. Thus, both the spiritual heart and the causal body signify the same entity. It is seated here that Īśvara, as the *Prājña* within each individual jīva, controls it. That the causal body is also the repository of the individual's vāsanas makes logical sense since, under the Prakṛti-Īśvara paradigm, Īśvara and vāsanas co-operate in controlling the jīva. The causal body is inaccessible to all outer layers of our personality, including the Mind-Intellect. Decision made in that inner most layer of our personality will not therefore be known to the M-I until the decision issues out as perceptible action or the intention to act is registered in the brain. This is in line with the general implication of the neuroscience experiments mentioned above also.

It will be recalled from our discussions in the previous chapter that all things and beings appear interconnected at their causal body or bliss sheath (*ānanda maya kośa*) level. A well known scripture echoes this thought when Sage Vasiṣṭa, in answer to a question from Lord Rāma, says: "*All creatures in this universe have two kinds of hearts-one to be taken note of and the other ignored. The one to be ignored is the physical organ which is situated in the chest as a part of the perishable body. The one to be taken note of is the Heart which is of the nature consciousness. It is both inside and outside of us and has neither an inside nor an outside*" [44]. The last sentence implies that the heart-space inside is continuous with the heart-space outside in a single unbroken continuum encompassing all creation.

Individuality of things and beings, it would thus appear, is confined to their outer (i.e. B-M-I) layers only. At the deepest level of *ānanda maya kośa* there is only totality, a totality that pervades and connects everything and every being. *Ānanda maya kośa* should not be seen merely as a sheath of ignorance into which the jīva withdraws in deep slumber forgetting for a while its sorrows. It is the seat of both Prakṛti's vāsanas and Īśvara's Will. As the powerhouse of vāsanas, it sets the world in motion in potentially different ways. At the same time, as the abode of *Īśvara,* it is from here that things and beings receive their command on which way to actually move. The interconnected causal realm must be also the secret wellspring from which "the finite receives the intimations of the infinite": The inspiration behind the creativity of artists, the intuition that informs scientists, and the revelations that enlighten the sages. The bliss sheath thus fully earns its title as the causal body. It is fitting that the ancient seer-poets saw Creation as the *ānanda taṇḍava (*Dance of Bliss) of the Lord. The cause for Creation, if we can hazard a guess at all, is *ānanda*, Bliss, just as a spontaneous brilliant dance is an act born of the joy of the dancer.

Ānanda is the mother of all vāsanas and creation continues to evolve guided by that *ānanda* as vāsanas. The "carrot view" of nature's forces introduced in the last chapter holds that things and beings follow nature's laws for the *ānanda* it brings. It is *ānanda* that brings out the bewildering, relentlessly changing world out of the changeless Brahman and it is also the same *ānanda* that makes the world go back to its source seeking peace and stability. Inert systems mechanically seek an equilibrium state; individual beings search for happiness and peace, and societies demand freedom, equality and justice for all its members. The world wants to merge back into that *ānanda* from which it arose. Ultimately, *mumukṣutva* -the craving for God that each jīva comes to feel sooner or later- is also due to the urge to return to *ānanda.*

Is it possible for a world of pain and pleasure to arise out of *ānanda*, the Pure Bliss? An analogy from physics seems appropriate as an answer to this question. Pure energy (the so-called gamma rays) is produced on annihilation of matter with antimatter. Conversely, from pure energy one can create matter and antimatter, i.e. electron – positron pairs [45]. *Ānanda*, is similar to Pure Energy: The world of pain and pleasure and all other dualities is projected by Īśvara out of *ānanda,* the primordial Non-Dual Pure Energy associated with Brahman. Creation is not for joy but out of joy. A poet can compose a tragic ballad while immersed in the joy of creativity. From Pure Bliss, a world of pain and pleasure is possible indeed.

In every bit of gross matter, there is pure energy. Even a partial manifestation of that energy requires the matter to be "burned" by subjecting it to chemical or nuclear reactions. When matter is totally annihilated by its exact opposite antimatter, pure energy is released. Individuality of the jīva is like a bit of gross matter. In every jīva is Pure Brahman, but the manifestation of that Brahman requires the individuality to be burned by spiritual *sādhanas* and the eventual total annihilation of vāsanas by contact with the antidote of *viveka* and *vairāgya* or Knowledge of Self. The *ānanda*, or the pure bliss of realization, is akin to the release of pure energy upon complete annihilation of gross matter.

Why Uncertainty?

Does uncertainty serve any purpose in creation, or is it just a source of frustration and anxiety? This is a question which science cannot answer, but Vedānta does. The answer lies in asking what a world in which everything is certain and predictable will be like. Hopes and dreams will have no rightful place in that world. It will be a rather dull, dreary and even fearful existence. For example, can one live in ease knowing the exact day and hour in future one will have an accident or will die? Uncertainty makes life more hopeful, spicy, interesting and challenging. On the other hand, if that world were totally uncertain, with not even the semblance of some law and order, existence will be a nightmare.

Fortunately, what we have instead is a mixture certainty and uncertainty that makes for a most enchanting creation[13]. Many things important to us in the world are predictable and even controllable to a large degree, thanks to advances in science and engineering. Yet, many other significant aspects of life remain uncertain. This is what makes the world entertaining and engaging like a lively sport. A sport must have predictable rules as well as unpredictable outcome in order to entertain. In football (US style), for example, when the offense does not complete 10 yards in four plays, it must turn over the ball to the other team. There can be no uncertainty here. But the game will lose all its fascination if there were no uncertainty about what happens in each of those four plays!

Vedāntic scriptures rightly call this world as God's *līla*, or sport, for its ceaseless entertainment value. It is a sport with the right mixture of certainty and unpredictability. It is often portrayed in philosophy and religion as a sport that pits good against evil. What then is the purpose of this sport called life? All sport, by definition, is really for pure entertainment. But not all spectators derive pure pleasure from watching a sporting event. Consider, for instance, a horse race in which a spectator bets big money on a horse. Having thus made his attachment to one horse and having expectation for its victory, this person is not in a position to truly enjoy the show in all its spectacular details. He will not watch with joy the strong, graceful run by another horse to win the race. Enjoying a sport requires non-identification with any particular player or team, and non- expectation regarding the outcome of the competition.

Life is also a sport but it is entertainment only for God, and for the fully-detached God-realized jīvas. For others who are not fully detached and are yet to realize, life has a different purpose. For them, the same arena of life serves as a classroom filled with tears and laughter that will slowly but surely teach them the way to god-realization and the wisdom to enjoy life as it comes.

13 The Planck's constant in Physics, which is a fundamental constant of our universe, provides a scientific basis to this statement suggesting that our universe has just the right degree of uncertainty. The world will be drearily deterministic if the Planck's constant were zero and bewilderingly uncertain if it had a large value. As it turns out, the Planck's constant is extremely small but not zero.

CHAPTER 4

The Logic of Vedānta

We examine in this chapter the Vedāntic concepts regarding Consciousness in the light of scientific theories as well as logic. Since the discussions are not necessary for following the rest of the book, the reader, if so inclined, may skip this chapter and proceed directly to Part II. It is being introduced here mainly to complete our discussion on Vedānta as a logical theory of spirituality.

Broadly speaking, there are three major views possible about Reality:

1) A materialistic philosophy asserting that matter alone is everything including mind and consciousness;
2) A dualistic approach which views matter as separate, and distinct, from mind and consciousness; and
3) A non-dualistic view holding Consciousness as the only reality behind both mind and matter.

Advaita Vedānta belongs of course to the third category and as such differs from both the materialistic and dualistic systems of thoughts. It does not agree with the presumption of the materialist that knowledge and consciousness are also products of matter and energy. We will discuss this issue further in detail as we review current scientific theories of consciousness. Regarding the dualistic view that matter and mind are different, we note that Vedānta also makes a distinction between the subtle mind and the gross body. But, by claiming that both are manifestations of the one underlying Reality, Brahman or

Pure Consciousness, it avoids a major criticism leveled against dualistic schools, namely the impossibility of mind and body functioning together if they are in fact two totally distinct realities.

Science of Consciousness

Science, as a rule, tends to adopt the materialistic view in investigating any phenomenon. Consciousness has been no exception to this rule. Neuroscientists studying the nature of consciousness have been attempting to determine how best to characterize it in terms of the chemical and electrical activities of the brain. This field of research is still young and active; it is aided these days by an array of sophisticated non-invasive techniques such as fMRI and PET scan. The techniques allow the scientists to see how the brain functions in people in response to a variety of sensory and mental stimuli. A rather large body of scientific literature related to brain and consciousness has been building up as a result of the work of the neuroscientists in collaboration with scholars from other disciplines such as psychology, philosophy, cognitive science, linguistics, etc. There is no need here to survey this vast literature, but only to broadly indicate the emerging views and how they relate to Vedānta.

The first and foremost fact to note is that scientists are far from forming a consensus at this time as to what consciousness is. Therefore, instead of a single, scientifically validated theory, what we have now is a large number of differing proposals and hypotheses awaiting further evaluation and validation. But there is no assurance that there will be a single fully validated theory emerging at any time. Notwithstanding this opening disclaimer, let us see what some of the leading hypotheses being proposed by the scientists are. It is helpful to note at the outset that, while most workers in the field do distinguish between awareness and consciousness just as Vedāntins do, some tend to use the term consciousness in contexts where the term awareness would have been more appropriate.

David Chalmers issued a basic challenge to scientists working on consciousness when he enunciated the now famous "Hard Problem" of Phenomenal Consciousness [46]. The term Phenomenal Consciousness or "P-Consciousness" is used to distinguish it from the other relatively easier problem of "A-Consciousness" or "Access Consciousness" which refers to our ability to store, retrieve, process, and act on information received through sensory organs. Chalmers accepts that neuroscientists may be able to formulate, in due course, A-Consciousness in terms of the physiological processes of the brain. However, he claims that the P-Consciousness- which refers to our capacity to *experience* life with all its qualities of colors, sounds, and flavors etc- cannot be similarly explained in materialistic terms.

Chalmer's hypothesis is supported by many who sympathize with the premise of the hard problem. But it is also opposed by those scientists and philosophers who, as a matter of principle, cannot accept that there is anything in the observed universe which is not a manifestation of physical matter and energy.

A good summary of the existing scientific theories of consciousness can be found in a book by neurologist Dr. Adam Zeman [47]. All scientists agree on some basic points as a starting point of their study, including the view that consciousness is bound up with brain activities, though not all the activity occurring in brain is subject to consciousness. An emerging general observation based on studies is that activity giving rise to consciousness is not localized to one area of the brain but is spread around its several areas. "Consciousness arises", says Zeman, "from the integration of activity across these areas .... entering into a unifying dialogue". Weiskrantz, discoverer of blindsight in neurological patients (who react to something shown to them but deny they saw anything), notes that in these patients the primitive faculty of sight or memory survives but the ability to 'comment' or reflect upon it, and to make use of it in thought or imagery is gone. A possible inference is that "making this commentary itself endows us with consciousness; it is what is meant by being aware and what gives rise to it." Philosopher David Rosenthal also suggests that to be conscious of what one is seeing is to be having the thought that one is seeing it: in other words, consciousness arises when thought illumines unconscious sensation [48].

There is general agreement too that mere sensation or perception is insufficient for awareness. Prof. Antonio Damasio says that perception "must be first transformed by a process which makes explicit the impact of the knowledge on the knower" [49]. For example, if an object perceived holds a potential threat to one self, then there must be a process in the brain which recognizes from memory the possibility of danger from the object and alerts us that it is to be avoided. These theories imply that awareness depends on "dialogue" between diverse regions of brain responsible for perception, memory etc. Scientists hypothesize that consciousness arises when individual neurons transmit information to one another about who they are and what they are seeing. More specifically, awareness occurs when a group of cells "which represent disparate features of a single object- which may be widely spread across the brain- are associated by firing at the same moment.", i.e., synchronous neuronal discharges, firing at gamma frequencies of 25 to 100 hertz, might generate awareness [50]. Physicist Roy John suggests this synchronous firing generates a 'resonating electronic field' in the brain leading to subjective awareness. Roger Penrose and others have tried approaches adapted from Quantum Mechanics to consciousness, but, admit that "subatomic particles and the workings of consciousness are equally mysterious" [51].

Dennett is among the most avid supporters of the view that the sense of "I" is a mere convenient abstraction to pull together and coordinate brain's various sensory, motor, memory, computational, linguistic and cognitive activities [52]. The sense of self is generated by this effort as much as to help this effort. There is constant verbalization of thoughts as the brain goes about its myriad tasks. It is as if the brain is loudly reporting to itself about what it is doing or finding. This creates awareness of awareness, that is, the notion of "I am doing this and this", "I am feeling this and this" and even "second-order thoughts" such as "I am thinking this and this". From all this constant narration inside the brain, says Dennett, emerges the sense of self. Dennett sees this self as the "Center of Narrative Gravity". Center of gravity, in mechanics, is only a mathematical abstraction of a material object and not a physical object itself. Similarly, the self at the center of the constant verbalization within our brain, is also only an abstraction without any reality. In other words, according to Dennett and others sharing his views, self is an illusion. Since consciousness is closely related to the sense of self, consciousness is also not real. Only the brain and its activities are real. This line of thought leads Dennet to believe that robots with human like qualities of intelligence and sense of self are possible. All they need is information processing power comparable to that of human brains. They do not need to be endowed with a separate faculty called consciousness imported from some outside source. Human beings are no different from such machines in their functionality and hence there is no need to assume that we have a special faculty called consciousness either. The conclusion that Dennett draws from this is that "We are all zombies", though he appears to have own reservations about this rather dismal conclusion.

Vedāntin's Critique of the Current Scientific Views on Consciousness

Clearly, the science of consciousness as it exists today is a grab bag of ideas and hypotheses which certainly will need more testing and debate. In a recent book, Alva Noe, a philosopher and cognitive scientist, sums up the current status of research thus: "*...only one proposition about how the brain makes us conscious...has emerged unchallenged: we don't have a clue*"[53]. Vedāntins also will readily find many contentious points in the current state of the science. We will discuss these under three headings.

a) The Hard Problem of Consciousness: Vedāntins will agree that it is not possible to explain experiences of color, sound etc in terms of the physical activities of the brain or any other part of the gross body. For the Vedāntin, the explanation lies instead with the subtle body, which includes the mind-intellect complex as well as the sense organs. Whereas the external sense organs of eyes, ears etc are gross, the corresponding internal sense organs are subtle. The rich qualitative nature of our life experiences, with its vivid sensation of colors and sounds, is made possible by the internal subtle sense organs. The subtle organs translate the gross stimuli received by the brain into the subtle sensations we experience. This is the brain-to-mind transition. Scientists may object that the subtle internal sense organs, or their functions, cannot be brought under observation of gross instruments that science uses today and hence the theory is not acceptable. But this objection can be raised against all theories pre-supposing a dualistic nature of matter and mind. It is no doubt difficult for a scientist to accept a dualistic view, yet some eminent neuroscientists such as Eccles [54] and Smythies [55] have found it necessary to do that. The idea may find greater support as future research point more and more towards a vindication of Chalmer's stand.

b) *The Neuroscience of Brain*: We saw that scientists are able to make many specific claims about the physical processes in the brain underlying sensory perceptions and motor functions. There is nothing invalid about these claims as they are based on scientifically sound observations. However, they make the mistake of identifying awareness with consciousness when they draw conclusions such as "consciousness arises when the neurons in many parts of the brain fire synchronously on perceiving an object". A Vedāntin will say that what arises is the awareness of the object. Further, as stated above, this awareness cannot happen until the gross neuronal activities are translated by the subtle sense organs into a complete mental picture of the object. Vedānta goes yet another step further when it says that the subtle body gets its power to do its cognitive and other functions only because of Consciousness, the Brahman. Thus, it is not that consciousness is generated out of the physical activities of the brain, but that Consciousness makes it possible for the subtle and gross bodies to function together to produce experiences we call life.

c) *Self as the Center of Narrative Gravity*: Dennett argues that the self is an illusory notion emerging out of the constant chatter in the brain as it goes about its daily business. Without a true self, he concludes that we must be all zombies. Now, zombies can act and talk intelligently, but by definition they lack the power to know anything, let alone really know that they are zombies. In other words, "we are all zombies" is a self-contradictory statement[14].

Curiously, for different reasons, Vedāntins also hold that the ego or self is an illusion, but they do not concur with the view that this makes a jīva an insentient zombie. Vedānta posits both a lower self and a higher Self in every jīva. The lower self, like everything else in the manifested world and of which it is a part, is not real. But the higher

14 See Appendix 2 at the end of this book.

Self of the jīva is real and of the nature of Consciousness itself. The lower self arises as the jīva, under the illusory power of *māyā*, falsely identifies with its own body and mind, its perceptions of the world, and with the chatter of its brain. All these prop up its image of individuality and cause it to experience the pains and pleasures of life. The higher Self, on the other hand, is untouched by the world, but whose nature as Pure Consciousness gives the lower self its power to experience the world. This higher Self is real and not an illusion.

The problem with the current scientific theories of brain, awareness, and self seems to be that the scientists are not willing to ask the hard question. For instance, if there is a constant narrative present in the brain, it is only fair to ask who the constant, ever present, listener of this narration is. There cannot be a real narration without a real listener. Similarly, if the self is an illusion, for whom is this illusion? It is not meaningful to talk of illusion when there is no one to get deluded by it. Again, when a neuroscientist says that such and such activities of the brain cause awareness of an outside object, who has this awareness? In all these cases the answer, according to Vedānta, is that there is something in a jīva with Consciousness that enables listening, delusion, and awareness. This is the Ātman or the Brahman which makes every jīva divine. Such a jīva cannot be a zombie.

The Sentient Robot

I am not a zombie, but who am I? Vedānta's answer to this deceptively simple question is contained in the symbolism we used earlier, namely:

$$\text{Jīva}_i = \text{Brahman} + \text{Prakṛti}_i$$

The "I", taken as the jīva, has both a real and apparent nature. Its real nature is that of Brahman, Pure Consciousness, as made clear in the Upaniṣadic statement *"tat tvam asi"* or "*Thou art That* (Brahman)". But when associated with Prakṛti (that is, when the Consciousness is conditioned by the individual body-mind-intellect equipment-), the "I" assumes its apparent lower nature as an ignorant jīva.

The jīva cannot be a zombie given that in reality it is Brahman. But its Prakṛti part does obey Prakṛti's laws and Īśvara's Will. The Prakṛti-Īśvara paradigm and the above symbolism together suggest that the jīva behaves somewhat like a "*sentient robot*" in its conditioned lower state[15]. The jīva is sentient, aware of its existence and of the world around it. But the jīva is also like a robot to the extent all thoughts, feelings and actions expressed through it are governed by Prakṛti's laws and executed at Īśvara's Will. We are but Īśvara's instruments, say the scriptures, and are advised to live in that knowledge. Scientists also are only supporting the same view when they report failure to see evidence of any "self" in the brain ("ghost in the machine") directing the brain's activities.

In summary, it is this author's belief that there is nothing in the current scientific views to cast a shadow of doubt on Vedānta. On the contrary, the Vedāntic views are logical and even help to resolve some of the conceptual problems that science has run into in its studies on consciousness and self. True, not all Vedāntic concepts are amenable to observation and verification in a laboratory as a scientist would ideally like to do. But the same is true also of many theories and hypotheses in modern physics such as String Theory and Parallel Universes.

Jīva as the "Quantum Monad"

This survey will not be complete without reference to the work of physicist Dr. Amit Goswami proposing a quantum mechanical basis for our spiritual nature [56]. While several other scientists like Roger Penrose have speculated on possible quantum processes in the brain giving rise to consciousness, Goswami's theory is arguably the most developed since it addresses consciousness as well as other major aspects of a jīva's spiritual life. Goswami attributes to a jīva five bodies: a physical body providing experience of an outside world, a vital body which is the seat of feelings, a mental body expressing thoughts, a supramental body from which arises creativity, and finally the bliss body which is of the nature of Consciousness. The theory is largely consistent with Advaita Vedānta though there are some differences in respect of the functions and roles attributed to the five bodies. The vital, mental, and supramental bodies together constitute the "*sūkṣma śarīra*" or the subtle body. Of the five bodies, the physical body alone has a concrete structure visible to others. The vital and mental bodies have no structure and are only functional;

15 A robot does not have personal will, being totally directed by the nature's laws affecting its hardware and software. Jīva's, on the other hand, have limited will power, as discussed in Chapter 7.

they are private in the sense that feelings of the vital body and thoughts of the mental body are known only to the concerned jīva and not to others. The supramental body is considered to be cosmic; its nature and role are similar to those of the *kāraṇa śarīra* (causal body) described in Chapter 2. The bliss body or Consciousness, also considered universal, is the "ground of being" in which the material world and all vital, mental, and supramental bodies exist as possibilities. In Goswami's theory, the roles of Brahman and Īśvara are attributed to the bliss body.

A jīva progresses spiritually through its experiences with the outside world. Goswami invokes quantum mechanical principles in describing how a jīva experiences the world and how those experiences alter its spiritual character. In his conception, the world as well as the physical, vital, mental, and supramental bodies are quantum systems, existing as "possibility waves" in Consciousness, the universal bliss body. The possibility waves collapse into a definite state in the presence of Consciousness. The physical brain and the world it sees through the sense organs form what is called a "tangled hierarchical" quantum system with correlated possibility waves. A specific experience of the world, along with the notions of "experienced object" and "experiencing subject", arises when this quantum system collapses in the presence of Consciousness into a definite state. The specific experience is recorded in the brain as a physical memory, just as sound is recorded in a magnetic tape. The possibility waves of the vital, mental, and supramental bodies also collapse producing definite feelings, thoughts, and creative insights. The impression left behind by the collapse in the subtle body is of the nature of "quantum memory". Whereas physical memory in the brain is that of the specific experience following the collapse, quantum memory is through alteration of possibility waves of the vital and mental bodies in such a way that the probability of experiencing the same feelings and thoughts in similar future encounters with the world is increased. In this manner quantum memories affect our spiritual character by changing our habitual patterns of feeling, thinking, and responding to the world.

Goswami uses his theory to explain many spiritual phenomena such as transmigration, clairvoyance, near-death experiences, past life memories, and spiritual progress towards final liberation. Goswami's work thus provides a scientific basis for many of the Vedāntic concepts used in this book.

A valuable addition to the growing literature on neurosciences and consciousness comes from Deshmukh [57]. The author has provided in this book a comprehensive and authoritative survey of the concepts and hypotheses relating to consciousness currently prevalent in neurosciences, while juxtaposing these concepts against declarations found in Vedānta regarding Consciousness as the Ground of all Being. While the author, himself a learned neuroscientist and Vedāntin, is content with a scholarly presentation of the facts, it is nevertheless significant that he does not suggest anywhere that the supreme status accorded to Consciousness in Vedānta is contradicted beyond doubt by neuroscience.

Theory Vs. Truth And Hierarchy Of Theories

Vedānta provides a logically consistent theory of spirituality. But is it the only theory possible or existent? Also, one could ask if Vedānta is a theory or is it the truth.

Swami Chinmayananda, in his commentary on Vivekachūḍāmaṇi, notes that all science and theories of the intellect, including Vedānta, are only "prattle" *(prajalpa)* of the mind [58]. This statement is made from the highest standpoint of truth and does not imply that the teachings of Vedānta are unreliable. It only reiterates the Upaniṣadic view that all theories involve mind whereas the ultimate Truth is beyond mind. Vedānta is a sure guide to Truth, but it is of no further use to the Realized jīva. We need to appreciate the fine distinctions between theory and truth in order to fully appreciate Vedānta's status as a reliable, logical guide to spirituality.

A theory about a phenomenon can be viewed as a set of sufficient conditions that logically explain the phenomenon. That is, *if* the theory is true *then* the behavior of the observed phenomena is explained. However a theory is not a necessary condition since the converse is not generally true. Given the laws of Physics one can explain (most of) the observed behavior of matter and energy. To this extent the laws of physics constitute a set of sufficient conditions. But these laws cannot be considered as "truth" unless Physicists can show that these laws are necessary and no other set of laws can explain the behavior of matter in our universe. It is usually difficult to argue and make this case. Therefore a theory is not in general *the* truth regarding the phenomenon. Stated another way, a theory is just one possible explanation and not itself necessarily the truth.

This leaves room for more than one theory that explains a phenomenon. In such a situation, one can rank the theories based on the following criteria:

a) *How universal and complete they are*: Relativity Physics explains the world of matter and energy more completely than Newtonian Physics does. Hence it is considered superior as a theory even though Newtonian Physics is still considered quite adequate for most day-to-day applications;
b) *How simple and parsimonious the concepts used are*: A theory that uses fewer, clearly defined concepts will be ranked higher over one which has ill-defined, redundant or irrelevant concepts;
c) *How intuitive or self-evident their axioms and assumptions are*: Most theories are founded upon explicit or implicit axioms and assumptions. The axioms may not be logically or experimentally provable, but must be self-evident or at least reasonable;
d) *The rigor of logic used*: theories that respect rules of logic are no doubt preferable to those which do not; and
e) *How well the theory promotes universal welfare*: This criterion may have no place in material science, but it can be important when judging the relative merits of different spiritual view-points. If two spiritual philosophies are about same with respect to the other criteria, we can justify preferring the one that is clearly more conducive to the welfare of the world. Gītā touts Vedānta, the "Royal Knowledge", as

"yat jñātvā mokṣyase aśubhāt"

that is, as the knowledge knowing which one shall be freed from all forms of inauspiciousness [59].

Proof vs. Realization: For Brahman, the Proof of the Pudding is in Eating

Vedānta offers a theory of existence and spirituality, explaining how the world and individual jīvas have come about from Brahman, the One Reality; how the jīvas gain awareness of the world and of themselves; how they suffer in the world due to ignorance of the true nature of their self; and how they may gain the knowledge that will end the suffering. As mentioned earlier, Vedānta adheres to the rules of logic in its reasoning but does accept axiomatically, i.e. based on *sabdha pramāṇam* or authority of scriptures, some basic statements found in the scriptures regarding Brahman, jīvas and the world.

In the eyes of its adherents, Vedānta is not merely *an* explanatory theory, but *the* truth. That is, its axioms and statements are sufficient and necessary conditions for explaining existence in its full compass, including all its material and spiritual manifestations. However, Vedānta explicitly acknowledges that the truth of Brahman, which is at the very core of its philosophy, cannot be proved by mere logic, words, thoughts, observation, or any other means. The Taittirīya Upaniṣad (II.4.1) expresses this truth thus:

"yato vāco nivartante aprāpya manasā saha..."

Brahman is That, failing to reach which, words, along with the mind, return in vain. That Brahman is, however, the essential nature of all beings. Therefore any jīva can *realize* this truth in own experience. In other words, for Brahman, the proof is indeed in eating the pudding.

Theory "A" is superior to a competing Theory "B", if B can be understood on the basis of A but not vice versa. This, for example, is the situation in the case of Relativity Physics and Newtonian or Classical Physics. The extent of validity of Newtonian laws can be well understood using Relativity Physics. But Relativity cannot be understood in terms of Newtonian model of time and space. In establishing Relativity Physics, Einstein had to look beyond the familiar Newtonian laws. Thus, Relativity Physics is superior to the Classical Physics. A similar situation applies to Vedānta, and more specifically to Advaita Vedānta. The concepts employed in Vedānta, such as *jñāna, bhakti and karma*, help one to understand what makes religious practices work. As we shall see later in this book, the *dvaitin*'s stand on the duality of Īśvara and Jīva also can be appreciated from the point of view of Advaita Vedānta as being valid within limits. However, it is not easy to appreciate the truth of Non-Duality of Advaita from the strictly dualistic stand point adopted by most religions.

There is a famous, if enigmatic, statement in the Upaniṣads to the effect that Vedānta's goal is to attain "The Knowledge by Knowing

Which Everything Else is Known" [60]. Read in the context of the above discussion, Vedānta's goal is to reach the highest mountain peak of Knowledge from which every other material and spiritual philosophy can be conveniently and comprehensively surveyed and understood. Having reached this peak, there is no higher heights to scale. The Knowledge that Vedānta leads to is Supreme.

This brings us to the conclusion of the first part of the book where we have reviewed the basic Vedāntic concepts. We have also discussed the Īśvara-Prakṛti paradigm in some detail. The next part of the book attempts a mathematical representation of the basic Vedāntic concepts in order to build a mathematical theory of spirituality.

PART II

Mathematical Representation

List of Mathematical Symbols

t		(cosmic) time
$\theta(t)$	Greek letter "theta"	Spiritual detachment at time t, in radians
θ^*		The spiritual detachment associated with *Brahmalok*
$\underline{h}_t$		State vector of the world at time t
H		The space spanned by $\underline{h}$, the space of all possible states for the world at all times
$\mathscr{M}$		The first quadrant of the space defined (t,θ), the *Mahat*, the Field of Experiences
λ	Greek letter "lambda"	The distance between two consecutive waves in the $\mathscr{M}$space, unit cosmic time
$\tau(t)$	Greek letter "tau"	Experienced time cumulated through *t*
$G(t)$		Accumulated merit through time t
$\zeta(t)$	Greek letter "zeta"	The complex variable $\tau(t) + i.G(t)$
$\gamma(t)$	Greek letter "gamma"	A random variable taking values 1 and 0 with probabilities $\sin^2\theta(t)$ and $\cos^2\theta(t)$ respectively
WP_S		Will power required to stay in Self
WP_{NS}		Will power required to stay in Non-Self
x		Vāsana x, in the range $0 \le x \le 1$
x^*		The limiting value for x, associated with *Brahmalok*
$V(x,t)$		Intensity of vāsana x at time t
$V'(x,t)$		Normalized $V(x,t)$
$E_o(t)$		Outward directed mental energy at time t
$E_{In}(t)$		Inward directed mental energy at time t
$E_T(t)$		Total mental energy at time t
$W_k(x,t)$		The perturbation caused by object (or action) k on vāsana x at time t
$W'_k(x,t)$		The perturbation of vāsana x expected from gaining the object k
$\hat{S}(t)$		Expected suffering at time t

CHAPTER 5

The Experiencer and the Experienced

The first part of the book was an overview of the various important concepts in Vedānta which together provided a logical basis for understanding human spirituality. In the following pages the concepts are given a mathematical representation in order to formulate a mathematical theory of spirituality. This is a task for which there is not very much by way of precedence. It appears that work done so far, such as the previously cited work by Goswami, has been limited to a few individual scholars working in isolation. A Unified Field Theory integrating the knower, the knowing process, and the known has been proposed by Hagelin [61]. Srivatsava [62] employs a set theoretic approach to characterize the nature of ultimate Reality and consciousness. Mention must be made also of Paul Budnik [63] who attempts to integrate spirituality and science by focusing on the mathematical structure that underlies scientific concepts and how it relates to the spiritual "essence" of our existence. These works represent a rigorous attempt to come to grips with the most elusive and mysterious of all phenomena, namely existence and consciousness. They have been done in relative isolation and, in the absence of an established forum for wide dissemination of the ideas, do not appear to have benefited from the critical cross-examination and vigorous discussion they deserve.

The approach taken in this book to spirituality is based on classical Vedāntic concepts discussed earlier and it differs from the previous works in its focus. We do not focus in this book on the nature of Consciousness or how it is related to the experienced world. We put our trust in the Upaniṣadic wisdom regarding these fundamental questions without trying to formulate that wisdom in mathematical terms. The focus instead is on the jīva and how it evolves spiritually while transacting with the world. It is this spiritual evolution that we strive to represent mathematically in the following chapters. We rely again on Vedānta, and also on science to some extent, for guiding us in the choice of a proper mathematical framework for this task.

The seen-seer distinction is fundamental to Vedānta philosophy and that is where we will commence the task of building a mathematical theory.

The Experienced: The World of Objects-Emotions-Thoughts (O-E-T)

The world is an ensemble of insentient objects and sentient beings (jīvas). The sentient jīvas are not only a part of the world, but they also experience the world. Objects possess only gross body whereas jīvas also possess conscious Mind and Intellect (M-I). A complete description of the world at a given moment will have to consider not only the physical state of all gross objects, but also the emotional and intellectual state of all its beings. Following Gurudev Swami Chinmayananda, the experienced world may be denoted by the acronym O-E-T (for Objects-Emotions-Thoughts). The O-E-T is thus the totality of the gross and subtle bodies; that is the *Virāṭ* and *Hiraṇyagarbha* aspects of Totality shown in Fig 2.1.

This world is in constant flux and moves from one state to another under the forces of change constantly operating on it. The position of a speeding automobile at the next moment depends on where it is at the present moment and the direction, speed and acceleration it is subject to now. Similarly, where the world will be at the next moment depends on where it is at present and the forces of change (their magnitude and directions) active now. In this sense, the present moment (meaning, the state of the world at present together with the present active forces of change) is the cause and the next moment its effect. Next moment is the cause for the (Next+1) moment and so on and so forth as indicated in Fig 5.1. The figure reflects what is often referred to as the "classical" or "Newtonian" view of the universe in as much as that it implies a clock work like world which moves along a well determined path of cause-effect changes. In this view, the laws of nature are such that the future can be unambiguously predicted.

	cause→	effect cause →effect cause → effect cause →effect			
WORLD	O_0--------------→	O_1----------------→	O_2-------------→	O_3------------→	O_t---
AT→	t=0	t=1	t=2		

Fig. 5.1: O_t, the World of Objects-Emotions-Thoughts at time **t**=0,1, 2,....

The State Description of the Experienced World

A complete description of the state of the world at any given time may never be practically possible, since it must include all information about the physical status of every gross particle in the cosmos as well as the subtle mental-intellectual state of every being. Notwithstanding this practical difficulty, it is possible conceptually to specify the state of the world by a vector $\underline{h}_t = \{h_{i,t}\}$ of N elements, where N is the total number of objects and beings, and the i-th element $h_{i,t}$ is itself a vector describing the gross and subtle states of the i-th individual object or jīva, at time t. The vector $\underline{h}_t$ defines the state of the world of all gross, and subtle bodies. We need not be daunted by the unimaginably large dimension of this vector, or by the difficulty in describing the emotional and intellectual state of jīvas, since, fortunately, there is no need to actually work with this vector in the models to be discussed. The main purpose of introducing the vector $\underline{h}_t$ is to lay down clearly the conceptual framework of the subsequent mathematical model. It will be noted that the state vector $\underline{h}_t$ takes into account the mental and intellectual perception of the world by each jīva. Even if the gross physical world seen by two different jīvas at a given time be the same, it can give rise to very different emotional and intellectual states in the minds of the jīvas.

Mind and matter are both forced to move from one state to another by nature, or *Prakṛti*. The forces of Prakṛti cannot be resisted by things and beings, says the Bhagavad Gītā:

"sadṛśam ceṣṭate svasyāḥ prakṛter jñānavānapi, prakṛtim yānti bhūtāni nigrahaḥ kim kariṣyati?"

"Even a wise man acts in accordance with his own nature; beings will follow their own nature; what can restraint do?" [64].

As a result of Prakṛti's forces, the vector $\underline{h}_t$ takes on different values as time progresses. The number of possible states the world can be in is immensely and immeasurably large; that is to say, the state vector $\underline{h}$ can potentially assume a large set of different values. We denote by

H the set, or space, of all possible values of h. In terms of Vedāntic concepts introduced in Part I of the book, **H** includes all possible states of *Hiraṇyagarbha* and *Virāṭ*. **H** represents all the possible worldly experiences that any jīva can have at any time[16].

The total causal body is not part of **H**. The total causal body refers to all natural laws and vāsanas in *Prakṛti*, which cause the moment-to-moment changes in h, the state of the world. The laws of nature themselves are considered universal, unchanging, applying to all, at all times. Further, the laws themselves are not directly "seen" or experienced; only their effects are experienced. For these reasons, the causal body is not considered a part of the changing, experienced O-E-T, or the set **H**.

Though the *Prakṛti*'s laws apply to all things and beings, the effect of these laws can depend on some characteristic of the object. These characteristics themselves may belong to the O-E-T, or not. For example, the law of gravity is universal and generally believed to be unchanging; but its effect depends on the mass of the object. The mass of an object is part of the description of O-E-T, and hence part of the vector h. On the contrary, *sāttvic, rajasic, and tamasic* vāsanas are also forces affecting all beings, but the extent of their effect on an individual being depends on that jīva's "vāsana make-up" (denoted by V_i in Fig 2.2)[17]. However, a jīva's vāsanas are not directly experienced and are not part of O-E-T.

The Concept of Time

Fig 5.1 depicts changes in the state of the world as a cause-effect chain. Cause does not transform into its effect instantaneously. To use an approximate analogy, a seed does not sprout instantly into the seedling, even if the conditions are right. Though the state of the world at the present moment, together with the forces acting on it now, is the cause of the next state of the world, there is an interval between the cause and effect as shown in Fig 5.1. Symbolically,

cause "+" time = effect

16 Vedānta and religions talk of heaven, hell, and other possible worlds which a jīva may experience due to its *karmas*. All such possible realms of experience are included in our concept of "world".

17 Chapter 8 will define what we mean by "vāsana make-up" and the laws describing how vāsanas affect a jīva's behavior.

where the "+" sign is read as "together with". We will refer to the interval between the world "now" (the cause) and the world "next" (the effect) as unit "cosmic time". In the mystic literature of Shaivism, the beat of Śiva's drum, *ḍamaru,* is sometimes associated with the creative process. If we assume that each beat of the drum signifies some change in the cosmos, then the interval between any two consecutive beats is the interval between two consecutive changes or one unit of cosmic time. By this definition, there can be no changes during the interval of silence between two consecutive beats[18].

The length of the interval between two consecutive moments in Fig 5.1 is assumed to be a constant, namely one unit of cosmic time. This amounts to assuming that the present progresses to the future at a constant rate. This is the most natural assumption one can make, especially since cosmic time cannot be measured. We cannot, and do not, specify the length of this interval; nor is it relevant to the discussions. In fact the interval could be considered to be arbitrarily small so that the cause-effect chain is seen as almost a continuous stream of changes.

Though we have chosen to call it cosmic time, it is not what jīvas experience as time. Cosmic time, as defined above, may be discrete or continuous. Time experienced by jīvas, however, does appear to be continuous. Nature of cosmic time, and its relation to experienced time, will be made clear as we proceed.

Experienced Time

We generally view changes as occurring *in* time, as in Fig. 5.1. In this view, Time has independent reality and is the substratum for changes. The cause-effect relationship, on the other hand, can also be interpreted to suggest that time is *born* of changes. Here, time is not the independent variable against which all changes are measured; rather it is the changes that give rise to the experience of time. In Vedānta, the Changeless Brahman is also considered Timeless. Concept of time has fazed many

18 This is also similar to the metaphor of *rāsa līla* used by Gurudev Swami Chinmayananda to explain the concept of time. In *rāsa līla* Krishna and the village maidens, *gopīs*, dance in a circle, with multiple forms of Krishna appearing magically to dance between every two *gopīs*. In this allegory, each *gopī* represents a "thought". The interval between two consecutive thoughts is time, in the form of the silent mind or the (unobservable) Brahman.

thinkers, but Sri Ramana, with his profound insight into Reality, has offered a simple definition. States the Sage of Aruṇacala [65]:

"*What is time? It posits a state, one's recognition of it, and also the changes that affect it. The interval between two states is called time.*"

This view accords with the statement found in a text of *Nyāya-Vaiśeṣika* school: "*.... time is not perceivable. Changes in objects make us infer the existence of time behind such changes*". There is also precedence in the Indian systems of philosophy, specifically the *Atharvaveda,* for dual concepts of time similar to the cosmic time and experienced time used in this book [66].

Sri Ramana's definition supplies the clue to understand time as experienced by jīvas. For time to be experienced there must be changes and also there must be recognition of the changes by some cognizant being. Where there is no change, there is no sense of time. From the perspective of the jīvas, the world of Objects-Emotions-Thoughts is always changing. Jīvas experience the successive states of the world and perceive the interval between experiences as time.

Two Issues with the Classical View of World

The classical view of Fig. 5.1 that we have discussed so far turns out to be unacceptable to both modern physics and Vedānta. There are primarily two problems that Vedāntins can have with the classical view. The first concern they have is regarding the presumption of a world that is entirely predicated on the cause-effect laws of nature. This leaves apparently no room for Īśvara's Will in the affairs of the world. Modern physics also has rejected the determinism of the classical Newtonian view based on experimental evidence in quantum mechanics. The second objection Vedānta will have is with the inadequacy of the model to explain how the world is experienced. In Fig. 5.1, the jīva is portrayed as part of the world, O-E-T. However, according to Vedāntic principles, the experienced O-E-T and the experiencing jīva cannot be the same. As Adi Sankara says in the Vedāntic text *Dṛg Dṛśya Viveka*

sākṣī dṛgeva na tu dṛsyate

meaning, the witnessing seer is not seen [67]. In other words, the experiencing aspect of the jīva must have its locus in something other than the experienced O-E-T.

We discuss each question separately and then propose a Vedāntic model that resolves these difficulties.

Uncertainty Inherent in Nature

Vāsanas (which also include all natural laws known to scientists affecting behavior of matter and mind) are the causal forces behind the changes in O-E-T from one moment to next. However, vāsanas do not completely determine the future course of the world as discussed at some length in Chapter 3. There is some uncertainty about the future even if we can know everything about the current state of the world and all the forces that are acting on it at this moment. This is due to uncertainty inherent in *Prakṛti* (nature.) To use the earlier example, the position of the automobile at the next moment depends on how the driver decides to steer it now. But human decisions are unpredictable and hence the future position of the car is also unpredictable. Generalizing this principle, vāsanas indicate only the probability of the various potential states the world can be at the next moment. The choice of the actual state is made at Īśvara's Will (Fig. 5.2.)

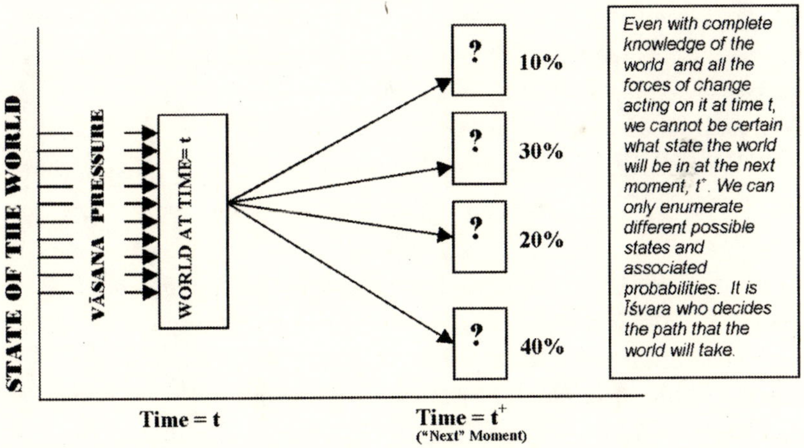

Fig. 5.2: Uncertain Evolution of the World Under *Prakrti's Vāsana* Pressures

We recall from the discussion on this subject in a previous chapter that, in determining O-E-T's evolution, the rule is "*Prakṛti* proposes and *Īśvara* disposes".

Predicting the state of the world is the goal and domain of science but not generally of spirituality. Spirituality is more concerned with prescribing processes by which jīvas may live a more fulfilled life regardless of the state of the world. Our task ahead is in fact made much easier because of this natural dichotomy between science and spirituality since the mathematical model developed in these chapters need not be concerned with the Herculean task of predicting the future states of the world. An additional benefit of the dichotomy is that what we have to say in these pages avoids any conflict with science.

The Experiencer

The model in Fig 5.2, while an improvement over Fig 5.1, is still an incomplete representation of reality. It may fit a scientist's view of the world, but will not appeal to a Vedāntin for one important reason. It would seem from this model that all things and beings are at the mercy of nature, being pushed relentlessly from change to change. All jīvas, according to this view, must necessarily suffer changes as the world changes. This is contrary to Advaita Vedānta's declaration that there is an alternative to suffering. In *Vivekachūḍāmaṇi*, for example, we find the disciple imploring the Master: *"I am being roasted in the blazing infernal fire of change; I am being tossed by the cruel storms of misfortune.... I seek refuge in thee"*. In response, the Master comforts the disciple *"Fear not, O learned one! There is a way to cross over this ocean of change..."*[68].

What exactly is missing from Fig 5.1 or Fig 5.2? The missing element is to be found in the statement of Adi Sankara we quoted in Chapter 1:

"asti kaścit svayaṁ nityaṁ, ahaṁ pratyayalambanaḥ
avastā traya sākṣī san, pañca kośaḥ vilakṣaṇaḥ"

The "something else", proclaims this verse, is the witness of jīva's experiences in all three states of waking, dreaming and deep sleep. The larger implication of statement here is that there is something more to this universe than the experienced world because of which jīvas witness all its states. As mentioned, a basic precept of Vedānta is that the witnessed (experienced) and the witness (experiencer) cannot be one and the same. Many examples of this principle can be given: A telescope can be used to see objects outside, but cannot be trained on itself. A weighing scale can be used to weigh other objects, but cannot weigh itself. The eyes can see everything, but cannot see themselves. Thus, the witness and the witnessed must be necessarily distinct. The experiencer is the "something else" in the presence of which jīvas experience changes in O-E-T. Fig 5.1 is a flawed representation of reality in that it makes no distinct reference to this experiencer.

How does one augment Fig 5.1 to represent the experiencer when it is not part of O-E-T and is therefore in another dimension of reality? Following the standard practice in mathematics we do this by adding a second dimension, orthogonal to the single horizontal axis of Fig 5.1. This leads us to a two-dimensional model of the world and its knower shown in Fig. 5.3. We will see in detail how this represents the experienced, the experiencer, *and* the experiences, and what the two axes and the space enclosed in between the two axes, signify.

TheVedāntic Model in Polar Coordinates (t,θ)

The one dimensional line which was the substratum for the changing world in Fig. 5.1 is replaced by a two-dimensional space $\mathscr{M}$, bound by two axes at right-angle. The changing states of the world, previously resembling beads strung on the time line, are now represented graphically by concentric "waves" radiating from the origin A. For example, the wave HD in Fig. 5.3 with the label t =1 indicates the state of the world at time 1, while the wave FE represents the state of the world at the "next" moment, namely t = 2. Each wave is a quarter-circle with its center at

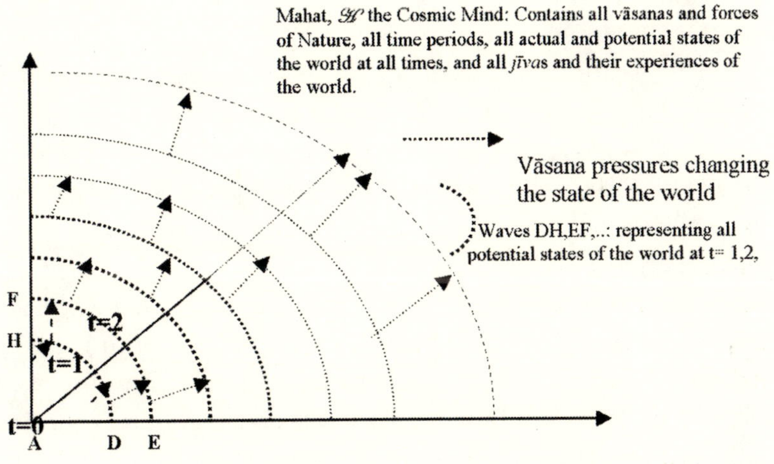
Mahat, $\mathscr{H}$ the Cosmic Mind: Contains all vāsanas and forces of Nature, all time periods, all actual and potential states of the world at all times, and all *jīvas* and their experiences of the world.
Vāsana pressures changing the state of the world
Waves DH,EF,..: representing all potential states of the world at t= 1,2,
F
H
t=2
t=1
t=0
A
D
E

Fig. 5.3: The $\mathscr{M}$-Space or Cosmic Mind

A, the origin, and radius = *t*. Thus the world at *t* =1 is represented by the quarter-circle DH with center at A and radius =1; the world at *t* =2 by the quarter-circle EF with center at A and radius =2, etc.

It is the vāsanas affecting both the gross physical matter and the subtle "mind-intellect" of sentient beings that cause the world to go from one state at t =1 to another state at t = 2. For example, under the pressure of the vāsanas in effect at t =1, the world moves to a different state, indicated by the wave EF, at t =2. To use a more suggestive language, we may say that the winds of vāsanas blowing at time t =1 changes the wave HD at time 1 into the wave FE at time 2. The arrows in Fig. 5.3 represent the innumerable vāsana pressures behind the waves. This picture of the cosmos echoes faithfully a beautiful simile employed by Adi Sankara [69]:

"mayyakhaṇḍa sukhāṁbhodhau bahudhā viśvavīcayaḥ
utpadyante vilīyante māyāmāruta vibhramāt"

"In me the ocean of unbroken Bliss, endless waves of the universe are created and destroyed by the play of the storm of Māyā"

The separation, or distance, between any two consecutive waves in Fig. 5.3 is one unit of cosmic time. We call this distance as "time" mainly to be consistent with the nomenclature used in the classical "Newtonian" representation of the changing world in Fig. 5.1. A more accurate description will be "one unit measure of distance in the $\mathscr{M}$-space". We will have occasion to comment more extensively on the nature of $\mathscr{M}$-space and what the distance in that space measures, but for now will continue to call it as "cosmic time".

Meaning of the Coordinate t: the Experienced World at time t

Two points need to be made to explain what the "waves" and the field in which they arise are. Each wave, *as a whole*, represents the state, $\underline{h}_t$, of the O-E-T at a particular time: for example the arc DH as a whole is the state of the world at t=1. The phrase "as a whole" is used to imply that segments or points on the arc do not have any significance with respect to the state of the world. In particular, they do not represent particular parts or elements of the world. Secondly, the state of the world includes not only an objective description of the physical world at a given time, but also a subjective description of that world from the point of view of each jīva. The physical world being the same, it is experienced by each jīva differently. What is a happy world to one jīva may be at the same time a sad one to another. This fact is conceptually accommodated in the model since the state description of the world includes the physical state as well as the emotions and thoughts specific to every jīva.

Employing the notation previously introduced, we are saying that the wave at time t stands for the vector $\underline{h}_t$. This vector, as noted there, is composed of sub-vectors $\{\underline{h}_{it}\}$, i = 1,…….N, where $\underline{h}_{it}$ stands for the physical-emotional-intellectual state of the i-th jīva or object. The total state of the world thus incorporates the world as experienced by each jīva. The space spanned by $\underline{h}_t$, as defined before, is **H**.

As mentioned earlier the vāsanas only suggest the different possible changes that could happen and their relative likelihood. The possibility actually realized is as willed by Īśvara. Thus, the evolution of the cosmos, shown as the expanding field of waves in the space $\mathscr{M}$, is the combined result of Prakṛti's forces and Īśvara's Will. The waves DH, FE etc shown in Fig. 5.3 can be viewed as the actual state of the world $\underline{h}_t$ that the jīvas experience. The space $\mathscr{M}$ in this case is the field of all experiences of all jīvas from time zero onwards. Alternatively, we can consider each wave to represent *all* possible states in which the world can be at that time, and not just the actual state decided by Īśvara. In this case, each wave can be associated with a probability distribution function over the space **H** and hence may be called,- to loosely borrow a term from physicists- a "probability-wave". The field $\mathscr{M}$ is now the field of all possible experiences of all jīvas from beginning of creation to its end.

The changing world, represented by the sequence of waves, is what is experienced by the sentient jīvas of the cosmos. The "experienced" is shown in our model by the waves at t=0, t=1, t=2 etc, etc. where the parameter *t* is a proxy for $\underline{h}_t$, the world experienced at time *t*. Those familiar with the polar coordinate system for two-dimensional spaces will recognize that *t* is the "radius vector" with A as the origin. The origin A itself is the world at t = 0, i.e. at the beginning of creation. The point A has no reference to any particular event like "Big Bang" since the world could have existed prior to that event. Nor does t=0 refer to any particular time, time itself having come into existence at point A.

Using a polar coordinate system, a point "P" in the space $\mathscr{M}$ can be designated by specifying the wave *t* on which it is located and the "vectorial angle" θ that the line AP makes to an "initial line" (or "horizontal axis") AE. See Fig. 5.4 below. But what does θ signify?

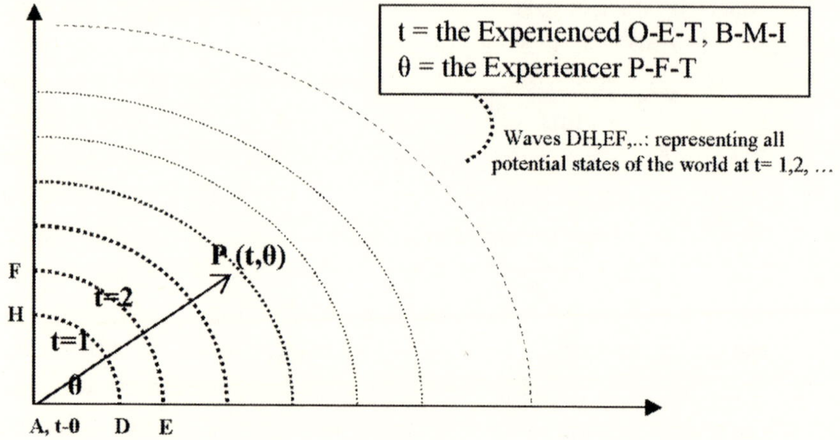

Fig. 5.4: Polar Coordinate Designation of $\mathscr{M}$, the Field of Experiences

Meaning of Coordinate θ: Spiritual Detachment of the Experiencer

Since *t* refers to the experienced, one may expect the other parameter θ to relate to the "experiencers", or jīvas. This indeed is the case, but we need to be clear about the sense in which this is so. The parameter θ does not refer to any physical, mental, or intellectual attributes of the jīva since, by our definition, these are part of the experienced O-E-T. Instead it refers to a jīva's spiritual detachment, a key characteristic of spiritual maturity of a being.

A jīva's encounters with the world produces its life experiences. The nature of the experience is determined not only by the state of the world encountered, but also by the jīva's spiritual detachment at that time. Spiritual detachment is a measure of the purity of mind attained by practices such as the four-fold spiritual disciplines ("*sādhanā catuṣṭayaṁ*") of discrimination (*viveka*), dispassion (*vairāgya*), control over mind and body (*samādhiṣaṭka saṁpatti*) and yearning for liberation (*mumukṣutva*) described in *Vivekachūḍāmaṇi*. The spiritual detachment in jīvas can vary over a wide spectrum, from the lowest level of ignorance to the highest level of Self-Knowledge. At the low end of the spectrum is the jīva which encounters the world in total ignorance. It takes the limited part of the cosmos it knows as the only reality. Unaware of the omnipotent, omniscient Īśvara, it takes itself to be the doer and enjoyer and experiences the resulting joys and sorrows. As the world changes in ways beyond its control, it is stressed by bouts of anxiety. In contrast, at the highest level of detachment is the jīva that has realized the Truth. It witnesses the world even while acting detachedly, with the full knowledge that it is all but a play of *māyā*. This jīva does not suffer, but revels in Bliss, no matter what the state of the world is. As Adi Sankara phrases it, not even a "whiff of suffering" affects the Realized jīva. In this respect this jīva is like the Creator itself.

Swami Tejomayananda

Spiritual detachment is arguably the single most important variable characterizing the level of spiritual maturity of a jīva. Sw. Tejomayananda observes how detachment increases with each of the seven stages of spiritual practice described in *Yoga Vasiṣṭa* and concludes that "one of the measuring rods of spiritual progress is our degree of detachment"[70]. In the chapter on Vāsanas, we will see in mathematical terms how the variable θ provides a summary, as it were, of a jīva's spiritual attributes at any point in time.

Inert matter is not sentient and hence we do not talk of spiritual detachment in their case. However, in Vedānta, animals and even plants are considered as jīvas though generally not as spiritually evolved as human beings. Birth in human form is considered a significant milestone in spiritual evolution of a jīva. Human beings usually have the capacity to witness and question the world around them. Therefore, a value of $\theta > 0$ is generally appropriate in their case.

As a jīva matures spiritually, its detachment, indicated by the second of the two polar coordinates θ, increases. In our model, θ, measured in radians, can take values from 0 to $\pi/2$. The horizontal and vertical axes in Fig. 5.3 or 5.4 correspond to the limiting values of $\theta=0$ and $\theta = \pi/2$ respectively. A jīva at the lower limit of $\theta = 0$ represents a being which is fully attached to the world, ignorant of the Self, and suffering the dualities of pain and pleasure etc. At the other end is $\theta = \pi/2$, which is a jīva living in full knowledge of Self, remaining in Bliss while merely witnessing the changing world. For reasons to be discussed later, the vertical axis can also be identified with *saguṇa Brahman*, or Īśvara. No jīva can have a greater spiritual detachment than Īśvara and hence it is sensible to limit θ to a maximum of π/2 radians.

In concluding this discussion on detachment, it could be asked if there are indeed degrees of spirituality as the model postulates. Is there anything like a halfway *Yogī*, one who is not Realized, yet not fully attached to *saṁsāra*? The idea of jīvas with different degrees of spiritual maturity is not a new fangled idea. For example, the aforementioned commentary by Swami Tejomayananda is supportive of this notion. Swami Vivekananda also makes this clear when he says

"In speaking of the soul, to say a human being is superior to the animal or plant, has no meaning; the whole universe is one. In plants the obstacle to soul-manifestation is very great; in animals little less; and in human beings still less; in cultured, spiritual persons still less and in perfect beings, it has vanished entirely"[71].

The Space defined by (t,θ): $\mathcal{M}$, the Field of Experiences

The space $\mathcal{M}$ defined by the coordinates (t,θ) {with $0 \le t < \infty$ and $0 \le \theta \le \pi/2$} is the first quadrant of a two dimensional space. P(t,θ) represents the point in the $\mathcal{M}$-space where a jīva with detachment θ encounters the world at time t. The result of an encounter of an experiencer with the experienced is an *experience.* The points in space $\mathcal{M}$ are thus points of experience and the space $\mathcal{M}$ as a whole is the field of all experiences of all jīvas from time 0 to infinity. In other words, the $\mathcal{M}$-space represents the entire creation and its evolution over time. According to Vedānta, creation is a projection on the Cosmic Mind, *Mahat*. Therefore the $\mathcal{M}$-space in our geometrical model can be identified with the *Mahat* which itself depends on Brahman for its existence. The field of experiences can also be the "mind-space" or "*mana-akaśaḥ*" mentioned by Sri Ramana. The mind-space, Sri Ramana says, is the support for the physical space.

In our Vedāntic model, time is in *Mahat*, but *Mahat* is not in time. The time-waves do not rise up and die one after another in the *Mahat*. Rather, all time waves- those of past, present, and future-exist simultaneously in that space. Many physicists today hold a nearly identical view about the cosmos but for entirely different reasons. There is evidence from both physics and the teachings of Vedānta that time is something that the individual jīvas experience but which does not exist in reality. The implications of this "stationary time" are profound and even mind boggling. A full discussion of this mystery of time will be taken up in Chapter 9.

Three Quarters are Puruṣa's Glory Only

In the polar coordinate system the parameters t and θ are non-negative; i.e. they cannot be less than zero. In our model, $t = 0$ denotes the beginning of time and creation. It makes no sense then to talk of a "negative time" or a time before the beginning of creation. Similarly, negative values for the parameter θ also do not make sense since a jīva can be only either totally attached to the O-E-T (in which case $\theta = 0$), or somewhat detached from it (in which case $\theta > 0$). The $\mathscr{M}$-space is defined by the region where $t \geq 0$, $\theta \geq 0$ and also $\theta \leq \pi/2$. The reason for restricting θ to a maximum of $\pi/2$ radians is less obvious. It has to do with the characterization of the horizontal and vertical axes that we will point out shortly. The restriction is also for a mathematical reason since otherwise certain variables to be introduced later will have meaningless negative values. Finally, allowing the other values for θ does not add to the explanatory power of the model.

With θ restricted to $(0,\pi/2)$, the $\mathscr{M}$-space, the Field of Experiences, occupies only the first quadrant, or one-fourth, of the total 2-dimensional space defined by the two parameters (t,θ) shown in Fig. 5.5.

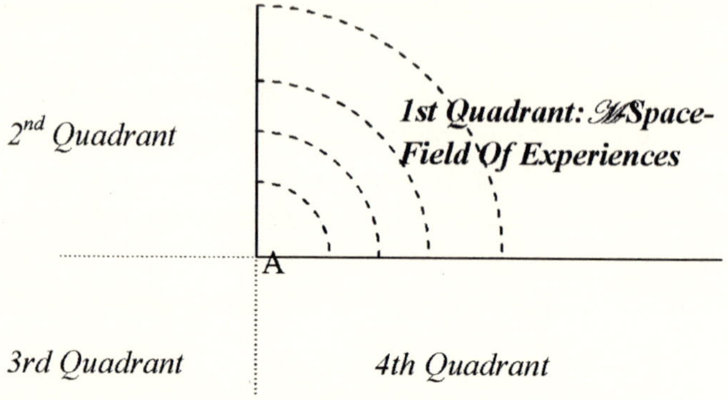

***The 2nd, 3rd, and 4th quadrants are beyond experience**

Fig 5.5: The Four Quadrants of the 2-Dimensional Space of (t,θ)

That is, the entire realm of all possible experiences from beginning to eternity occupy only one fourth of the space. Stated differently, the second, third, and fourth quadrants are beyond anything experiencable and therefore not subject to analysis of any kind.

The above observation will ring a bell in the minds of readers familiar with the famous *Puruṣa Sūktam,* (Hymn to the Cosmic Person) in *Rg Veda* describing the process of creation. There we find the following lines:

"etāvānasya mahimā, ato jyāyāmśca pūruṣaḥ,
pādosya viśvā bhūtāni, tripādasya amṛtam divi

"This much is His Glory only. And Puruṣa is much more than all these. The entire universe of happenings and creatures constitute but a quarter of Him. The remaining three quarters of his Glory consists of Immutable Consciousness" [72].

To summarize the ideas presented so far, the Vedāntic model portrayed in Figs. 5.3, 5.4 and 5.5 is based on the concept of the *"tripuṭi"* of experienced, experience and experiencer. It reflects the Vedāntic views on cause-effects and time and conforms to teachings regarding world, jīvas, spiritual detachment and Īśvara. Representing the cause-effect chain as waves in the Total Mind, is almost a literal interpretation of Advaita Vedāntic thinking. In short, the model we are proposing is consistent with the teachings in the Upaniṣads and *Vedas*.

Spiritual Significance of the Two Axes, $\theta = 0$ and $\theta = \pi/2$

The two axes in Fig. 5.4 describe two diametrically opposite poles, as it were, of the spiritual world. As pointed out earlier, the horizontal axis defined by $\theta = 0$ signifies the spiritual condition of an ignorant jīva. Identifying totally with its body-mind-intellect complex, it arrogates to itself the sense of doer ship and actively indulges in its joys and sorrows. Bound to the changing vicissitudes of life, it leads the life of a time bound mortal being. The vertical axis defined by $\theta = \pi/2$ stands in direct contrast to the horizontal axis. It signifies the spiritual condition of a jīva which has cast-off every last vestige of its ignorance in its Knowledge of Self. It no longer takes the world to be real or its body-mind-intellect to be its true self. It witnesses the world and its own actions with detachment born out of the knowledge that all these are the manifestations of Prakṛti's vāsanas and Īśvara's Will. Not affected in the least by the changes, it remains beyond time in the changeless, immortal, Blissful Self. This is the state of the Realized jīva.

The Realized jīva is in many respects like *Īśvara*, the Creator, in his immanent aspect. The Creator has infinite knowledge. There cannot be anything in the cosmos It is not aware of. It is under Īśvara's direction that the Prakṛti creates. Yet, Īśvara is not attached to anything in the world, but is ever established in the Bliss of Self. As Lord Krishna says:

"Under Me as supervisor, Prakṛti (nature) produces the moving and unmoving; because of this, O Kaunteya, the world revolves".

"These acts do not bind Me, O Dhananjaya, sitting like one indifferent, unattached to those acts" [73].

Īśvara's relationship with the world is said to be both transcendent and immanent. That is, Īśvara pervades the creation, yet is above it all. Fig 2.1 in an earlier chapter brought this out clearly: There Īśvara is shown as being outside the *Mahat* as well as in the "heart space" or causal body of each and every thing in the world. Seated in the heart, Īśvara controls everything in the world, yet remains at all times in its Pure Blissful state by means of this "relation-less relationship" with the world.

Īśvara, in Its immanent aspect, thus truly exemplifies the totally detached Blissful state signified by the vertical axis. For this reason we view the vertical axis as representing the very abode of Īśvara, the *saguṇa* Brahman, the Brahman with attributes of Infinite Knowledge and Universal Love. In terms of Hindu mythology, it is the "*Vaikuṇṭh* " or "*Kailās*" where the Lord dwells and to which all jīvas aspire. The vertical axis reached by a jīva through total detachment is the axis of Knowledge and Love.

The table below is a comparison of the spiritual significance of the two axes.

HORIZONTAL AXIS/ JĪVAS ATTACHED TO WORLD/AXIS OF IGNORANCE & SUFFERING	**VERTICAL AXIS** / ABODE OF ĪŚVARA / AXIS OF KNOWLEDGE & BLISS
Time bound, changes from moment to moment	Timeless, Changeless
In Ignorance; limited in knowledge; finite	Total Knowledge; Infinite
Controlled by vāsanas, natural laws	Controller, Complete Freedom of Will
Ego and selfish interests	Universal, Unconditional Love
Suffering pain and pleasures	Established in constant Bliss

Table 5.1: **HORIZONTAL AND VERTICAL AXES**

Thus in Figs. 5.3, 5.4 etc, the vertical axis is the axis of Perfect Knowledge and Goodness, as opposed to the horizontal axis which one could call the "axis of evil". But, in deference to Vedānta which generally eschews the term "evil", it is more appropriately referred to as the "axis of suffering".

Jīva's Spiritual Progress and The Function θ(t)

Spiritual progress for a jīva is the process by which it makes the transition from the finite, ignorant, suffering, O-E-T bound existence (the horizontal axis) to the all-knowing, all-loving, infinite abode of Īśvara (the vertical axis.) It makes this progress by learning from life itself. Swami Chinmayanandaji has very appropriately defined life as the "**L**imitless **I**ncessant **F**low of **E**xperience". For a jīva, the flow of experiences never stops from the beginning of time to the time of its final liberation from the *samsār*. Every experience of life has the potential to advance the jīva along the spiritual path. Because of this, a jīva's detachment, θ, is not a constant but a variable that will change and generally increase with time over the long term.

A jīva's position in $\mathscr{M}$ is represented geometrically by the coordinates (t,θ) where *t* = time and θ = the jīva's spiritual detachment. The degree of detachment changes with time due to the experiences it has of the world, including, in particular, its spiritual practices. The varying θ can be mathematically represented by a function θ(t) of *t*. We call θ(t) the jīva's "*spiritual progress function*", or simply as the "*progress function*". The function can be plotted as a curve in the $\mathscr{M}$-space as illustrated in Fig. 5.6. The plot is the graphical representation of the spiritual growth of the jīva and may be referred to as the jīva's spiritual "*progress curve*".

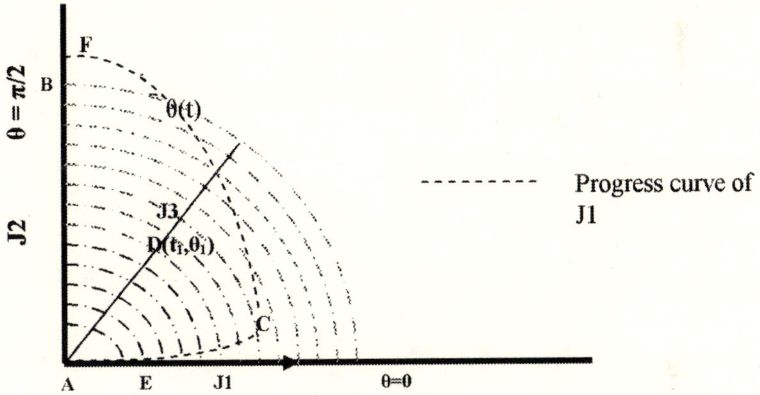

Fig. 5.6: Progress Function θ(t) of a Jīva

In Fig 5.6, the curve connecting the points AECF represents a function θ(t) that consistently increases with t. This is the progress curve of a jīva that has shown steady spiritual progress. In reality, the spiritual evolution of a jīva may be marked by progress as well as setbacks. The curve θ(t) will therefore zigzag. A special case of theoretical interest is the jīva with constant, or unchanging, spiritual detachment. Its progress curve will be a straight line going through the origin A. For example, the line AD is the progress curve of a jīva J3 with a constant detachment θ_1 given by the angle EAD. If the detachment is higher, the line showing the evolution will be higher (making a larger angle with the horizontal axis).

The Origin and the Destination

The point of intersection of the horizontal and vertical axes, the point A in Figs. 5.5 and 5.6, is customarily referred to as the "origin". In our polar coordinate system, origin is the point where $t=0$. That is, origin is the point of beginning of time or creation. The spiritual journey of all jīvas also begins at A, if jīvas are assumed to be born simultaneous with the creation of the cosmos. The wave at $t=0$ is just a point, a point where both horizontal and vertical axis come together. Therefore all jīvas can claim the vertical axis to be the source from which their spiritual journey starts. The "fall" from the vertical axis, that is ignorance of Self, accompanies birth. Indeed some define the birth of the jīva as the effect of this ignorance, the Vedāntic equivalent of the "original sin". The spiritual journey of the jīva starts soon after birth, as it laboriously climbs its way back to the source from which it was born. As mentioned in the earlier chapters on Vedānta, all jīvas eventually reach the abode of Īśvara, though each jīva takes its own time and route through the *samsār* in completing the journey.

The progress function $\theta(t)$ is the mathematical description of the route a jīva takes. It begins at A at $t=0$ and ends at the vertical axis at some future time, t^*, when it Realizes the Self; i.e. when $\theta(t^*) = \pi/2$. The path between time 0 and t^* can meander depending on the ups and downs in the jīva's spiritual progress over its many life times. But once having reached the blissful destination of the vertical axis, the jīva does not fall back, but stays in the realized state. As Lord Krishna says:

"yat gatvā na nivartante tat dhāma paramam mama"

or *".. to which having gone they return not, that is my Supreme Abode"* [74].

By this it is clearly indicated that there is no return for a jīva to worldly life after having reached the supreme abode of Īśvara. In our notation, if $\theta(t^*) = \pi/2$ then $\theta(t) = \pi/2$ for all $t > t^*$.

Attachment to Higher and Detachment from Lower

An obvious and immediate property of the 2-dimensional model is that as a jīva moves away from the lower self (by increasing detachment θ) it must necessarily get closer to the Higher. Therefore, detachment from the world and attachment to the Self are not two independent processes, but a single one. Gurudev Sw. Chinmayananda often compared this process of detachment with the technique of a caterpillar as it moves around on a tree. The creature stretches itself and attaches to the next leaf before it does let go of the one it is on. Similarly, suggests Gurudev, a jīva must reach out to the Higher even as it renounces the lower.

Plotting Progress curve of Multiple Jīvas

The path, $\theta(t)$, of more than one jīva can be shown in Fig. 5.6 without causing confusion since generally each will have a distinct progress function $\theta_1(t)$, and $\theta_2(t)$, etc. In fact in Fig 5.6 we are showing the path of three jīvas, one with varying spiritual detachment, a second one with $\theta(t) = 0$ for all t and the third with $\theta(t) = \pi/2$ for all t. Now, it is possible that two jīvas can have the same detachment at a given time t. That is, $\theta_1(t) = \theta_2(t)$. In this case their progress curves will cross in the graph and the two jīvas will be shown collocated in Fig. 5.6 at the point $(t, \theta_1(t))$. Since each point in $\mathscr{M}$-space represents an experience of a jīva, does it mean that the two jīvas have the same experience at time t? The answer is: "No". Many, many jīvas no doubt contact the world at any given time, but each jīva sees only its own selected part of the world and not the whole world. Even if they see the same part of the world, each jīva brings its own perspective to what it sees and therefore experiences essentially a different world. This is particularly the case with mind-intellect component of the O-E-T, where the emotions and thoughts encountered by each jīva is all its own. Thus when we say each point P in the $\mathscr{M}$-space represents the experience of a jīva with a certain detachment, it does allow for multiple jīvas of same detachment to have different personal experiences.

Experiences From Jīva's Contacts With the World

In Figs. 5.1 and 5.2, the polar coordinates t and θ are used to represent respectively the experienced world at time t and the experiencing jīva with detachment θ. Each point (t, θ) in the space $\mathscr{M}$ signifies an encounter or experience the jīva has with the world at time t. Let us pause for a moment here and see what exactly the words "experiences from contacts with the world" might mean.

A jīva is alive to the world around it. As shown schematically in

Fig. 2.5, it perceives the world, and reacts and acts in response to its perceptions. The sentient mind of the jīva makes all this interaction possible. The dynamics behind this interaction has been explained by Swami Chinmayananda using the analogy of the "*havan*"[19]. In this ritual the priest invokes various *deva*s as he pours clarified butter, grain, etc into the sacred fire[20]. The fire flares up and roars into life as it comes into contact with the offerings. Similarly, a jīva's sentient mind flares up when it comes into contact with the sensual stimulus poured into it through the five sense organs. In Vedānta, each sense organ is said to be presided over by a *deva* and therefore what a sense organ channels into the mind is like an offering in the name of that *deva*.

The nature of the contact depends on what is being poured in (namely, the material aspects of the specific worldly contact) as well as the nature of the receiving mind and the vāsanas. There is no end to the variety and complexity of these contacts or the different ways in which the mind can get stimulated. These experiences after all define life itself with its rich, unpredictable variety. But, following the insight given in a Bhagavad Gītā verse noted earlier[21], we understand that finally it is the dualities of pain and pleasure at the body level, joy and sorrow at the mind level, and honor and dishonor at the intellect level that is produced by contacts with the world. The simple truth behind this statement should be clear if only we think for a minute about what our life at any given moment really boils down to. What we experience ultimately as a result of contact with objects of the world, and contact with our own emotions and thoughts, is a state of being that is somewhere between extreme pain and extreme pleasure at the physical level, between extreme joy and extreme sorrow at the emotional level, and between high regard and low self-esteem at the intellect level. It is safe to say that normally we spend most of our time somewhere in the middle of these extremes.

The world changes from moment to moment and hence our experience also can change from moment to moment. Our mind and intellect, which are part of the experienced world, also change as our attention shifts from one thought to another. A pleasant thought can

19 *Havan:* the Vedic ritual of offering oblations in the sacred fire.

20 *Deva:* a demi-god such as *Indra*, *Varuna*.

21 *"mātrā sparśāstu kaunteya ....."* quoted in Chapter 2 of this book.

be interrupted without warning by a painful memory as we suddenly recall some unpleasant event of the past. Thus we pass through countless number of experiences during our waking and dreaming hours. The second line of the Gītā verse points out to the momentary, transient *(anitya)* nature of our experiences and advises us to cultivate forbearance.

Obviously, it is impossible to predict what the experience of a jīva will be at any given time. Fortunately, however, our task does not call for such prediction; instead we focus only on the spiritually significant aspect of each jīva-world encounter. As indicated in Fig. 2.6, there are two possible spiritual outcomes from each worldly experience: "suffering" and "knowledge". In what follows, our attempt will be to model mathematically these twin outcomes as a function of the jīva's spiritual detachment. Once again, we find the wisdom of the Upaniṣads readily available to help us in this key task.

The Twin –Birds Of Muṇḍaka Upaniṣad

The approach used for representing the spiritual detachment and its effects on the jīva's experience of O-E-T is best explained from the well known metaphor of twin birds found in the *Muṇḍaka Upaniṣad* [75]:

"Two birds, bound one to the other in close friendship, perch on the self-same tree. One of them eats the fruits of the tree with relish, while the other looks on without eating.

"Seated on the self-same tree, one of them- the Ego- sunk in ignorance and deluded, grieves his impotence. But when he sees the other- the Lord, the Worshipful- and also His Glory, he becomes free from dejection."

The tree referred to is the tree of *samsār* or O-E-T. The two birds "bound one to the other in close friendship" are the two selves of a jīva: one is the lower self that eats the fruits of the tree (i.e. experiences the changes in O-E-T) and the other is the "higher self" that simply witnesses the scene. Using this imagery, the scripture drives home the point that both the mundane and the divine are within each jīva.

In Fig. 5.6, the lower self of the jīva, fully attached to the world, is perched on the lower branch, namely the horizontal axis $\theta=0$; the fully detached witnessing higher self is on the higher branch, the vertical axis $\theta = \pi/2$. Spread between these two axes or branches, is the $\mathscr{M}$-space, the tree of *samsār*. A jīva's spiritual detachment at any time measures how much it is identified with the higher self rather than its lower self. If the identification with lower self is complete, $\theta=0$ and the jīva is located on the horizontal axis. In Fig. 5.6, J1 is such a jīva. If the identification is fully with the higher self, $\theta = \pi/2$ and the jīva is located on the vertical axis; J2 in Fig. 5.6 is an example. For a jīva partially identified with the lower self, $0 < \theta < \pi/2$ and the jīva's location is somewhere above the horizontal axis and to the right of the vertical axis; for example, J3 in Fig. 5.6.

The higher self in each jīva is identical in nature with Īśvara as evidenced by the second verse of the above Upaniṣad *mantra* which addresses it as the "Lord, Worshipful". Sri Ramana also makes this explicit in the following verse in *Upadeśa Sāram*:

īśajīvayor veṣadhī bhidā, satsvabhāvato vastu kevalaṁ

Īśvara and jīva differ in form only; by nature of their Self they are of one substance [76].

Modeling Spiritual Outcome of Contacts with World

The twin-bird imagery of the Upaniṣad gives us a straight forward way to capture geometrically the spiritual outcome of contacts with O-E-T. Consider a jīva with a constant detachment θ during the time interval (t_1,t_2). The progress curve for this jīva is the line PQ shown in Fig. 5.7, making an angle θ with the horizontal axis. The jīva may have a large number of contacts with the world during the time interval (t1, t2). Our objective is to model the effects of jīva's experiences during this time interval on its suffering and knowledge.

The twin bird analogy suggests a very important simplifying feature: The spiritual outcome does not depend on the nature and intensity of the worldly experiences, but only on how much of that experience the jīva "eats". To recall what we saw in the previous chapters, a jīva which has the "I, mine, I want, I do, and I enjoy" notions during a contact with the world, considers the pain-pleasure dualities produced by the contact as its own and suffers thereby. It does not matter if the fruits of the tree are sweet or bitter; the bird eating a fruit is bound to suffer compared to the witnessing bird. Similarly, it does not matter whether the worldly experience is painful or pleasurable, joyful or sorrowful, honorable or dishonorable; the jīva "eating" these experiences suffers as a result. The jīva J1 in Fig. 5.6 suffers while J3, which merely witnesses its experiences, is free from suffering.

Based on this Upaniṣadic insight, we propose that the two spiritual outcomes of suffering and knowledge are the projections of PQ on the horizontal and vertical axis respectively. In Fig. 5.7, projection on horizontal axis is PR = PQ cosθ and projection on vertical axis is RQ= PQ sinθ. The reasoning behind this suggestion will be obvious to the mathematically versed reader and goes as follows. *Cosθ* measures the extent of the jīva's identification to the lower self. When θ =0, cosθ = 1 indicating that the jīva is totally identified with the lower self

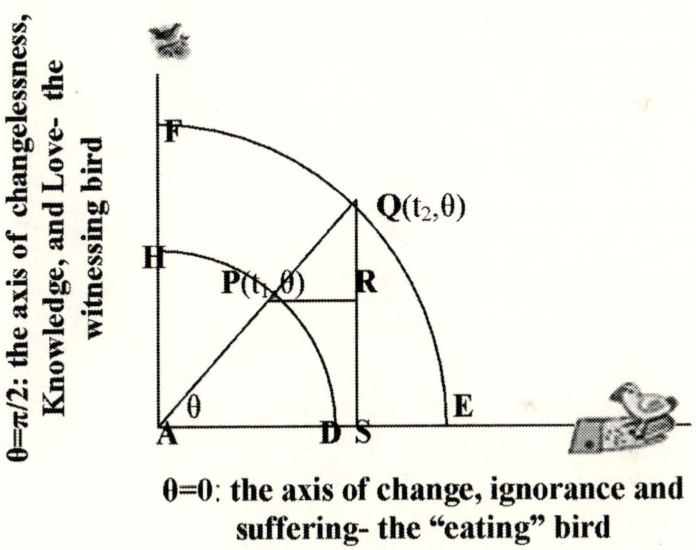

Fig. 5.7: Spiritual Components of Contact With O-E-T

and the world of constant change it "eats" from. As θ increases, cosθ decreases, signifying growing detachment from the world of the lower self. Finally, when θ reaches its maximum at π/2, cosθ = 0, indicating complete dissociation with the lower self. The projection PQ.cosθ is thus appropriate for measuring how much the jīva eats the fruits of its experiences during (t1, t2), that is to say, how much it "suffers" the dualities of pain-pleasure etc. In this sense, PQ.cosθ is a measure of the jīva's "suffering" during the time interval (t_1, t_2).

Similarly *sinθ* measures the jīva's identification with the Higher

Self. For $\theta = 0$, $\sin\theta = 0$, indicating "zero projection" on the vertical axis; that is a jīva with no knowledge of the Higher Self at all. Such a jīva is considered ignorant (i.e. ignorant of the Reality, even if very learned in worldly matters) and also lacking in the higher virtues of universal, unconditional love that comes from this knowledge. As θ increases, $\sin\theta$ also increases and the jīva gets increasingly identified with, or "established in", the Higher Self. *Muṇḍaka Upaniṣad* says the jīva attains proximity and similarity to the Supreme ("*paramaṁ sāmyaṁ upaiti*") as it grows spiritually more detached [77]. The jīva manifests more and more of the Knowledge and Goodness of the Higher Self in its transactions with the world. Such transactions are considered "meritorious" as it helps in the spiritual advancement and at the same time the jīva derives a sense of deep contentment (*saṁtoṣ*) as a result. As the earlier quote from the *Muṇḍaka Upaniṣad* puts it, "*When he sees the other- the Lord, the Worshipful- and also His Glory, he becomes free from dejection*". This contentment is quite different and apart from, any happiness that the jīva may obtain from the material aspects of the transaction. The happiness at the material level is quite transient, as we know from our experience. But the spiritual merit accrued, we are told, stays with the jīva even from one life to next as mental impressions (*saṁskāras*) which modify the jīva's vāsanas for the better. The projection QR = PQ. $\sin\theta$ is a measure of this merit gained by the jīva from its encounter at P. PQ.$\sin\theta$ is the "merit" part of the experience during (t1, t2), contributing to exhaustion of the jīva's vāsanas and increased spiritual knowledge.

Relative Goodness, r_A, of a Jīva

It was pointed out earlier that Knowledge and Goodness are viewed by Vedāntins as essentially one and the same. What is meant by "goodness" is the universal, unconditional love that a Realized jīva exhibits towards all beings; we had earlier referred to this as the acme of Goodness. This unconditional love can be sustained only by a deep, intuitive understanding (*vijñāna)* of Reality, and not by mere intellectual comprehension (*jñāna*) of Vedāntic theory. Intellectual knowledge matures into true understanding when the knowledge has become the very nature of the jīva. We therefore use the phrase "*Universal, unconditional love and understanding*" in referring to the Knowledge and Goodness expected of a Realized jīva.

Knowledge and Goodness cannot be measured in absolute terms, but can be compared to that of a Realized jīva. In our model, a jīva's "Relative Goodness", r_A, is indicated by $\sin\theta$. The maximum r_A can be is 1 when $\theta = \pi/2$, that is on total detachment or Realization. For other jīvas, r_A is less than 1. Therefore, r_A is an appropriate measure of a jīva's Knowledge and Goodness compared to that of a fully Realized jīva; it is the level of "universal, unconditional love and understanding" attained by the jīva. $r_{A,}$ being dependent on θ, can vary with time.

JĪVAS OF UNIFORM SPIRITUAL DETACHMENT

Typically, a jīva's spiritual detachment changes with time; therefore the function $\theta(t)$ is not constant. Our analysis must therefore eventually deal with the time-varying $\theta(t)$. But it will help to start with a simple, even if unrealistic, case so as to understand the steps involved in the analysis. This is the special case of jīvas whose spiritual detachment is unchanged, or uniform, over time. For such a jīva $\theta(t) = \theta$ for all t and the progress curve is a straight line; for example the line APQR in Fig. 5.8.

In this uniform case, the jīva's suffering due to all its experiences from time 0 through time t, is given by $t.\cos\theta$. To illustrate, in Fig. 5.8, AB= $t1.\cos\theta$, AC = $t2.\cos\theta$, and AD = $t3.\cos\theta$ measure the suffering component from time t=0 through t1, t2, and t3 respectively.

Similarly, the projections BP = $t1.\sin\theta$, CQ = $t2.\sin\theta$, and DR = $t3.\sin\theta$ represent the merit component of the jīva's experiences from time t=0 through time t1, t2, and t3 respectively. In general, the "accumulated merit through time t" is given by $t.\sin\theta$.

(See Fig. 5.8 in the next page)

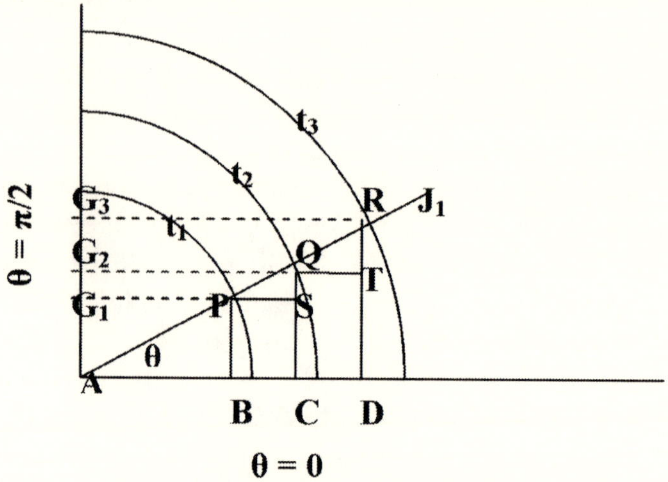

Fig. 5.8 Jīva of Uniform Spiritual Detachment

In the sequel we will use the notation $\tau(t)$, and G(t) to denote "suffering through time t", and "accumulated merit through time t". In the uniform detachment case, we just saw that

$$\tau(t) = t.\cos\theta \text{ and } G(t) = t.\sin\theta$$

In the range $(0<\theta<\pi/2)$, cosθ and sinθ are positive and hence the functions G(t) and $\tau(t)$ are positive, increasing functions of time t. It will be noted that (τ,G) are the Cartesian coordinates corresponding to the polar coordinates (t,θ). The spiritual significance of the two Cartesian coordinates is examined next in some detail.

τ(t) as Experienced Time

In the discussions above, t.cosθ is taken as a measure of the suffering of the jīva through time t. However, mathematically, t.cosθ has the same dimensions as *t* since cosθ is just a dimensionless number. We are therefore calling something which has characteristics of time as a measure of jīva's suffering. This is justified since time and suffering are related, as pointed out in Upaniṣads. For example, Kathopaniṣad [78] describes the ordinary jīva living in duality as going "from death to death".

"mṛtyoḥ sa mṛtyuṁ gacchati, ya iha nāneva paśyati"

The term "death" as often used in Vedānta refers to change; every change in the world is the death of one state and the birth of the next. With this understanding, the Upaniṣad is simply stating that a jīva living in duality suffers change after change. Suffering includes both the joy of positive changes and pain of negative changes.

Time, we had observed earlier, is also defined in terms of changes: The interval between two changes is one unit of time. The jīva experiences time as it goes from change to change. The experienced time, as the Upaniṣad *mantra* hints, is dependent on how much the jīva is bound to duality, that is, on its spiritual detachment θ. In fact, $\cos\theta$ is just such a measure of the degree of attachment to O-E-T and $t.\cos\theta$, denoted by $\tau(t)$, the experienced time, is the sum effect of living with detachment θ during (0, t). $\tau(t)$ also serves as a proxy for "suffering" because of the relation between suffering and time noted above. By "proxy" we mean that suffering is related to $t.\cos\theta$, and not that it is $t.\cos\theta$ [22]. If detachment is totally lacking, $\theta = 0$, the jīva moves with changing cosmos along the horizontal axis. The experienced time for this jīva is $\tau = t.\cos(0) = t$; that is experienced time and cosmic time are same. This is the maximum that experienced time can be. At the other extreme, a jīva which is totally detached has $\theta = \pi/2$. The experienced time for this jīva is $\tau = t.\cos \pi/2 = 0$. That is, this jīva does not experience time; it, like Īśvara, is beyond time.

"Doing time" is a U.S. slang for incarceration. When a criminal is sentenced to jail, the severity of the crime is primarily reflected in the length of time behind bars. For a prisoner, "doing time" is suffering. Against the background of this analogy, the term "*bandha*" or bondage used in Vedānta for the state of the ignorant jīva is very appropriate. Such a jīva is indeed "doing time" incarcerated in this world and its suffering (experienced time) is proportionate to the severity of its "sin", namely attachment to world as measured by $\cos\theta$. Spiritual goal is to secure release, *mokṣa*, from this bondage.

G(t), Accumulated Merit vs. r_A, Goodness

In Hinduism there is the concept of "accumulated merit" representing the sum effect of all good deeds done over all lifetimes by a jīva until the

22 We will see in the Chapter 8 a more complete characterization of suffering that explicitly considers the role of vāsanas in determining suffering.

present moment. We view G(t) also as the cumulative merit of the jīva at time t, but must qualify it with some important clarification regarding the meaning of the term "merit".

Meritorious deeds can be of two different kinds. In the first category are good deeds (*karmas*) performed for the sake of some definite material gain in this world or in heaven. We may call these "materially good" actions. For example: charity and service done with some selfish motive such as for fame here or for heaven hereafter. Such selfish actions do not exhaust the vāsanas, and, as explained in Gītā, merit gained from them can in fact bind the jīva to *samsār* even if they lead it temporarily to heaven [79]. The accumulated results of good (*puṇya)* and bad (*pāpa)* actions can make one go back and forth between heaven, earth and hell as per the laws of *karma.* This is not to condemn good *karmas* of this kind as totally worthless; they can encourage the jīva to undertake later more truly beneficial spiritual efforts. In the second category are what we may call as "spiritually good" acts of selfless service and other spiritual practices which are undertaken for no material goal, but only for the sake of Liberation from the material realm. They reduce the vāsanas, purify the mind, and increase the spiritual knowledge, while bestowing the peace of contentment on the jīva. They eventually lead to the full Knowledge of the Self and Bliss of Realization which is vastly superior to any excitement a heaven has to offer [80].

The term "accumulated merit" as used in these pages refers to the second category only, namely the results of spiritually good actions. It is the cumulative spiritual result of transacting with the world while established, to some degree, in Goodness; that is, with a degree of detachment. Note that we are making here a fine distinction between merit and Goodness which is clearly brought out by the mathematical equivalents of these two concepts. Mathematically, the relative Goodness of a jīva, r_A, is $sin\theta$, which depends on θ, the jīva's spiritual detachment and purity of mind. On the other hand, accumulated merit, G(t), is $t.sin\theta$, and represents the direct result of transacting with the world for t units of time with spiritual detachment θ. G(t) is an increasing function of time as long as $\theta > 0$. The distinction between merit acquired and Goodness is easily understood by comparing these in physical terms to distance traveled and speed respectively. Distance traveled equals *t*.speed. Increasing the speed increases the distance traveled. But speed does not necessarily increase just by traveling even for long distances. Speed can be increased only by the force of acceleration. Similarly, increasing Goodness, i.e. $\sin\theta$, increases accumulated merit $G(t)$, but Goodness does not necessarily increase by accumulating more and more merit. Goodness and Knowledge can be increased only by bringing to bear the required will power to purify the mind and increase the detachment.

Referring to Fig. 5.8, the jīva J_1's accumulated merit at time t_1, t_2, and t_3 are respectively G_1, G_2, and G_3. The projection of J_1's progress curve on the vertical axis steadily climbs up as time goes by. But this does not mean that J_1 is climbing higher in Goodness and Knowledge. Increasing Goodness and Knowledge requires increasing detachment so that the jīva's progress curve- the line AR- shifts to the left and get closer to vertical axis. To attain Realization, the jīva's progress curve must coincide with the vertical axis; it is not enough if its projection G on the vertical axis is very large. This subtle difference arises because we are using polar coordinate system where Goodness and Knowledge is represented by $\theta = \pi/2$, the *entire* vertical axis. Projections on this axis do not measure Goodness and Knowledge.

This distinction between merit and Goodness introduced by mathematical considerations agrees with the Vedāntic view that liberation does not come about by only performing spiritually good actions for a long time, without making the effort to achieve higher levels of detachment. One might ask what accumulated merit is good for, if it does not automatically lead to Liberation. Is the conjecture shown in Fig. 2.6- that meeting life's experiences in detachment leads to increased spiritual knowledge- invalid? This is not so. Performing actions in detachment brings about certain peace and contentment. Higher the detachment we show in our transactions, the more the contentment in life. This is the immediate reward, here and now, of living a spiritual life. Additionally, the accumulated merit, which is the cumulative effect of living in Goodness, serves also as the "spiritual reserve" a jīva has within itself at a given time to meet intelligently the coming encounters with the world. In other words, armed with its acquired merit, the jīva is more prepared to meet future challenges of life and hence is less fearful and anxious.

But more important than the above immediate reward is the

potential "vāsana reduction" that takes place when a jīva transacts with a degree of detachment. This process is amply explained by Gurudev Sri Chinmayananda in his many commentaries, especially on *Karma Yoga*. As we perform an act with detachment, -that is, act not with desire for the fruits of action, but as a sacred duty to be performed accepting whatever the resulting material gains and losses might be-, then the vāsanas associated with that desire are reduced. To act with attachment, on the other hand, is to only reinforce the vāsanas. Mind gets purified by reducing the vāsanas and the purified mind leads to increased Goodness and Knowledge. This is the logic behind the assertion in Fig. 2.6 that transacting with detachment leads to increased spiritual knowledge. In reply to a query from Arjuna, Lord Krishna says that the good deeds of a jīva are not wasted even if they fail to bring liberation in the present life [81]. That jīva takes birth in a noble family of *yogīs* or afforded other similar conducive opportunities to gain Knowledge and advance spiritually in its future life.

While accumulated merit G(t) has been related mathematically in simple terms to detachment, modeling mathematically the above processes of vāsana reduction and increase in spiritual knowledge remains a goal yet to be achieved. We will have occasion to comment further on this issue later in the book.

Contraction of Experienced Time With Increasing Spiritual Detachment

As θ increases in the range $(0,\pi/2)$, $\cos\theta$ decreases and therefore, $t.\cos\theta$ also decreases. In words, this says that as spiritual detachment grows, experienced time decreases. Fig. 5.9 below illustrates this graphically and may help in visualizing the result better. J1 and J2 are two jīvas with uniform detachment θ_1 and θ_2 respectively, θ_2 being greater than θ_1. P and Q are their points of contact with the world at time t. The time experienced by J1 and J2 over the time interval (0,t) are $AC = t.\cos\theta_1$ and $AB = t.\cos\theta_2$ respectively. It is readily seen that AB is less than AC. That is, experienced time is less for the jīva with higher detachment. Generalizing, we conclude that higher the detachment of a jīva, less is its experienced time.

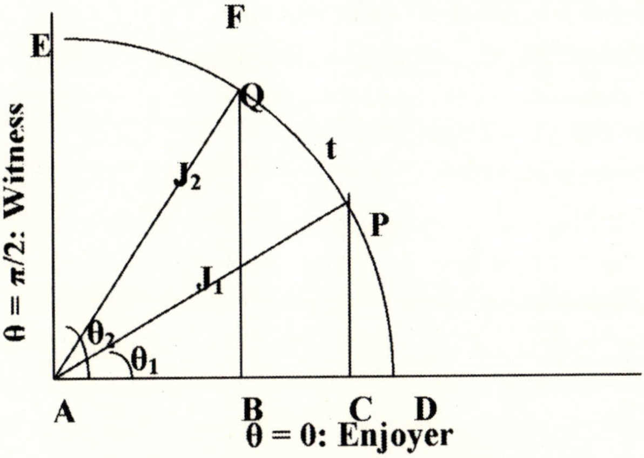

Fig 5.9 Contraction of Experienced Time with Increasing Spiritual Detachment

An Analogy Using Jet Travel

An analogy may help to illustrate the above important observation. Imagine motoring at the (unrealistically) high speed of 400 mph along a highway flanked by towns, buildings, farms, hills etc on either side. The visual impact of the scenery rushing by on both sides at such high speed, as well as the noise and motion of the vehicle, can overwhelm the senses of the traveler inside. With adrenal flowing, the motorist may feel thrilled by the high speed and at the same time also very apprehensive. Imagine now another person traveling also at 400 mph, but in a plane thousands of feet above the same highway. The same terrain of cities and mountains pass by below but there is for her none of the overpowering sense of rapid changes that the earth-bound traveler feels. Everything else being equal, the jet passenger is more serene than the motorist in the car even though both are in effect traversing the same changing terrain at the same speed.

A jīva with some spiritual detachment from O-E-T is like the jet passenger, except that we are dealing with travel over the space of experiences rather than the material space. Higher the detachment of a jīva, higher above the world of changes is its "flight path" (i.e. the line AQ in the case J2, and AP for J1), and more its serenity compared to a worldly being traveling hugging the horizontal axis. The spiritually detached jīva subjectively experiences fewer changes than the worldly being even while witnessing the same changing O-E-T. This is the basic result demonstrated above.

Practical Verification of Contraction of Experienced Time

In spiritual literature of any tradition, including Vedānta, there is usually no attempt to quantify the degree of spirituality of a jīva, or measure the effects of spirituality on that being's experiences. However, mystic traditions do claim that time comes to a standstill for one fully established in the Self. To quote Swami Sivananda:

"There is neither darkness nor void in this experience (of samādhi). It is all light. There is neither sound nor touch nor form. It is a tremendous experience of unity and oneness. There is neither time nor causation here" [82].

There are some insightful references to relativity of time in Sri Ramana's teachings also. For example we find the following conversation with Sri Ramana recorded by a disciple:

"There was a reference to reincarnation... The latest case reported of a boy of seven is different, however. He recalls his past births. Inquiries go to show that the previous body was given up ten months ago. The question arises how the matter stood for six years and two months previous to the death of the former body. Did the soul occupy two bodies at the same time? Sri Bhagavan pointed out that the seven years is according to the boy; ten months is according to the observer. The difference is due to these two different upadhis. The boy's experience, extending to seven years, has been calculated by the observer to cover only ten months of his own time"[83].

Sri Ramana himself had experienced contraction in time. In recounting his early days, it has been recorded that he took shelter in a lamb pen which was hardly tall enough for him to sit erect or long enough to stretch. When it rained he remained wet on a sodden ground. Yet he did not feel any inconvenience because he had no body sense. "*Time and Space did not exist for him. He felt that sunrise and sunset came in quick succession."* [84]

More direct to the theme of our discussion is the following excerpt from Gurudev Swami Chinmayanandaji's commentary on a verse in Bhagavad Gītā referring to the length of a day and night of the Creator [85]:

"Einstein's "Theory of Relativity" has pricked the bubble and it has been accepted even in the West that the concepts of time and space depend upon individual factors governing their measurements. Time hangs heavily and moves at a snail's pace when one is in agitation or anxiously waiting for something; while, to the same individual, time flies when he is quite at ease with himself, under circumstances happy, pleasant and entertaining. One

playing cards knows not when the night was spent and he is surprised when he notices the early dawn peeping through the windows. The same person will complain that each moment has lengthened itself to become hours, when he is at some unpleasant work or in pains. One who is enjoying the homogeneous experience of sleep, has no concept of time at all, while he is sleeping.

From the above, it has been logically concluded in the philosophy of the Hindus that time truly is the measure of interval between two experiences. The greater the number of experiences that flood the mind to agitate it, the slower time moves; while the longer the same experience continues faster moves the time. In a given single experience there is no perception of time just as there is no concept of distance when there is only one point; distances can be measured only between two or more points. Basing their calculations upon this theory, the Pauranic Poets rightly conceived that their Gods had a larger dial for their divine watches. In the Upaniṣads also, we find a scale of relative intensity of Bliss-experience from a mortal, healthy young man living in conducive environments, up to the very Creator Himself. This ascending scale of joy experienced in different realms of Consciousness has been found there as showing the relative mental equipoise and tranquility at those different levels of existence."

The insightful views expressed above by the great Vedāntin agree with our mathematical model in the way time is defined: time is interval between consecutive experiences. The relationship indicated between subjective time and state of mind also concurs with the observations based on our model[23]. Further, in the next chapter, we will see how the model supports the Upaniṣadic statement referred to above regarding the "ascending scale of joy".

---

23 The statement that time *flies* for a jīva in a relaxed state of mind may appear, at first reading, to contradict our observation that experienced time *slows* as detachment grows. However there is really no such contradiction. Consider the example of a person playing cards who feels he has been playing for only a couple of hours. When he looks up at the clock on the wall which tells him that he has been at the card table for six hours, he exclaims "How time flies!" By this he means that a time-duration of six hours was experienced by him as only two hours. It is as though the hour-hand of his subjective mental clock advanced by only two while the hour-hand on the wall clock advanced by six. In other words, his mental clock had slowed down compared to the wall clock. What actually "flew" was the time as shown by the wall clock compared to which the mental clock registering his experienced time slowed down.

Thus, other than the novelty of geometric representation, there is not anything in the mathematical model contradictory, or new, to Vedānta. In the next chapter we will further study the time contraction phenomenon and its rather surprising similarity to the space-time relationship in Einstein's Relativity Theory.

CHAPTER 6

Universal Love and the Fundamental Law of Spirituality

"Such a realized one, in this state of his experience (of the Oneness of the universe) alone, can break away from all his identifications with his own body, home, community, state, nation, and world and come to live as a Universal Lover of All. He alone can cry out truly, "May the entire living world be happy!" Him the world of creatures cannot but love and adore." - Swami Chinmayananda.

We commence the discussions in this chapter by examining the relationship between contraction in experienced time and Relative Awareness. We continue to use the case of jīvas with uniform spiritual detachment, deferring the more general case of varying $\theta(t)$ to a later section of the chapter.

Time Contraction and Relative Awareness

Consider a jīva J2 with detachment = α. In Fig. 6.1 below, the line AC represents the progress curve of this jīva. The experienced time for the jīva is $\tau(t) = t. \cos\alpha$. Had J2 been fully bound to O-E-T, its experienced time would have been t. Therefore we may say that experienced time is compressed by a factor $\cos\alpha$ for J2 relative to the time experienced by a worldly "totally ignorant-of-Self" jīva like J1. In all these comparisons involving two or more jīvas, we tacitly assume there is no difference between the two jīva*s* other than in their spiritual detachment[24]. Let T_{J2} = time experienced by J2 during the interval (0,*t*), and T_{J1}= time experienced by J1 in the same duration. As reasoned earlier in Chapter 5

T_{J2} = AB, T_{J1} = AE, and the Relative Awareness r_A of jīva J2 = sin (α)

The *time- compression ratio* T_{J2} / T_{J1} = AB / AE = AB/ AC = cos(α).
Since cos(α) = √ (1- sin²(α)) we have the relation, reasoned from principles of Vedānta,

$$T_{J2} / T_{J1} = \sqrt{(1- (r_A)^2)} \qquad \text{Eq. (6.1)}$$

where T_{J1}= time for a worldly {i.e. "ignorant of the Self"} jīva J1, T_{J2} = time for a jīva J2 with some Knowledge of Self, and r_A = Self-Knowledge of J2 relative to that of the Perfect Being (maximum possible Knowledge of Self of one fully established in Self).

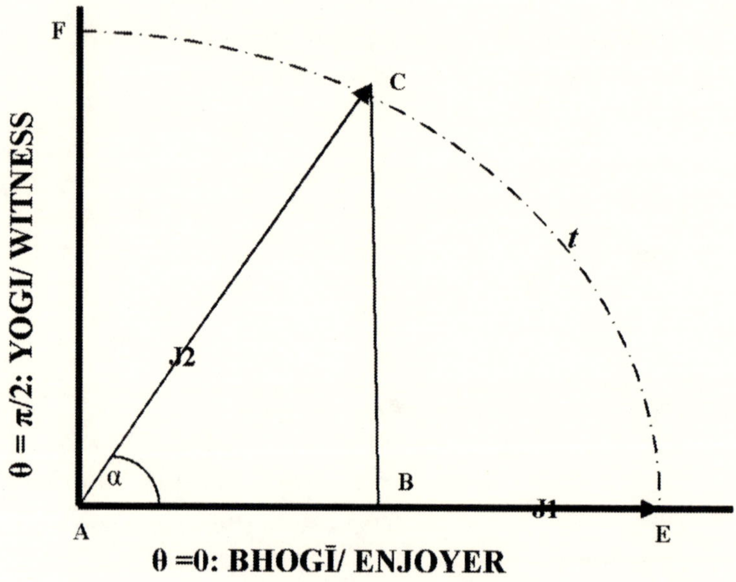

Fig. 6.1 Time Contraction

Eq. 6.1 indicates that as r_A increases, experienced time of the jīva

24 For example, comparison between two jīvas can be invalid if one of them is in deep sleep during (0,t) while the other is awake to the world and its experiences.

decreases. Recall from discussions in previous chapter that experienced time and suffering are two effects caused by the same phenomenon of changes in the world. Also, r_A is the degree of "universal, unconditional love and understanding" the jīva has gained relative to that of a Perfect Being. Therefore, Eq. 6.1 is a statement of the inverse relationship between a jīva's spiritual maturity and its suffering. This is the "Law of Love" expressed as follows:

"As a jīva *grows more and more in Universal, Unconditional Love and Understanding, it suffers less and less in the world"*

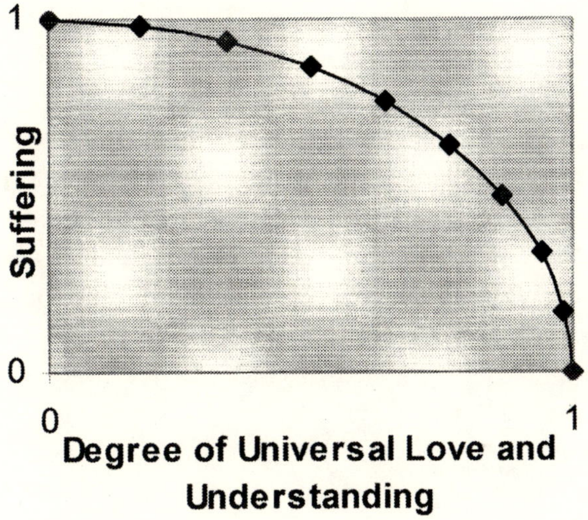

Fig. 6.2 Love & Understanding vs. Suffering

Fig. 6.2 presents the Eq. (6.1) graphically. This relation between Love and Suffering can be called, with some justification, *"The Fundamental Law of Spirituality"*. Unconditional Love is at the core of spiritual teachings in most religious traditions. Selfless love is viewed as the hallmark character of a saint. The terms used in different religions may differ, but the message is the same. Some religions call it Love for God. In Vedānta the seeker is exhorted to develop the vision of Oneness, *samadarśanaṁ,* by which one sees one's own self in every being. This vision underscores the seeker's unconditional love for all beings.

Universal, Unconditional Love: the Goal and the Means of Spiritual Practice

Universal Love is one of the truly unifying principles common to all religions. The fact is that no two individuals are alike when it comes to practicing spirituality. This is especially true in a religion like Hinduism which allows considerable personal freedom of expression. Some find joy in pilgrimage to various temples, some in singing *bhajan*s in fellowship with other devotees, and yet others prefer a *pūja* performed in the privacy of their home. Some sit quietly for hours in meditation, while others believe in fasting and dietary restrictions. Then there are those who find fulfillment in chanting *veda mantras* and in performing *havans* and other rituals. Some spend years learning the Bhagavad Gītā and the Upaniṣads and learn these well enough to give scholarly discourses. What, one may ask, can be the common spiritual goal pursued by practices which are apparently so dissimilar? Which practice, if any, among the above is mandatory to achieve that goal? If nothing by itself is indispensable, can one do away with all of them and still be considered a true seeker?

Asked another way, is there anything which is absolutely necessary? Are there basic truths in spirituality showing which way the goal lies, and providing criteria by which to judge the worthiness of the various practices? The answer is a definite "Yes". The ultimate goal and the absolute imperative to achieve that goal are both stated in the above fundamental law of spirituality. The worthiness of a spiritual practice is given by the extent to which it increases the universal, unconditional love and understanding in the practitioner.

The statement captures an essential teaching of most religions. Religions may vary widely in their view of life and concepts of God, but it is safe to say that they all acknowledge the power of Love. However, what religions promise the jīva as a reward for its virtuous life is not always the same. Some may promise the joys of Paradise, but this promised joy is only after death. In contrast, the above "Law of Love" suggests that the reward for a life lived in Love is not in some distant place, at some uncertain future date after death, but it is greater happiness here and now. The jīva does not have to look elsewhere for happiness, the very Love it has manifests as happiness. Love, it is correctly observed, is its own reward.

Selfless Love is the means for the liberation of the individual and the reward is the peace and happiness it confers. Apart from spirituality at the individual level, Love is also equally significant at the collective level for the society as a whole. Part III of the book is devoted to discussing the Law of Love as it relates to the larger social and economic issues.

We now turn our attention to a fascinating aspect of the Fundamental Law of Spirituality stated in Eq. 6.1: Its striking similarity with an equally fundamental law in the material realm.

Correspondence with Special Relativity Theory

Eq. 6.1 is repeated below, highlighting certain key terms needed for making a subsequent comparison:

$$\mathbf{T_{J2} / T_{J1} = \sqrt{(1 - (r_A)^2)}} \qquad \text{Eq. 6.1 .... } (\textit{Vedānta})$$

where T_{J1} *= time for a worldly {i.e.* ***"ignorant of the Self"****} jīva J1,* T_{J2} *= time for a jīva J2 with* ***some Knowledge of Self****, and* r_A *=* ***Self-Knowledge of J2*** *relative to that of the Perfect Being (****maximum possible Knowledge of Self*** *of one fully established in Self).*

Note that we have not used anything other than elementary geometry and principles of Vedānta in deriving Eq. 6.1. Yet it bears a striking resemblance in form and content to a basic result in special relativity theory:

$$\mathbf{T_{J2} / T_{J1} = \sqrt{(1 - (r_C)^2)}} \qquad \text{Eq. 6.2.... } (\textit{Physics})$$

where T_{J1} *= time for a stationary {i.e.* ***"immobile in space"****} observer J1,* T_{J2} *= time for an observer J2 moving through space at* ***some constant speed****, and* r_C *=* ***speed of J2*** *relative to speed of light (****maximum possible speed in space****).*

The remarkable similarity between Eq. 6.1 and Eq. 6.2 gets all the more impressive when it is recalled that Vedānta often speaks of **Self** (i.e. Consciousness) and **Space** in the same breath as though the two are indeed one. Terms such as "*cidākāśaḥ*", (meaning consciousness-space) abound in Vedāntic literature. The spiritual "Self" is routinely compared to "Space" in the material realm. Space is the first and subtlest of the five great elements and closest to the Brahman by virtue of its attributes: homogeneous, pure, beyond the grasp of the five senses, pervading the universe, without beginning or end, and supporting or accommodating all matter. Similarly, "**Knowledge**" and **"Light**" are almost synonyms in Vedānta and other religious traditions as well. In modern physics, light is of fundamental importance for the reason that it represents the maximum speed for information transmission over space. We also note the Upaniṣadic definition of State of Realization as the "Highest Knowledge" or "That by knowing which everything else is known". The Realized Master (one established in Full Knowledge of Self) possesses this Maximum Knowledge. Such great jīvas, *Mahātmas*, are spoken of as Light itself. Indeed they are universally referred to as the "Enlightened" ones. Thus, a *Mahātmā* with Maximum Knowledge of Self is likened to Light which has the maximum speed in space. Setting the following rules for translation of terms from Vedānta into Physics

LANGUAGE OF VEDĀNTA		LANGUAGE OF PHYSICS
Self	=	***Space***
Maximum Knowledge of Self	=	***Maximum Speed in Space***
Knowledge of Self[25]	=	***Speed in Space***

we see that Eq. 6.1 of Vedānta transforms readily into Eq. 6.2 of Relativity. Vedānta and Physics seem to speak of the same Truth but using different languages appropriate for the spiritual and material realms.

The fact that such a close correspondence in language and results exists is remarkable in itself. But there is something more involved here than just an interchange of words. In deriving Eq. 6.1 from Fig 6.1, we did not use results from Relativity Theory and substitute words from Vedānta in place of terms in Physics. The way we abstracted reality in Figures 5.1-5.6 is quite different from the conventions used in Physics. Our approach was simple and straight forward based on well known

25 Recall that, for jīvas striving for Realization, Knowledge is measured by the purity of their mind-intellect. It is valid to speak of degrees of Self-Knowledge since the purity of mind has a wide spectrum of levels from the most gross to the most immaculate.

Vedāntic principles such as the *tripuṭi* of experiencer-experienced-experiences.

Since the 1920's when Relativity Theory and Quantum Mechanics revolutionized modern thinking, a growing number of scientists and philosophers have been speculating on the convergence of science and spiritual traditions based on eastern philosophies [86]. The correspondence noted between Eq. (6.1) and Eq. (6.2) is an indication that these speculations are on the right track.

Interpretation of the Concordance Result Using Minkowski's Metric

The correspondence between Vedānta and Relativity Theory stands out more clearly when the Minkowski's Metric for time-space continuum is used. To start the discussions, consider Fig. 6.3 below with a jīva of uniform detachment θ.

Let AB and CD be two time arcs and PQ the radius vector at angle θ intersecting the two time arcs at P and Q respectively. PQ = is the "distance" between P and Q in the *ℳspace*. We denote PQ by δΛ.

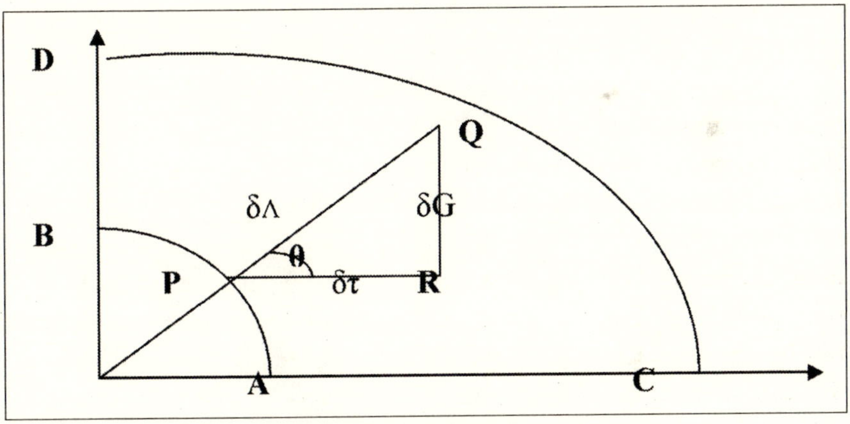

Fig. 6.3: *ℳ: Cosmic Mind Space*

Following the notations introduced in the last chapter, PR= δΛ.cosθ is the incremental experienced time, denoted by δτ, over the time interval

$\delta\Lambda$. RQ = $\delta\Lambda.\sin\theta$, denoted by δG, is the incremental "merit" over the same time interval.

We have the relation

$$\delta\Lambda^2 - \delta\tau^2 = \delta G^2 \text{ .... } (6.3)$$

This is similar to the Minkowski's Metric in Relativity Theory for the 4 dimensional time-space continuum:

$$\delta s^2 - \delta t^2 = \delta d^2 \text{ ------- } (6.4)$$

where δs = the distance in the ordinary three dimensional Euclidean space, $\delta t = c$.time, δd = the metric (distance or time) in the 4 dimensional time-space continuum, and c being the speed of light. For convenience, the units of measurement of time and space may be set such that $c = 1$. This equation shows how time and space are related and why two observers moving in the Euclidean space relative to each other experience time and space in different ways.

Physicists sometimes explain the relationship (6.4) between time and space in a way that is particularly helpful to our discussions [87]. Everybody and everything in this universe, they point out, is constantly moving through the time-space continuum at the speed of light. Even objects stationary in space are also traveling at that speed, except that their travel is in the dimension of time only. They are moving through time at the fastest speed possible, namely speed of light. We may say that time moves fastest for these objects. When something or somebody is moving also through space, it is in fact diverting part of its speed in time dimension to accomplish travel in the three dimensional space. Because of this diversion, its speed in time is reduced; that is "time slows down" for it. In the extreme, time stops for an object moving through space itself at the speed of light. All these observations are of course cast in robust mathematical terms in relativity physics.

We can re-write Eq. (6.4) as follows:

$$\delta d^2 - (i\delta t)^2 = \delta s^2 \text{ ------- } (6.5)$$

where $i = \sqrt{-1}$ is the unit imaginary number. Comparing equations

(6.3) and (6.5), we see the correspondence between the following pairs of terms:

a) the four dimensional time-space continuum **d** with the space $\mathscr{M}$;
b) the imaginary time **i.t** with experienced time τ on the horizontal axis; and
c) the distance in three dimensional Euclidean space **s** with the increased merit **G**, on the vertical axis

The time-space relationship of Special Relativity Theory can be readily translated now in the following spiritual terms:

Everything and every jīva is in the *Mahat* ($\mathscr{M}$ space) and all move at a uniform speed from wave to wave, just as everything is moving at the speed of light in the time-space continuum. This is the message conveyed when the Upaniṣad extols the Supreme Self with the words *"yasmin lokā nihitā lokinaśca"*, meaning " *wherein exist all worlds and worldly beings***"** [88], or when Jesus exclaims *"For in him we live, and move, and have our being* **...**" [89]. In Fig. 6.3, the universe, which is in the arc AB at a certain time, is in the arc CD after the elapse of δΛ in cosmic time. All things and beings must also necessarily move with the universe. However, jīvas, possessing some spiritual detachment, divert part of this speed to advance in the dimension of G, along the vertical axis. This reduces their speed in the dimension of "experienced time" τ (along the horizontal axis) or suffering.

The speed component along the vertical axis is δG/δΛ. This equals sinθ which we defined as the "Relative Awareness", a comparative measure of the Goodness and Knowledge of the jīva relative to that of a fully Realized "Perfect Being". Higher the vertical speed component, lower is the horizontal speed component. Stated differently, more the jīva's relative awareness, less is its suffering. This is the inverse relationship between Love and Suffering, the "fundamental law of spirituality".

Plot of G(t) against t

There is yet another way to illustrate the correspondence between the Vedāntic concepts and Special Relativity notions. Figure 6.4 below

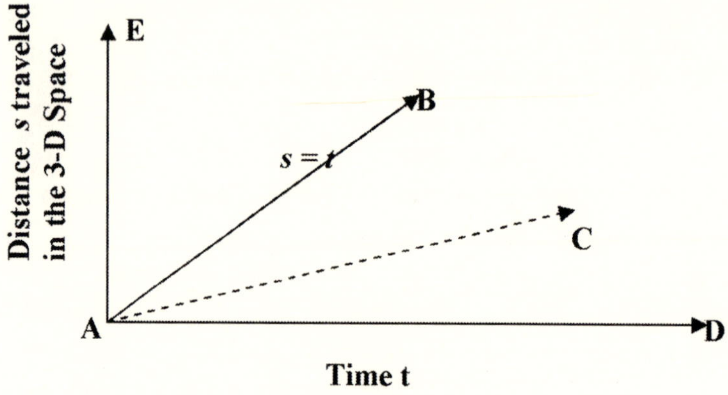

Fig. 6.4 Plots of Distance Traveled in Space vs. Time

plots *s*, the distance traveled in the 3-dimensional space, against time t where the units for space and time are so chosen that speed of light = 1; for example if t is in seconds, the vertical axis is in light-seconds, the distance light travels in one second. In this configuration, the line AB, given by the equation s = *t*, represents the motion in space of an object at the speed of light. The object will move one unit distance per unit time along AB. Since this is the maximum speed allowed, any other uniform motion will be a line below AB. In particular, a stationary object will lie on line AD and it can be thought of as moving along this axis at the same speed as AB, that is one unit per unit time along AD. A third object which is not stationary but moving uniformly at less than the speed of light will move one unit distance per unit time along a path such as AC. Assume that all these motions are relative to a stationary object on AD.

Relativity Theory says that the clocks will run slower (that is, time experienced will be shorter) as the speed in space increases. Time will be significantly slower for the observer in AC compared to that in AD. Clocks will get slower and slower as speed in space increases until time will come to a standstill for an observer in AB moving at the speed of light. This observer experiences all time as "now". Further, the theory suggests that space (in the direction of the motion) also will effectively shrink to zero to such an observer. This is because speed of light must remain constant for all observers and therefore space must shrink to zero when time is at a standstill. So for this observer, all space is "here". It is hard to relate to this experience from our usual understanding, but one may say that all space has been conquered by this observer in an instant.

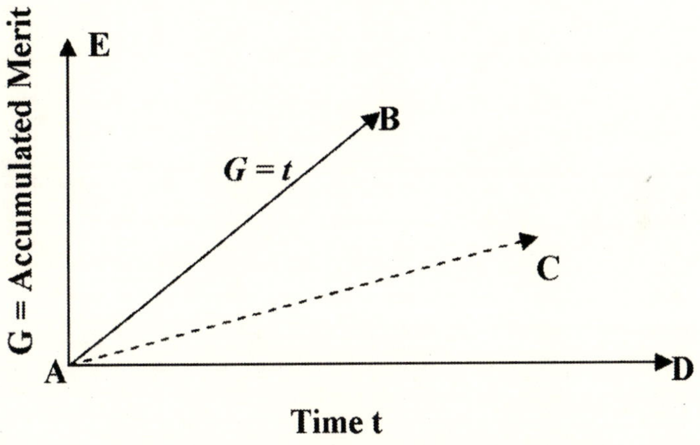

Fig. 6.5 Plot of Accumulated Merit vs. Time

We can now draw another important parallel between the physical world and the Vedāntic concepts of Knowledge and Self. Fig 6.5 shows plots of $G(t) = t.\sin\theta$ against t. G(t) is the "distance traveled" in time t along the vertical axis by a jīva with uniform spiritual detachment θ. The vertical axis, $\theta = \pi/2$, represents the "space" of Knowledge and Goodness and G(t), the "distance traveled" in that space corresponds to accumulated merit. The rate at which G(t) grows is dependent on θ, with the maximum occurring at $\theta = \pi/2$ when the jīva is totally detached and totally identified with Self. This is a realized soul with full Knowledge of Self. In this case $G(t) = t.\sin\pi/2 = t$, or the line AB in Fig. 6.5. The realized jīva moves along the line AB at one unit per unit time. At the other extreme, a jīva with $\theta = 0$ is fully attached to the world and moves along AD at the same unit speed. This jīva experiences time (that is to say, suffers the changes in O-E-T) in its full measure due to its total ignorance of Self. As spiritual detachment of the jīva, θ, increases, the time experienced and associated suffering decrease. At the maximum speed, or detachment of $\theta = \pi/2$, the jīva is released from the bondage of time (i.e. experienced time stops) and suffering ends. Further, says Vedānta, this jīva, living as a "*jīvanmukta*" also stops accumulating merit and knowledge since it now possesses "the knowledge by which everything else is known". That is, this jīva has now conquered the entire space of Knowledge and Goodness.

Conquest of Space Not Possible by Travel, nor Knowledge of Self by Actions

In the above comparisons, merit acquired, $t.\sin\theta$, is the spiritual equivalent of "distance traveled in space". To "conquer" space, it is not enough if we keep traveling far in space, space being infinite. We can be only at a single point in space no matter how far we have traveled. Instead one must increase the speed to the speed of light at which point space and time shrink to nothingness. Then, it is as though one is everywhere in space; one has become space. To achieve this feat, an accelerating force is needed to boost the speed in space. In the physical world, the force required is higher if the object to be accelerated has more mass.

Similarly, simply by engaging in meritorious act and acquiring merit (i.e. by increasing G, the accumulated merit), one does not "conquer" the Self. Self is Infinite, but results of actions are limited. Adi Sankara, as quoted earlier, repeatedly reminds us that actions, however meritorious, cannot by themselves destroy ignorance. One must increase the "speed", $\sin\theta$, to do that. That is, one must increase the detachment θ. When the detachment is total, then one is established in the Self, and one becomes Knowledge itself. All this is possible only with consistent spiritual practice. But consistent practice requires will power on the part of the jīva. Will power is the force that accelerates the progress towards the goal of Realization. The will power required is higher if the jīva's ego (its "mass") is higher, as shown later in Chapter 8.

Mathematical Similarities between the Space- Time Continuum and the $\mathscr{M}$-Space

A number of remarkable similarities between the spiritual realm and material realm thus stand revealed by comparing the equations (6.1) and (6.2). The table below summarizes the similarities:

Concept in the Material Realm of Relativity Physics	Concept in the Spiritual Realm of Vedanta
Space-Time Continuum or Field of Events with co-existing past, present, and future	*Mahat* or Field of Experiences, with co-existing past, present, and future
Space (3-dimensional)	The vertical axis of Knowledge, and Goodness (associated with Self or Consciousness)
Speed in space	Extent of establishment in Self, or Knowledge of Self, given by $\sin\theta$
Distance traveled in Space = t.speed	G =Merit acquired = $t.\sin\theta$
Stationary in Space	Ignorant of Self, totally attached to world, $\theta=0$
Maximum speed in space, c=1, is attained by light	Fully established state in Self, $\sin \pi/2 = 1$, is attained by the Realized (Enlightened.)
To attain speed of light, a particle must have no mass	To attain Enlightenment, a jiva must have no ego
An observer stationary in space is in the domain of time. But time comes to a stop for one moving at speed of light*	A jiva ignorant of Self, is bound to time and suffers the changes that time brings. But an Enlightened jiva goes beyond time and attains immortality.
Space contracts to zero in the direction of travel for one traveling at speed of light. Thus, there is no further forward to go.*	Everything is known by a jiva that realizes Self. Thus, there is nothing more to be known.

(* relative to some fixed frame of reference)

Table 6.1: **Comparison of Space-time Continuum and $\mathscr{M}$-space**
(* relative to some fixed frame of reference)

Two Important Differences

Notwithstanding the many similarities noted so far, the spiritual realm is not the same as the material realm in all respects. There are differences. One difference is that motion in space is not absolute, but relative. That is, we can say that an object is in motion only in relation to a frame of reference. Therefore we talk of only relative motion and not absolute motion in space. But in the spiritual realm, detachment has no relative reference and there appears to be no need to invoke a frame of reference. A second important difference is that no object with mass can attain speed of light, since such a feat will require infinite energy. The material world does not seem to have a source for providing infinite energy. But, in the spiritual realm, a jīva can attain Realization mostly by exercising its personal will and staying steadfast in its spiritual practices. Even here the very final step before Liberation depends on the infinite grace of Īśvara, which *is* available. A full discussion of these ideas is to be found in the next three chapters.

Temporal and Spatial Components of Spiritual Imperfection

The correspondence relationship does not mean that the Self of Vedānta is identical to the Space of the physicists or that State of Perfection is same as physical light. This is not what the results demonstrate. After all, a piece of inert matter when accelerated to speed of light does not become a Realized Being. To interpret the similarities as identities is stretching the analogy too far.

The concept of "time experienced" in Eq. (6.1) is not identical to the time in Relativity Theory. Further, Consciousness is different from space, in spite of obvious similarities. In fact, space and everything else is in the $\mathscr{M}$-space, or Cosmic Mind, which itself is in Brahman, the Pure Consciousness.

Eq. (6.2) describes a law of nature governing "physical time" affecting physical processes. Physical time is objective and can be measured by clocks. On the other hand, Eq. (6.1) is about experienced time which is subjective and not measurable by a clock[26]. What can experienced time be if it is not measurable? Experienced time, we saw, is related to a jīva's suffering, which in turn is dependent on the degree of "spiritual perfection" the jīva has attained. Therefore, we may infer that experienced time is somehow related to the jīva's state of imperfection. We introduce the concepts of "spatial" and "temporal" components of imperfection in order to explore this connection.

Temporal imperfection is associated with how a jīva feels about its individuality. It may help here to think about how we perceive ourselves as we reminisce about our past. We generally feel that we are not now exactly what we were years ago and that we, as a person, have been changing as our body-mind-intellect changed over time. At any given time I feel almost identical to what I was a second ago. But if I look back 1 day, 1

26 Cosmic time also cannot be measured and is different from both physical time and experienced time. This is a subject of discussion in Chapter 9.

month, 1 year or 10 years earlier, I progressively lose some of this sense of identification with myself. I identify far less with who I was as a child than with myself a second ago. This is due to the enormous number of changes I feel *I have* (i.e. myself, and not just my B-M-I, has) undergone since my childhood. This notion of change to my personality induces a feeling of alienation or distancing, from what I was in the past. Past feels subjectively very far (i.e. subjective time is very long) if the number of changes and the degree of alienation with own self is higher. An individual under anesthesia, on waking up, has nearly 100% identification with his self just before being put to sleep. No change was perceived while under anesthesia and hence there is no sense of elapsed time.

This reasoning leads to a different and more interesting interpretation of Eq. (6.1). A hallmark of The Perfect Being is its identification with all beings at all times. As an imperfect jīva, my state of awareness falls short of this ideal. Not only I do not identify with other jīvas with whom I share my existence at the present moment, but I cannot totally identify with what I myself was in previous moments. We call the former as the *spatial component of imperfection* since it is space that differentiates me from others at the present moment. Incomplete identification with my past self is the *temporal component* of my imperfection since it is time that separates my present self from past self.

In Eq. 6.1, T_{j2} indicates the temporal component of imperfection of jīva J2, while $(1- r_A)$ reflects its spatial component of imperfection. As θ increases, r_A increases while both $(1-r_A)$ and T_{j2} decrease. Eq. (6.1) thus demonstrates how, as one gets progressively more detached, both components of imperfection diminish. In the limit, subjective time is zero. The Perfect Being which is firmly "established in Self" has no concept of change in Its self. Notions of "I was" or "I will be" do not prevail here but it is always "I AM". This view of an unchanging Self is maintained by a *Yogī* even while seeing the physical clock tick and the O-E-T changing.

Concepts Of Brahma And Brahmalok

We now return to a topic last seen in Chapter 5, namely, the probabilistic nature of the changes in O-E-T and discuss how it dovetails with the concepts of Īśvara and Brahma found in Vedānta. In Fig. 5.3, the wave at time *t* represents all possible states the world could be at that time following Prakṛti's laws. Conceptually, one could assign a probability to each possible state of the world. With this understanding, the wave at time *t* could be referred to as the "probability wave" of the world at time *t*, though this is not necessarily the "probability waves" a Quantum Physicist talks about.

A jīva does not however bump into probability waves in life as it contacts the world; rather it experiences very definite objects, emotions and thoughts. In Fig. 5.4, for example, P(t,θ) represents a definite experience the jīva has with the world at time t. Nothing in the $\mathscr{M}$ -space can be experienced, if it remains merely as a field of possibilities. This raises a question: How and when does the field of possibilities become the field of actual experiences for jīvas?

Īśvara's role in the process of creation was discussed as part of the Prakṛti- Īśvara Paradigm in Chapter 3. Scriptures speak of the twin roles for the Supreme Being, one as Brahman, the Pure Consciousness, and another as Īśvara, the Lord or the Controller. As befits the title "Controller", it is Īśvara who chooses one state for the world out of the many possible states. The same Supreme Being, as Brahman or Pure Consciousness, illumines the experience for the jīvas as they contact the selected state of the world. As previously discussed in presenting Fig. 2.4, jīva experiences the world only with the help of the illumination provided by the reflection of the Pure Consciousness on its intellect. The scriptures also talk of sound, (*"nāda"*) and light (*"bindu"*) as the accompaniment of creation [90]. It is as though the world moves from one state to the next to the accompaniment of a steady drum beat while a strobe light illumines those changes to jīvas. Every flash of the strobe reveals the world in a different state willed by Īśvara which then the jīvas experience.

There are clues in the Vedāntic literature that allow us to add some quantitative and qualitative details to the above picture. One key is provided by the concept of "*brahma*-day" found in scriptures. Brahma, Viṣnu and Śiva are the three aspects of Īśvara, with *Brahmāji* being the creative aspect[27]. There are countless number of universes and associated with each universe is a different *Brahmāji* who supervises it over a life time of 100 *Brahma*-years. Thus, while Īśvara is truly eternal,

27 We add the respectful suffix "–ji" to Brahma, to help avoid confusion with Brahman.

Brahmāji may be thought of as Īśvara's "representative" for a particular universe over its lifetime. *Brahmāji* is viewed as the most evolved jīva of that universe and also as the grandsire, "*pitāmaha*", of all its jīvas. It is also said that the abode of *Brahmāji*, called the *Brahmalok*, is the penultimate stop in a jīva's spiritual evolution. *Brahmāji* is identified with the *Hiraṇyagarbha* in some texts, and as the first one born of the Cosmic Mind.

Brahmāji's Path or The Brahmalok

The Hindu concepts of time in terms of *yuga*s and *kalpa*s are well known to those familiar with its scriptures and mythology. One day of *Brahmāji* is called a *kalpa* and equals 1000 *yugas*, each *yuga* being 4.32 million human-years. *Brahmāji's* night is as long as His day. Thus one *brahma*-day, consisting of one day and one night, corresponds to 8.64 billion human-years, or $3.15576 * 10^{12}$ human day-night cycles, assuming each year to be 365.25 days. On this basis, each *Brahma*-second turns out to be 100,000 human-years. In other words, 100,000 human-years is experienced by *Brahmāji* as 1 second. This huge difference in the time as experienced by *Brahmāji* and ordinary mortals is consistent with *Brahmāji*'s stature as the most spiritually evolved jīva in the universe. From the information we have on brahma-days, we can in fact determine how close *Brahmāji* is to Perfection.

Following the previously introduced notations, let T_{Brahma} be the time experienced by *Brahmāji* and T_{J1} the time experienced by a worldly jīva.

$$T_{Brahma} / T_{J1} = (1 \div 3.15576 * 10^{12}) \approx 0.317 \times 10^{-12}$$

We can calculate $r_{A,\,Brahma}$, the relative goodness of *Brahmāji* using the inverse relation of Eq. (6.1), namely

$$\mathbf{r_A = \sqrt{(1 - (T_{J2} / T_{J1})^2)}}$$

$r_{A,Brahma,}$ is thus

$$\sqrt{(1 - (T_{Brahma} / T_{J1})^2)} = \sqrt{(1 - (0.317 \times 10^{-12})^2)}$$

which is approximately equal to 0.99999999999999999999999995; that is, 25 nines followed by 5 in the 26th decimal position. Relative Goodness of *Brahmāji* is thus very close to 1, signifying *Brahmāji's* virtual identity with the State of Perfection as shown in Fig 6.6. The angle CAF {which is approximately $\sin^{-1}(0.317*10^{-12})$ radians} is much smaller than shown in the graph, with the line AC lying practically on the vertical axis, AF. The vertical axis AF and the line AC are representative of the abode of Īśvara (*Viṣṇulok* or *Śivalok*) and abode of *Brahmāji* (*Brahmalok*) respectively. The former is Perfection itself, while the latter is nearly Perfect. The angle CAE is $(\pi/2-(0.317*10^{-12}))$ radians and will be denoted by θ^* in the sequel.

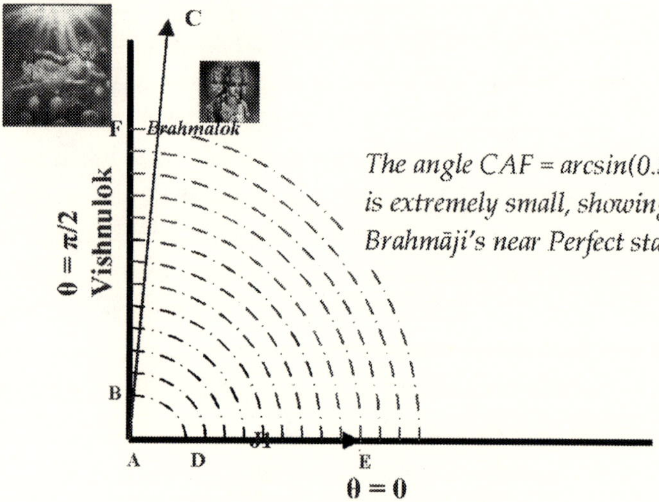

Fig. 6.6: *Brahmāji*'s State

Vedāntic texts indicate that it is not possible for a jīva to advance spiritually beyond *Brahmalok* and yet not be in *Viṣṇulok*. - i.e., a jīva can be on AC or AF, but cannot be in the narrow region between these two lines. This is consistent with the view that *Brahmāji*, the grandsire of all jīvas, is spiritually more evolved than any in His creation, with the exception of those who have attained Perfection (*jīvanmukta*). In Vedānta, the penultimate stop for a jīva before Liberation is said to be the *Brahmalok*.

This is where the jīva acquires further spiritual knowledge under the tutelage of *Brahmāji* Himself. In Fig. 6.6, the jīva, by stint of own efforts, can go up to AC (i.e. *Brahmalok*), but not any closer to AF. That is, the progress function can increase up to θ* by own effort. Transition from AC to AF requires no further effort on the part of the jīva (nor possible by its further effort), but by Īśvara's grace alone. As Adi Sankara says, "*the man of realization crosses over by the illumination and Grace of God.*"[91] Other religious traditions also hold that a jīva is conveyed to its final destination only by Divine Grace appearing in the form of angels etc.

A Grain of Distraction in the Creator

The very small magnitude of the angle FAC in Fig 6.6 suggests that there is a grain of imperfection in the creator, *Brahmāji*. Is this consistent with the scriptures and if so what is its explanation?

Traditionally, *Brahmāji*, though part of the divine trinity, is not accorded quite the same status as Viṣnu or Śiva. Whereas Viṣnu and Śiva are considered eternal, *Brahmāji*'s life is limited to 100 Brahma-years, or 320 trillion human years. It is no doubt very long by human reckoning, but finite nevertheless. It is a fact too that there are fewer temples dedicated to *Brahmāji* than for Viṣnu or Śiva. Viṣṇulok (*Vaikuṇṭh*) or Śivalok (*Kailās*) is the final destination for a realized jīva, but *Brahmalok* is only a stop on the way to that final destination. As such it is considered a part of the transient *saṁsāra* subject to birth and death. Lord Krishna, in Gītā, says:

ābrahma bhuvanāllokāḥ punarāvartinorjuna,
māmupetya tu kaunteya punarjanma na vidyate

"Worlds up to the 'world of Brahma' are subject to rebirth, O Arjuna, but one who reaches Me, O Kaunteya, has no re-birth." [92]

The final abode indicated by Lord Krishna, "reaching which there is no return", is the vertical axis AF in Fig. 6.6. For this reason this axis can as well be labeled as "*Viṣṇulok*" or "*Śivalok*". The "*Brahmalok*", represented by the line AC, is very close and to the right of *Viṣṇulok.*

Brahmāji, we may thus surmise, is a very special jīva, one that is very highly evolved, and fully divine but for a miniscule degree of imperfection. The tiny imperfection in *Brahmāji* can be attributed to the distraction occasioned by the need to attend to the affairs of creation.

Sw. Dheerananda relates a very picturesque analogy provided by Gurudev Sw. Chinmayananda to indicate qualitatively the magnitude of this distraction. Gurudev asks us to imagine a king riding his chariot at a high speed, with all attention focused on his task ahead, namely to confront the enemy at the battlefield. Resplendent in his royal gear, the king sports a long scarf, *aṅgavastra* around his neck that streams behind him as the chariot charges forward. Tassels at the fringe of the *aṅgavastra* are fluttering in the wind. The king is aware of the fluttering tassels, but the fraction of attention bestowed on them is tiny. Affairs pertaining to creation distract Creator's concentration on the Self to the same infinitesimal degree, says Gurudev.

Sw. Dheerananda

Brahmāji's Role in the Creative Process

Īśvara, according to the Prakṛti-Īśvara paradigm, transforms the world from its many probable states to one definite state. But, when does the transition from probable states to actual state happen? And, what is the special role of *Brahmāji* in the creative process to earn Him the title of "creator" or "grandsire"? I am not sure Vedānta answers these questions directly, but we can describe the creative process in a manner that is essentially consistent with the various suggestions found in the scriptures.

All potential and actual experiences of jīvas from the beginning of creation to its end co-exist in Īśvara's Cosmic Mind. We portray this graphically by showing potential experiences as probability waves in the $\mathscr{M}$-space. Neither time nor experience is there for the Īśvara, but both are (apparently) very real for the jīvas. All jīvas, including *Brahmāji*, encounter one wave after another.

It is noted that *Brahmāji* is the first, in terms of own *experienced time*, to encounter each wave in the Cosmic Mind. In other words, each wave, representing all possible states of the world at the time, "collapses" to one actual state even as *Brahmāji's* path intersects it. For example, referring to Fig. 6.7, the probability wave GG' collapses to some actual definite state G* of the world when *Brahmāji*'s path AC intersects the wave at the point G_1[28]. The state G* is as chosen by Īśvara, but it is as though *Brahmāji* executes Īśvara's Will. After all, it is Īśvara alone who works through all jīvas and *Brahmāji* is no exception. *Brahmāji* has the distinguishing role of causing the one world willed by the Lord to manifest, thus earning His title as the "Creator".

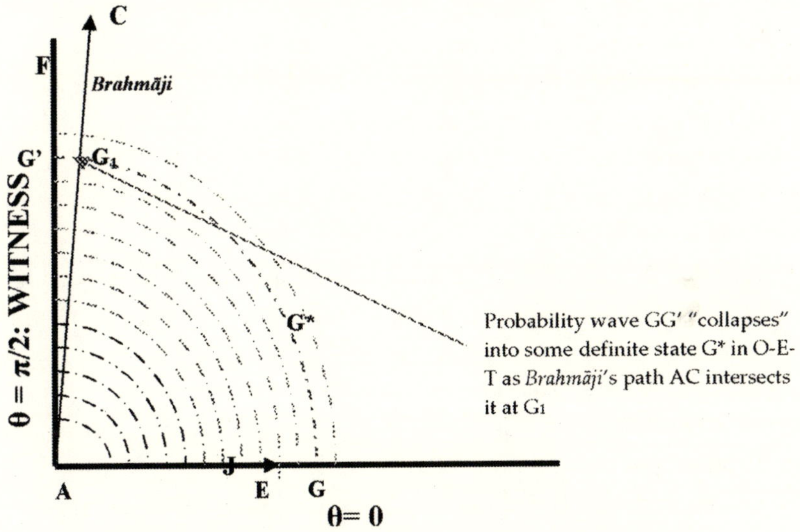

Fig. 6.7: *Choice of a Definite State For the World*

The Passage to Future

Brahmāji's spiritual detachment is higher than that of any jīva. Hence, the time experienced by *Brahmāji* is much shorter than that for other jīvas. This of course is the implication of the vast difference between Brahma-days and human-days. Interpreted another way, *Brahmāji* seemingly experiences His act of creation before other jīvas get to experience that world. This is as it should be since law of causality requires that the world be first created before it can be experienced. Because of this, all jīvas find the O-E-T in a definite state rather than as a "cloud of probabilities". The exception again is the Realized jīva, who has conquered time itself. Such a jīva is said to be a "*trikālajñāni*"

28 This does not mean that the wave reduces to just one point G* in our graph. G* is the new designation for the wave with the understanding that it is not a "probability wave" any more, but a wave representing some definite state of the world.

or knower of all three periods of time. That jīva can know the future before *Brahmāji* has created it.

JĪVAS WITH NON-UNIFORM SPIRITUAL DETACHMENT

We have considered so far in this chapter jīvas having a uniform (i.e. steady) spiritual detachment. In this case jīvas are in what we may call a spiritually inertial field; i.e. a field where no forces are present to either increase or decrease the spiritual detachment. This is similar to the situation in the material world where bodies move in space relative to each other at constant velocity which happens only if they are free from all forces of acceleration. We considered this special case in order to present many important concepts required in the general case. Further, the special case is important in its own right since it applies to *Brahmāji*.

We now address the general case of jīvas with non-uniform (i.e. varying with time t) spiritual detachment. To simplify the mathematics, we consider for the purpose of our analysis that cosmic time t is a continuous variable. But the concepts and results should extend to the discrete case.

The spiritual progress of jīvas can be graphically shown by plotting the spiritual detachment, $\theta(t)$ against t. We have previously referred to this graph as the jīva's "progress curve" and the function $\theta(t)$ as the "progress function".

In real life, the spiritual disposition of a jīva can vary over the short term and long term. Even hourly variations are possible, for example, with higher detachment in the morning hours than at mid-day. Long-term variations occur due to a) the *sādhanas* (i.e. spiritual practices) undertaken by the jīva and b) lessons learned by the jīva in its encounters with the world. The jīva may regress spiritually at times, but the overall long-term trend is expected to be one of increasing detachment. This optimistic view is based on the assumption that jīvas do learn from their experiences sooner or later. Thus, while interacting with the world, the jīva is in a spiritually dynamic field of accelerating and decelerating forces. It may be that jīvas begin their "*samsār*" (transmigratory journey) in lower forms of life such as plants and animals, and progressively evolve over several birth-death cycles until they take a human (or other spiritually equivalent) form. Having assumed human form, a jīva is generally expected to progress further until, at the end, it attains Realization. This in essence is what Vedāntic scriptures teach. When plotted, the chart for such a jīva will be a curve instead of straight line. The curve can zigzag if the jīva has periods of spiritual progress as well as regress.

Fig 6.8 illustrates the progress curve A-E-C-B of a jīva J3 which starts its journey bound 100% to O-E-T from t=0 through t=t1. It then makes modest progress from time t=t1 through t= t2, probably as it gains some wisdom (*viveka*) from experiences over several human lives. Point C is a turning point for this jīva, possibly as a result of meeting at last a Guru to guide it in its *sādhana*. From t=t2 onwards, the jīva makes steady progress as indicated by the steadily increasing value of θ. Finally at t= t*, when θ = 90°, J3 attains realization. A journey spanning many life times ends here.

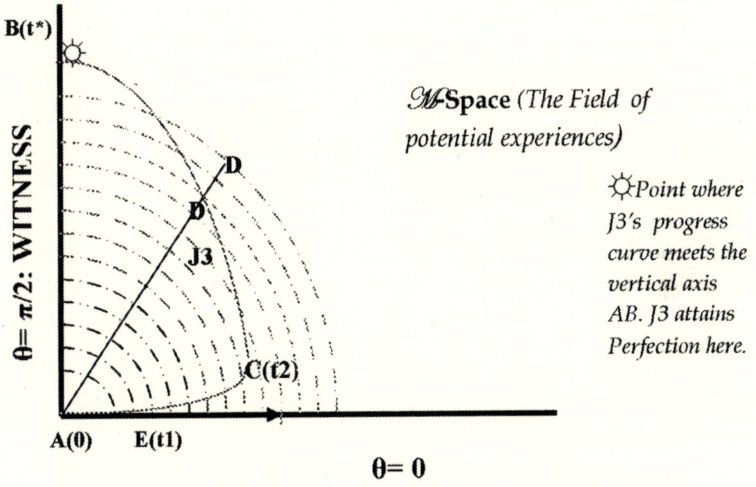

Fig. 6.8 Progress Curve of a Jīva with Varying Detachment

Experienced Time and Merit Acquired in the Case of Variable θ(t)

The time experienced by J3 during a specified time interval cannot be read off the horizontal axis in Fig 6.8, as was the case for jīvas with uniform spiritual detachment. It has to be computed using methods of calculus, assuming that θ(t) has the necessary mathematical properties. θ(*t*) represents the instantaneous spiritual detachment at time t. Over a small time interval $(t, t+\delta t)$, with δt being arbitrarily small, $\theta(t)$ can be assumed to be constant. In the uniform case, experienced time is the projection on the horizontal axis. Hence the time experienced by the jīva over $(t, t+\delta t)$, is $\delta t \cos(\theta(t))$. The total time experienced over a time interval $(0,t)$ is given by

$$\tau(t) = \int \cos(\theta(t))dt\ldots\ldots \text{ Eq. (6.6)}$$

The experienced time over a time interval (a,b) is now $\tau(b)-\tau(a)$. Since $0 \leq \theta(t) \leq \pi/2$ for all t, it follows that $0 \leq \cos(\theta(t)) \leq 1$, and $\tau(b)-\tau(a) \leq (b-a)$. The ratio $\{\tau(b)-\tau(a)\} / (b-a)$ is less than 1 and is the time contraction experienced by the jīva over the time interval (a,b).

In a similar fashion, the merit acquired over the interval $(0,t)$ can be shown to be

$$G(t) = \int \sin(\theta(t))dt\ldots\ldots\ldots\text{Eq. (6.7)}$$

Both $\tau(t)$ and $G(t)$ are increasing functions of t just as in the uniform case. The interpretation of the functions $\tau(t)$ and $G(t)$ also remains the same: $\tau(t)$ is experienced time and a proxy for the jīva's suffering from time 0 through t; $G(t)$ is the merit accumulated from time 0 through t.

Path of the Jīva in the $\mathscr{M}$- Space:

The coordinate pair $((\tau(t), G(t))$ provides a summary, as it were, of the jīva's spiritual history from beginning till time t: $\tau(t)$, the "suffering" through time t, is a statistic showing how intelligently the jīva has lived its life in the past, while $G(t)$ shows the accumulated merit it has now to meet future challenges of *samsār*. This suggests another possible graphical representation of a jīva's spiritual evolution. Having computed $\tau(t)$ and $G(t)$ using Eqs. (6.6) and (6.7), we may plot $G(t)$ against $\tau(t)$ as in Fig. 6.9 in Cartesian coordinates. Experienced time can be read off the horizontal axis of this graph. We call this plot of G against τ the "spiritual path", or simply as the "path", of a jīva, to distinguish it from the progress curve $\theta(t)$. Eqs. (6.6) and (6.7) suggest that the derivative of G with respect to τ is $\tan(\theta(t))$. This implies that the tangent of the spiritual path at time t is a line making an angle $\theta(t)$ with the horizontal axis. Therefore $\theta(t)$ is the direction of the jīva's path at time t. Or, equivalently, spiritual path of a jīva is the trajectory of a point which, starting from the origin, moves in the $\mathscr{M}$-space at an angle $\theta(t)$ to the horizontal axis at time t.

In the special case of uniform detachment, θ(t) is a constant, and hence the spiritual path will be the straight-line through origin making an angle θ to the horizontal axis. This line being also the progress curve, we see that the progress curve and spiritual path are one and the same in this special case.

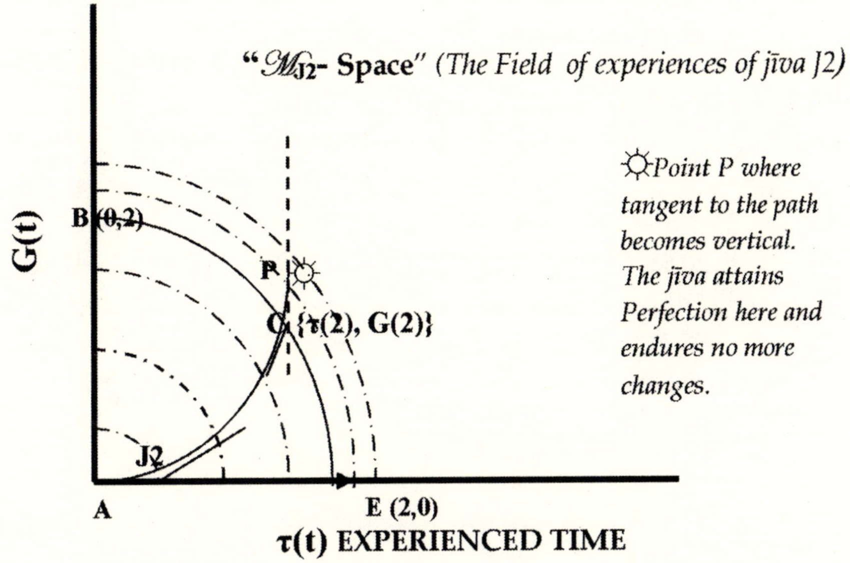

Fig. 6.9 Path of a Jīva

In Fig. 6.9, let P be the point of Realization for the jīva J2. At this point, θ = π/2, and the slope of the jīva's spiritual path, tan(θ(t)), becomes infinite, remaining infinite thereafter. We have here the mathematical equivalent of the statement that the jīva has contacted Brahman or Infinity. Since the slope of G(τ) becomes infinite with respect to the horizontal axis τ, the path becomes vertical at that point. Therefore τ, the experienced time, does not change after that point, implying that the jīva has progressed beyond the realm of time and change. This conclusion is in perfect agreement with Vedāntic views on Realization.

Besides the spiritual path, we can also show in such a diagram the cosmic time "waves" as concentric waves. For example, if C is the point on the path which corresponds to {τ(2),G(2)}, then the time wave at t= 2, can be shown as the quarter circle BCE shown in solid line. It must be noted however that when using the Cartesian coordinate system as in Fig. 6.9, the radius of the wave BCE is not necessarily 2, even though it represents the wave at t=2 for the jīva J2. The radius, given by $\sqrt{(\tau^2(2) + G^2(2))}$, is dependent on θ(t). The time value assigned to BCE, or any other wave, varies depending on the jīva's progress function. Therefore, while it is possible to show the path of multiple jīvas in a graph such as Fig. 6.9, no single time value can be associated with any time wave in such a configuration.

"Warping" of ℳ- Space with Accelerating Spiritual Detachment

The circles representing the time waves need not be equally spaced when the jīva's detachment is not constant. For example, during periods of increasing detachment, the time waves will become more closely spaced reflecting the increasing time compression. This is illustrated below through a numerical example where we plot the path of a jīva with progress function θ(*t*)= 0.01848 x *t* radians (or 1.05882 x *t* degrees).

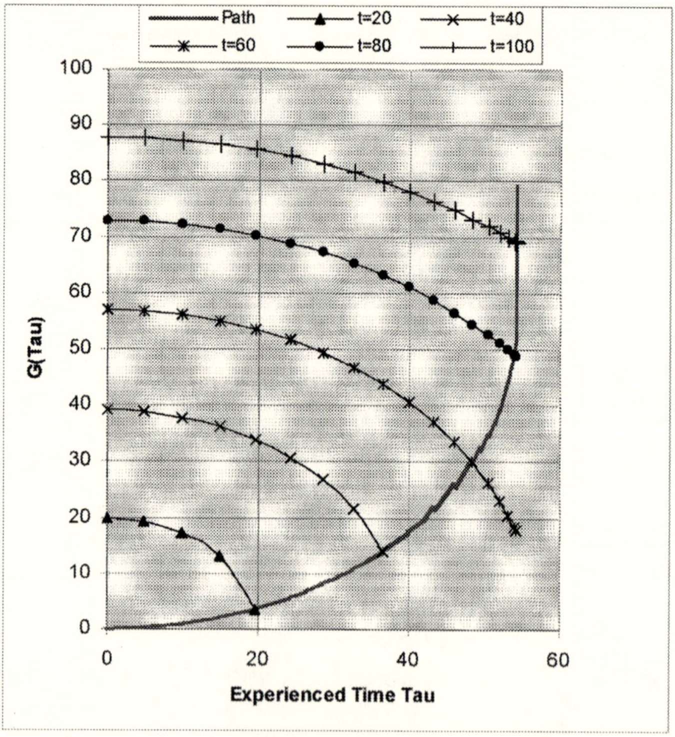

Fig. 6.10: Plot of (G(*t*),τ(*t*)) and Timelines for θ(*t*) = 0.01848 X *t* Radians

In this example, G(t) and τ(t) can be readily calculated using the integrals in Eqs. (6.6) and (6.7). Fig. 6.10 is the plot of the path (i.e. G(t) against τ(t)) and the time waves at t = 20, 40, 60, 80, and 100. This is a jīva with steadily increasing spiritual detachment reaching Realization (i.e. $\theta = \pi/2$) at t= 85 when τ(t) = 54. The path is seen to become vertical at t = 85 and τ(t) remains unchanged at 54 for all t ≥ 85. The separation between the time waves get progressively smaller as t increases from 0 to 85. For example, the lines representing t= 20 and t=40 are wider apart than the lines representing t= 60 and t = 80. The accelerating spiritual detachment of a jīva has the effect of compressing the time waves in the $\mathscr{M}$- space. We may call it the "warping" of the $\mathscr{M}$-space, borrowing a term from General Relativity Theory where time-space warping occurs due to gravity and other accelerating forces. Warping of time-space does not occur in the absence of accelerating forces and similarly $\mathscr{M}$-space does not warp in case of jīvas with uniform detachment. We must not, however, read too much into this perceived similarity since the mechanism underlying gravity and time-space warping is very different involving complex mathematics.

A Mathematical Note: It will be noted that both G(t) and τ(t) have same value, 54, at t = 85, the instant of Realization. That is, Realization occurs at a point in time when the G(t), the merit accrued, catches up with τ(t), the cumulative suffering. Having caught up with suffering, G(t) zooms to infinity relative to suffering as shown by the vertical path in the graph above. This is an interesting result, but one whose exact spiritual significance is not clear, especially since it is not known at this time how general the result is.

Length vs. Depth of Meditation

During meditation, a spiritual seeker endeavors to stay at a higher level of detachment for a short period of time by keeping contacts with the world to a minimum. Sw. Chinmayananda used to remind his students that the word "meditation" is a noun signifying the state of the mind achieved by this practice. During the meditative state, the mind is withdrawn from the external world and focused on the inner self. The "depth" of meditation is the degree to which this withdrawal is complete and can be related to the detachment θ achieved during meditation. The "length" of meditation is its time duration measured by some physical clock. To be effective, meditation should have no doubt both length and depth, but is one more important than the other? The theory developed in the previous pages allows us to answer this question, but we need to define first a measure of effectiveness.

The efficiency of the meditation can be measured by the ratio "experienced time/ time", a lower value for the ratio indicating higher efficiency. In the following illustration, we compare the efficiency of two individuals J1 and J2, both starting meditation at some time denoted by t_0. The starting point is B in the Fig. 6.11 which shows the path (G,τ) of the jīvas. Starting at t_0, J1 maintains a constant detachment of θ during an interval of t units of time. Its path during (t_0, t_0+t) is the line segment BD. The experienced time for J1 is $t.\cos\theta$ and its meditation efficiency is $(t.\cos\theta/t)$ or $\cos\theta$. Consider now another jīva J2 which maintains perfect detachment (i.e. $\theta = \pi/2$) from time t_0 to $t_0+t.\sin\theta$ and total attachment (i.e. $\theta=0$) over the next $t.\cos\theta$ units of time. That is, compared to J1 who maintains a constant, but not totally absorbed, meditative state over t units of time, J2 spends $t.\sin\theta$ units of time in total absorption, and the next $t.\cos\theta$ units in total attachment to the world.

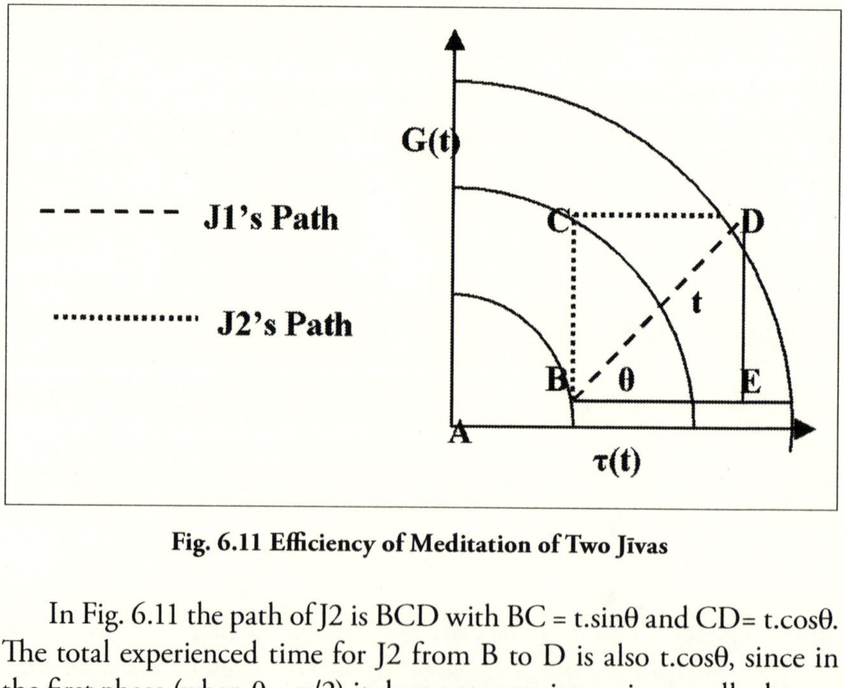

Fig. 6.11 Efficiency of Meditation of Two Jīvas

In Fig. 6.11 the path of J2 is BCD with $BC = t.\sin\theta$ and $CD= t.\cos\theta$. The total experienced time for J2 from B to D is also $t.\cos\theta$, since in the first phase (when $\theta = \pi/2$) it does not experience time at all whereas during the second phase (when $\theta = 0$) it is $t.\cos\theta$. The efficiency of meditation for J2 is $(t.\cos\theta/ (t.\sin\theta+t.\cos\theta))$. Since $\sin\theta+\cos\theta$ is greater than 1 for $0 < \theta < \pi/2$, this ratio is smaller than $\cos\theta$, J1's meditation efficiency. Thus, in this example, the short, intense meditation of J2 is more efficient than J1's longer, but shallower, meditation. It may be possible with further work to generalize this result to show that in meditation the depth is more important than the duration.

Fig. 6.11 also illustrates the problem with showing the path of multiple jīvas and time waves in the Cartesian coordinates of (G,τ). Specifically we see that the wave going through the point D represents the time wave at t_0+t for J1 whereas, for J2, it is the time wave at $t_0+t.(\sin\theta+\cos\theta)$. The disparity arises because J2 has non-uniform detachment. To avoid any potential confusion, we should not attach a time tag to the waves when there are two or more jīvas shown in these (G,τ) plots and at least one of them has non-uniform detachment.

Complex Variable Representation

Both $G(t)$ and $\tau(t)$ are real valued functions, but representation of these in terms of complex variables lends greater elegance and simplicity to the model[29]. Defining the complex variable $\zeta(t) = \tau(t) + i.G(t)$, we can express the relationship between $\zeta(t)$ and $\theta(t)$ by the relation

$$\zeta'(t) = e^{i\theta(t)} \quad \ldots\ldots \text{Eq. (6.9)}$$

where $\zeta'(t)$ is the derivative of $\zeta(t)$ with respect to t.

To see how this notation simplifies the analysis, let t^* be the time of Realization. $\theta(t^*)=\pi/2$ and $\zeta'(t^*)= e^{i\pi/2}$ which, since $e^{i\pi}+1 = 0$, is the complex number 0+1.i. The real and imaginary parts of $\zeta'(t)$ are $\tau'(t)$ and $G'(t)$. Hence we infer that at time of realization, $\tau(t)$ has zero gradient; signifying that experienced time freezes for the realized jīva. Also the rate of increase of $G(t)$ reaches 1, which is the maximum it can be and attained only by a jīva of Perfection.

---

29 The possibility of complex variable representation was raised during discussions of the mathematical model with Professor V.Krishnamurthy online at advaitins@yahoogroups.com

The Mystical Euler's Formula

There is one point worth noting here. We see that the expression $e^{i\pi/2}$ appears as the value of the ζ'(t) at the time of Realization and that consequently the relation

$$e^{i\pi} + 1 = 0$$

Leonhard Euler

is relevant to understanding the implications of Realization on experienced time. This relation is well known in mathematics as the Euler's Formula or Euler's Identity, in honor of the legendary mathematician Leonhard Euler (1707-1783) who first enunciated it in this form. The relation ties together five fundamental mathematical concepts into one simple, elegant formula: 0, 1, e, i, and π. The five constants surface unavoidably in almost all branches of mathematical, scientific, and engineering studies. The beauty of this curious formula continues to evoke near mystical exhilaration in those who try to ponder its meaning [93]. No wonder, it is considered by many mathematicians as the most famous, beautiful and mystical of all mathematical formulas [94]. It is therefore very appealing, and even gratifying, that it should show up in our mathematical model of spirituality and that too in relation to the value of a key expression specifying the spiritual path of a jīva at the moment of its Realization.

CHAPTER 7

Sri Ramana's Principle of Personal Will

"To be, or not to be; that is the question."
"To be with the Self, or the Not-Self; that is the choice."

The first quotation, from Shakespeare's Hamlet, is world famous and rightly so. Stunningly eloquent in its simplicity, the question captures an essential dilemma of human condition in the world. We want "to be", but find at times the "slings and arrows of outrageous fortune" so unbearable we would rather "not be". Nevertheless, the question is based on a false premise. Lord Krishna tells Arjuna at the very outset of His teaching that

"na caiva na bhaviṣyāmaḥ sarve vayaṁ ataḥ paraṁ"

meaning all jīvas are in truth indestructible and eternal [95]. Therefore "not to be" is not really an option available to Hamlet or any other jīva.

The solution to the sorrows of the world has to be sought elsewhere, not in non-existence. Had Hamlet approached Mahārṣi Sri Ramana with his short, cryptic question, he may have received the answer also in an equally terse language: "*You Be, Not Be You*".

Bhagawan Sri Ramana often taught his devotees that everything in the world happens at the Will of Īśvara only and not at the will of the individual jīva. But there is one notable exception, Bhagawan used to observe: It is up to each jīva to decide whether to identify with the world (i.e. with the Non-Self) or with the Self. Following is one such occasion when Bhagavan answers a specific question from a devotee [96]:

Referring to Sri Krishna's telling Arjuna: "Deluded by Māyā you refuse to fight, but your own nature will force you to fight;" a devotee asked Bhagavan whether we have no free will at all.

Bhagavan replied: "You always have freedom not to identify yourself with the body and the pleasures and pains that come to it as its prārabdha."

Sri Ramana

One summer afternoon I was sitting opposite Sri Bhagavan in the Old Hall with a fan in my hand and said to him: "I can understand that the outstanding events in a man's life, such as his country, nationality, family, career or profession, marriage, death, etc., are all predestined by his karma, but can it be that all the details of his life, down to the minutest, have already been determined? Now, for instance, I put this fan that is in my hand down on the floor here. Can it be that it was already decided that on such and such a day, at such and such an hour, I would move the fan like this and put it down here?"

Bhagavan replied: "Certainly." He continued: "Whatever this body is to do and whatever experiences it is to pass through was already decided when it came into existence."

Thereupon I naturally exclaimed: "What becomes then of man's freedom and responsibility for his actions?"

Bhagavan explained: "The only freedom one has is to strive for and acquire Jñāna which will enable him not to identify himself with the body. The body will go through the actions rendered inevitable by prārabdha (destiny) based on the balance sheet of past lives, and man is free either to identify himself with the body and be attached to the fruits of its actions or to be detached from it and be a mere witness of its activities."

The decision to be with the Self, or with the Non-Self, is thus made at the personal will of the jīva. All other decisions, by virtue of which the world changes from moment to moment, are made by the Will of Īśvara, says the sage. The general implication of Sri Ramana's profound insight is that a jīva has no control over the external material domain of which Īśvara is the sole supreme ruler, but has some control over its own spiritual destiny. Swami Chinmayananda reiterates the same view when he says that "What you meet in life is *prārabdha*, destiny. How you meet it is *puruṣārtha*, free will."[97] The present chapter examines this principle of personal will in the context of the mathematical model discussed previously.

The model posited that all changes in the world are the result of the interplay of Prakṛti's Wish (expressed as probabilistic laws) and Īśvara's Will. The spiritual evolution of a jīva was captured in the model using a function $\theta(t)$, representing the jīva's degree of spiritual detachment at time t, varying in the range $(0,\pi/2$ radians). The lowest level of detachment, $\theta(t)= 0$, indicates a jīva that is fully identified with the world, the Non-Self. At the other end of the range, $\theta(t)= \pi/2$ signifies a jīva that is completely detached from the world and fully absorbed in the Self. The spiritual progress of a jīva over its many life times is shown by plotting $(t, \theta(t))$ in polar coordinates (Fig 7.1).

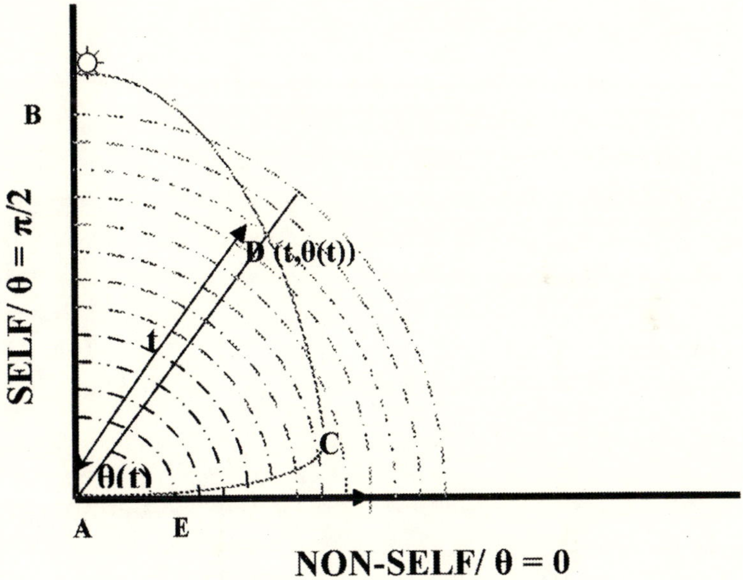

Fig. 7.1: Progress Curve (t, θ(t))

As a jīva becomes increasingly detached from the world through *sādhanas*, it suffers less and less from worldly concerns and at the same time gains more and more in purity of mind as its selfish desires are replaced by universal love. These twin effects of spiritual detachment on a jīva's life are described in the mathematical model by the complex function $\zeta(t)$ with

$$\zeta(t) = \int e^{i\theta(t)}\, dt$$

where the real part of $\zeta(t)$, represented by $\tau(t)$, is a measure of the jīva's "suffering" cumulated over the period 0 to t, while the imaginary part, G(t) is interpreted as the jīva's accumulated merit over the same period. That is,

$$\zeta(t) = \tau(t) + i.G(t) = \int e^{i\theta(t)}\, dt \ldots\ldots \text{ Eq. (7.1)}$$

A graph of G(t) plotted against $\tau(t)$ provides an overall view of the spiritual life or "path" of the jīva (Fig. 6.9). It was further explained using the model that a jīva attains Realization when its detachment $\theta(t)$ reaches the maximum possible value of $\pi/2$ radians.

Three aspects of the above model are open to legitimate questions:

a) The model admits any value for detachment in the range (0, $\pi/2$). But can a jīva be neither with Self, nor with the Non-Self, but somewhere in between? If so, what is this "in between"?
b) The model views the material and spiritual domains somewhat differently. Changes in the material domain are incorporated using a probabilistic approach based on the Prakṛti- Īśvara partnership mentioned earlier. That is, the material realm is recognized to be inherently uncertain. However, the spiritual evolution of the jīva, given by Eq. 7.1, is modeled without any explicit probabilistic elements. Are there no uncertainties associated with spiritual evolution?
c) Sri Ramana's teaching gives a large role to personal free will in a jīva's spiritual unfoldment. How is it reflected in the model?

All three are valid points and all three can be resolved by giving a probabilistic equivalent of Eq. 7.1.

The Probabilistic Approach

To see how Sri Ramana's Principle may be incorporated into Eq. (7.1), we introduce the complex variable z(t) whose gradient z'(t) (i.e. derivative with respect to *t*) is defined by

$$z'(t) = \{1-\gamma(t)\}/\cos\theta(t) + i.\ \gamma(t)/\sin\theta(t) \text{ Eq. (7.2)}$$

where $\gamma(t)$ is a random variable taking the values 1 or 0 with probability $\sin^2\theta(t)$ and $\cos^2\theta(t)$ respectively: 1 if the jīva identifies itself with the Self at time *t* and 0 if it identifies with the Non-Self. z(t) and z'(t) are random functions of *t*.

The expected value of z'(t), denoted by E{z'(t)}, can be computed easily and is $\cos\theta(t) + i.\sin\theta(t)$ or $e^{i\theta(t)}$. Hence

$$E\{z(t)\} = E\{\int z'(t)\,dt\} = \int E(z'(t))\,dt = \int e^{i\theta(t)}\,dt \quad \ldots \text{Eq. (7.3)}$$

Comparing Eq.(7.3) with Eq.(7.1), ζ(t) in the deterministic case and the expected path of z(t) in the probabilistic case are seen to be the same. Therefore we conclude that ζ(t) can be viewed as the expected path of a jīva which, at time t, identifies itself with either Non-Self or with Self with probabilities $\cos^2\theta(t)$ and $\sin^2\theta(t)$ respectively.

At any point in time, the gradient with respect to time of the path ζ(t) (which is the expected path in the probabilistic case) is $\cos\theta(t) + i.\sin\theta(t)$. Of this complex number, the real part $\cos\theta(t)$ is the time derivative of τ(t) and the imaginary part $\sin\theta(t)$ is the time derivative of G(t). A plot of G(t) against τ(t) is what we called as the "jīva's path". We also saw that the tangent of this path at any point is the derivative of G with respect to τ and is equal to $G'(t)/\tau'(t) = \sin\theta(t)/\cos\theta(t)$ or $\tan\theta(t)$. Fig. 7.2 below can be used to visualize geometrically the deterministic and probabilistic cases.

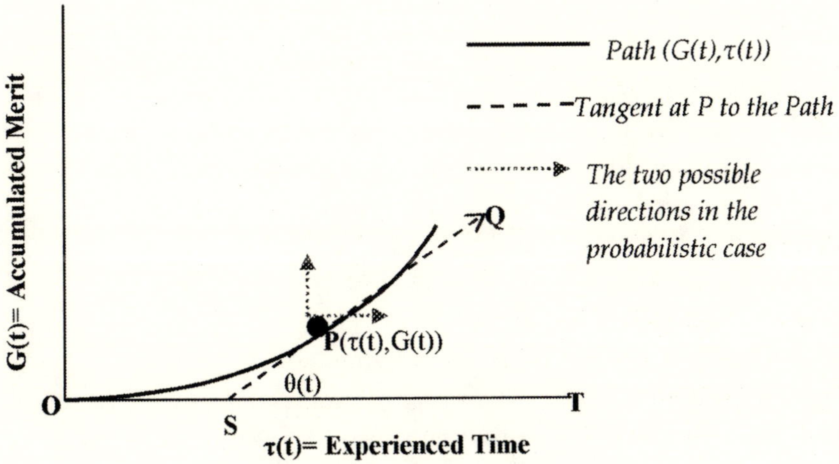

Fig. 7.2: Probabilistic Equivalent

In Fig. 7.2, let P ($\tau(t)$,G(t)) be a point corresponding to time t in the path of a jīva and SQ the tangent to the path at point P. The gradient at P is $dG/d\tau = \tan\theta(t)$ = tangent of the angle QST. Thus, in the deterministic case, the direction of the jīva at time t is PQ.

In the probabilistic case, as per Eq. (7.2), the gradient z'(t) is either $\{1/\cos\theta(t) + i.\ 0)$ if $\gamma(t) = 0$ or $\{0+i/\sin\theta(t)\}$ if $\gamma(t) = 1$. As before, since the real part of z'(t) is $d\tau(t)/dt$ and imaginary part is dG(t)/dt, the gradient $dG/d\tau$ is either

$$0/(1/\cos\theta(t)) = 0^{*}\cos\theta(t) = 0 \text{ if } \gamma(t)=0 \ \underline{\mathit{OR}}$$
$$(1/\sin\theta(t))/0 = \infty \text{ if } \gamma(t) = 1$$

That is, the gradient of G with respect to τ is either 0 or ∞, implying that in the probabilistic case the instantaneous direction of the jīva at any time t is either along the horizontal axis (if the jīva identifies with Non-Self) or the vertical axis (when it identifies with the Self). As just demonstrated, the *expected* direction is along PQ which is the same as in the deterministic case.

The three problems we noted with deterministic model get resolved by adopting this probabilistic approach. Firstly, the jīva is either with the Self or with the Non-Self at any given instant and not somewhere in between. Secondly, the direction of the spiritual path at any moment depends on the choice the jīva makes and hence is unpredictable. This choice is indeed as willed freely by the jīva. We will now see how exactly the personal will of the jīva is reflected in Eq. 7.2.

The Meaning Of γ(t) In Eq. (7.2)

The freedom to choose between Self and Non-Self is presumably available to jīvas all the time. It is reasonable to assume that a jīva's choice at time *t* between these two alternatives depends on its spiritual detachment $\theta(t)$: higher the detachment, more likely that it will choose to identify with the Self. Choosing to identify with Self, the jīva is a pure witness, *sākṣī*, untouched by the suffering at that moment. Choosing to identify with the Non-Self, it is a suffering jīva.

The random function $\gamma(t)$ in Eq. (7.2) represents this fundamental, and (according to Sri Ramana) *only*, freedom a jīva has. It takes the value 0 when the choice is Non-Self and the value 1 when the choice is Self. The probabilities of taking these values are $\cos^2\theta(t)$ and $\sin^2\theta(t)$, which does imply higher probability of identifying with the Self as $\theta(t)$ increases. $\theta(t)$ is a variable ranging between 0 and $\pi/2$ radians and, if and when $\theta(t)$ reaches $\pi/2$, the probability of choosing the Self becomes 1. The jīva does not waver between Self and Non-Self any more. Instead it chooses Self over the Non-Self decisively, with not even a trace of uncertainty. It has attained Realization. As pointed out earlier, $\theta(t)$ does not revert to a lower value once it reaches $\pi/2$ and the jīva remains in Self only thereafter.

Eq. (7.2) implies that a jīva can be in the witness mode ("*sākṣī bhāva*") even if it has not yet attained final Realization. The likelihood of assuming the witness mode is low when $\theta(t)$ is small and staying in that mode for any appreciable length of time is even more difficult and less likely. This is our common experience too. Abidance in the witness mode is permanent only in the case of a Realized jīva.

What exactly is required of a jīva to identify with the Self? Sri Ramana's principle suggests that a jīva must exercise its "will power". A jīva with a low degree of detachment will need very strong will power to lift itself up and identify with the Self, since such a jīva has to contend with the very strong vāsanas, or attachment, it has for the world. But a jīva that has acquired a high degree of purity of mind through *sādhanas* will do it relatively more easily. We discuss below how Eq. (7.2) can be interpreted in terms of the jīva's personal free will.

Choice, Will Power and Probabilities

Concepts of disorder, entropy, chance events, and intelligent effort are interrelated and have been the subject of discussion among physicists and philosophers alike for over a century, beginning with the formulation of the concept of entropy and the second law of thermodynamics in the 19th century [98]. A concrete example will help in understanding these concepts and their mutual relationship. Think of a typical office desktop with many objects- books, coffee mug, stacks of paper, pen, computer, etc. - as a system. Suppose, at some particular time we find this desktop to be in a bit of disorganized state. Most books are neatly stacked, but one of them is kept open with the coffee mug on top. Most papers are in a single pile and the computer monitor is clean of dust, but the pen is left uncapped on the desktop. Altogether, this is a state we may find a desktop if the person working there had stepped out of the office briefly.

But, suppose the person has actually just left the office on vacation for a couple of weeks. If no one steps into the office in the meantime to tidy it up, in what state is the person likely to find the desktop on return from the vacation? Any number of changes could have happened: the coffee mug may have rolled off the book and is now lying somewhere on the desktop with a spot of coffee stain on the book; the pile of papers may have been blown off the desktop by a puff of random breeze and some pages are now found strewn haphazardly around on the floor. The monitor most likely has a coat of dust on it. We cannot be sure any of these will happen, but can expect the desktop and office to be in a more disorderly state than before. Should the desktop be found better organized than before, one would suspect that someone has been into the office to tidy it up.

The above scenario can be applied to any system. Generally speaking, states of disorder are more likely than states of order for a system. Therefore, left to itself, a system is expected to move into states of higher disorder with the progress of time. Stated another way, probability of finding a system in a highly ordered state is correspondingly small; higher the order of the state, lower the *a priori* probability. However, there are situations, such as the above office desktop example, where intelligent and willful efforts can and do restore a measure of order, at least to a part of a system. In such instances the degree of order found in the system reflects the amount of willed effort spent on it. Since the degree of order in a state is inversely related to its probability, the amount of willed effort implicit in the state of a system is also inversely related to the *a priori* probability of that state. Greater willpower is required to bring about a low probability state.

This principle is applicable to decision-making situations involving multiple choices. It applies both to Īśvara who wills the state of the world and to jīvas choosing between Self and Non-Self. As an illustration, consider a situation where the laws of Prakṛti dictate that one of two events, A or B, happens with probabilities 99.9999% and 0.0001%, respectively. In the ordinary course of events A is far, far more likely than B. But it is Īśvara's Will that determines which event actually happens. Should B happen in spite of the great odds, we recognize a "miracle" i.e. a display of Divine Will at work. On the other hand, when A happens there is less recognition of that Īśvara's Will, though in reality neither A nor B can happen without that Will. It is just that Īśvara's Will power *on display* is much stronger- and hence more discernible- when the lower probability event B happens.

Let us apply this reasoning to the jīva which must choose between the "attached mode" { i.e. $\gamma(t) = 0$}and "witness mode" {$\gamma(t) = 1$}. The *a priori* probability of these two modes are $\cos^2 \theta(t)$ and $\sin^2 \theta(t)$ respectively. If $\theta(t)$ is low, $\sin^2\theta(t)$, the probability of identifying with the Self, is also low. The jīva can nevertheless still choose to be in the witness mode, but the will power required is correspondingly high. On the other hand, for a sagely jīva with deep detachment, $\theta(t)$ is high and the will power needed to stay identified with the Non-Self is high. Sri Ramakrishna went relatively easily into *samādhi* but it was a challenge for the disciples to bring him back to ordinary consciousness [99].

For a realized soul (*jīvanmukta)*, $\theta = \pi/2$, and infinite personal will power is required to identify with Non-Self. Seldom, if ever, this jīva identifies with the world even while living here; on leaving its body, unlike other jīvas, it is not born again. In other words, It has reached the supreme state from which there is no return. At the other end, when $\theta = 0$, there is seldom a moment when the jīva identifies with the Self. It can be argued that most, if not all, human beings have a modicum of detachment and hence do not fall into this low, practically insentient, category. Therefore, there is hope for spiritual advancement for all.

Mathematically expressed, we are saying that the will power required to stay with the Self varies inversely with $\sin^2\theta(t)$; that is varies as $(1/\sin^2\theta(t))$. Similarly, the will power needed to stay attached to Non-Self varies as $\{1/\cos^2\theta(t)\}$.

Eq.(7.2) can be therefore rewritten as

$$z'(t) = \{1-\gamma(t)\}\sqrt{WP_{ns}} + i.\ \gamma(t)\ \sqrt{WP_s} \ldots \text{ Eq.(7.4)}$$

where the weights WP_{ns} and WP_s are variables related to the will power needed to identify with the Non-Self and Self respectively. The words "related" and "needed" are significant in correctly interpreting the two variables. First of all, we indicate by these variables the will-power the jīva <u>needs</u> to identify with the Self or Non-Self; they do not represent the will power the jīva <u>possesses</u>. Secondly, WP_{ns} and WP_s are variables which increase or decrease as the will power needed increases or decreases. It is in this sense that we say they are "related" to the will power needed; it is not suggested that they are an exact measure of the will power needed.

The possible dual representation of z'(t) seen from Eqs. (7.2) and (7.4) reflects Sri Ramana's Principle that a jīva's will power is an essential determinant of its spiritual evolution. The same essential principle is also expressed in Gītā when Arjuna famously notes that the fickle, *"cañcala"*, mind is as difficult to control as the wind *("tasyāhaṁ nigrahaṁ manye vāyoriva suduṣkaraṁ ".)* By what means can one bring such a mind to single pointed attention on the Self? To this question from Arjuna, the Lord answers simply

abhyāsena tu kaunteya vairāgyeṇa ca gṛhyate

that is, it is by repeated practice and detachment that one learns to hold the mind still [100]. Since will power is a prerequisite to diligent, consistent practice, it can be surmised that both will power and spiritual detachment are required for meditating on the Self. With higher detachment, the will power needed to stay established in the Self is easier for the yogī to muster, but that will power still must be exercised.

The main result of this chapter- namely that the probabilities of identification with Self and Non-Self are $\sin^2\theta(t)$ and $\cos^2\theta(t)$- is key to establishing the mathematical relationship between vāsanas and spiritual detachment in the next chapter.

In concluding this chapter, we note the curious case of a neuroscientist, Dr. Jill Taylor, who suffered a stroke affecting the left hemisphere of her brain. Such events often leave the patient with serious physical and mental disabilities at least in the short term. In Dr. Taylor's case she not only recovered from the stroke, but found that it brought on, inexplicably, a significant spiritual change in her. She felt a strange detachment from her body and a loss of individuality. In its place she felt connected to everything in and around her, making her outlook on life more peaceful. One may question the manner in which Dr. Taylor gained detachment, but the effect she describes of that detachment on life and suffering, are unquestionably Vedāntic. In a book recounting her experience, Dr. Taylor asks:

"So who are we? We have the power to choose it, moment by moment. I can step into a consciousness where we are the life-force-power of the universe and of all the 50 trillion molecules that make up my form. Or I can choose to step into a consciousness where I become a single individual- a solid, separate from the flow, separate from you. Which would you choose? [101]".

Indeed, who would you rather be? Would you be "you, the suffering individual", or would you rather just "Be", the witness in Bliss? Following Sri Ramana, Dr. Taylor also seems to suggest:

"You Be, Not Be You."

CHAPTER 8

A Theory of Vāsanas

Previous chapters discussed spiritual detachment over time and its relation to suffering, will power, and *mokṣa* (salvation) of a jīva. We also had talked on several occasions about the importance of vāsanas in our spiritual life, but did not include them explicitly in the mathematical model. Detachment being the barometer of spiritual progress, one may ask how vāsanas relate to spiritual detachment. Vāsanas are the driving force determining the thought, desires, actions, and experience of a jīva. Developing a satisfactory mathematical model of vāsanas and their expression in a jīva's spiritual life is no doubt a daunting task. What is presented below is one possible approach to that task in a manner consistent with Vedāntic teachings.

The Double Life of a Jīva

Jīvas lead, as it were, two lives simultaneously: a worldly or material (*laukīka)* life and a spiritual (*adhyātmic)* life. Our material life involves worldly transactions in order to satisfy the many demands and obligations we have at the body, mind, and intellect levels. The spiritual life, of which spiritual detachment is a major characteristic, is defined by our understanding of who we are, what the world is, and our role in the world. The jīva's happiness has much to do with its spiritual life rather than the material life.

Though the two aspects of our selves are to a degree distinct, they do interact constantly, mainly at the level of mind and intellect. Mind-Intellect is the instrument for experiencing the material world; it is also the instrument for turning those experiences into spiritual knowledge. In comparison, the role of the physical body in spiritual matters is less significant.

The Vāsana Spectrum

In Fig. 2.6, the worldly life of a jīva was conceived of as a continuous series of transactions, or encounters, with the world. In its dealings with the world, a jīva is engaged in mainly three types of transactions: wishing, willing (i.e. acting), and experiencing. Typically, though not necessarily, the three transaction types occur in that sequence: we first entertain a wish, then we act to satisfy that wish, and finally we experience the consequences of our action. There are exceptions to this rule. A wish is not always followed by action, remaining merely as a thought instead. But this thought itself is experienced. Similarly, what we experience at times is determined by the actions of others with no input from ourselves. Vāsanas play a key role in all three types of our dealings with the world, but in different ways. Vāsanas being part of Prakṛti, the suggestion that a jīva's wishing, willing, and experiencing are affected by its vāsanas does not contradict the Īśvara-Prakṛti paradigm.

The number and variety of vāsanas potentially affecting a jīva in its daily activities are far too numerous and diverse to be neatly cataloged or listed exhaustively. Yet we need to find a way to address them in some systematic way in order to build a conceptual model.

One way to accomplish this is to conceive the totality of vāsanas as a "spectrum" ranging from the "lowest vāsana" to the "highest vāsana". Vedānta philosophy does help to a great extent in defining this spectrum. All of nature is governed by the three qualities of *tamas*, *rajas*, and *sattva*. Jīvas are also subject to these *guṇas*. Fig. 8.1 is a representation of the vāsana spectrum along a vertical line with the bottom of the line representing the lowest vāsana and the top representing the highest vāsana.

[See next page for Fig. 8.1]

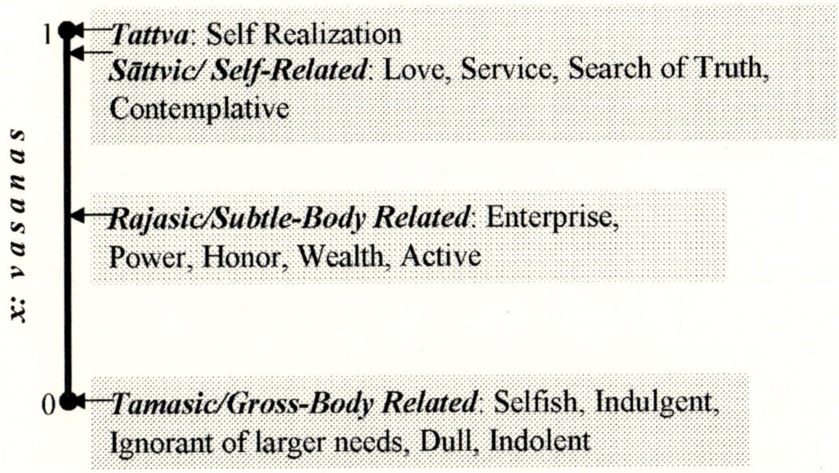

Fig. 8.1: The Vāsana Spectrum ***x: (0,1)***

At the lowest level are the "*tamasic*" vāsanas which have to do with merely appeasing the needs of the gross body by actions such as eating, sleeping, mating, and generally catering to a jīva's bodily comfort and survival. A jīva with only such vāsanas is in the lowest rung of spiritual evolution, a level that is non-distinct from one normally associated with animals and plants.

It is safe to say that most human beings have vāsanas which are "higher" than the purely gross-body oriented ones. There are "*rajasic*" vāsanas at the subtle body (mind and intellect) level which impel a jīva to seek wealth, power and knowledge and gain satisfaction in entertainment, education, arts, games, politics etc. The colorful history of human beings bears testimony to the power of these vāsanas. Truly human traits such as appreciation of beauty, curiosity for worldly knowledge, etc also manifest because of these vāsanas.

Then there are vāsanas that appeal to a jīva's sense of identification with progressively larger groups such as family, community, nation, and finally the entire universe of beings. Larger the group identified with, broader is the vision of the jīva and "higher" the associated vāsanas. Noble traits, such as altruistic love, sacrifice, self-less work, and philanthropy, are the results.

Further up the scale are the "*sāttvic*" vāsanas that speak to the spiritual self of the jīva. Propelled by these, the jīva seeks Truth regarding its own self and the world around it. It practices various *sādhana*s as a means to realize the truth. At the very highest level of the spectrum are divine vāsanas- if they can be called vāsanas- because of which the jīva, detaching itself from mind and matter and everything subtle and gross, seeks abidance in the Self that is beyond the dualities. In fact, the point x = 1 in Fig. 8.1 is representative of "*tattva*" or Self. Progress in spiritual evolution consists in moving from

tamas → *rajas* → *sattva* → (and finally) *tattva*.

We assume, based on the above brief description, that all vāsanas affecting jīvas can be represented by a point on this spectrum. Further, without loss of generality, we may assign the value zero to the lowest point of this line segment and 1 to the highest so that all vāsanas can be assigned a value x, in the range (0,1). Subsequently a more specific meaning will be attributed to the variable x justifying this choice. "Higher" the vāsana, closer is its assigned value to 1.

The Vāsana Function V(x,t)

The vāsanas affecting a jīva change with time; further multiple vāsanas are usually at work at any given time. A jīva has mostly low level vāsanas in the early stages of its evolution. It spends most of its time and energy in body oriented pursuits, survival being its main pre-occupation. Higher level vāsanas are acquired over many lives as the jīva evolves through intelligent living. Typically, a jīva is affected by a mix of vāsanas, some lower and some higher. Even one spiritually advanced must keep the body nourished and hence the corresponding vāsanas are active in that jīva also. But these vāsanas have less urgency or intensity in the evolved jīva compared to others. What makes one jīva spiritually different from another, or the same jīva different at different times, is the level of intensity of various vāsanas, or the "vāsana function".

The Vāsana Function, V(x,t), of a jīva specifies the intensity of its vāsana x at time t. Mathematically, it is a single-valued real function defined for all values of x in the range (0,1). When plotted it is a curve of general form in two dimensions with x, the vāsana, on the x-axis and V, the intensity of the vāsana on the y-axis (Figure 8.2). We restrict the intensity V(x,t) to non-negative values only.

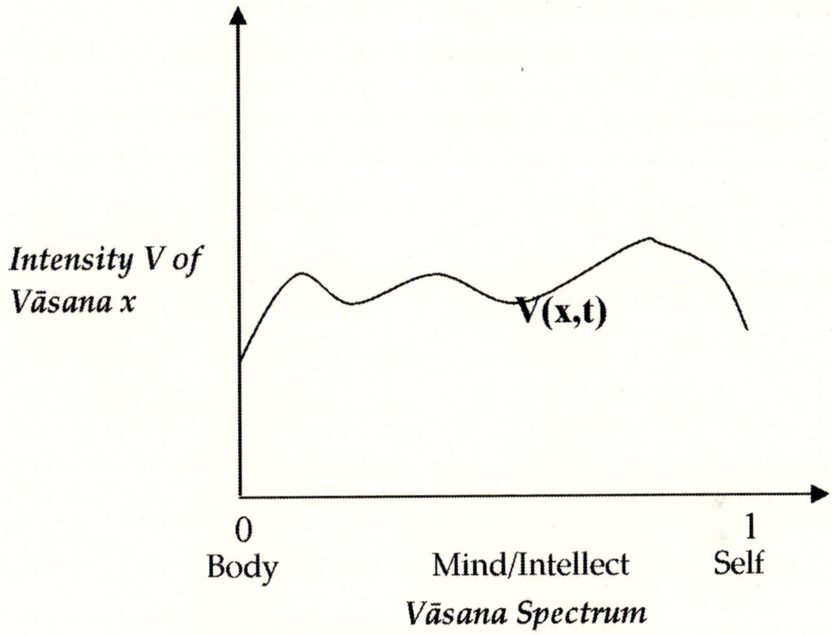

Fig. 8.2: Vāsana Function of a Jīva at time t

The intensity V(x,t) is a measure of the force the vāsanas can *potentially* exert at time t. We use the qualification "potential" in deference to the fact that most of the time some or the other of our vāsanas remain latent and are not called into play. The set of vāsanas that become active at a given time depends on what transaction the jīva is engaged in. For example, in a health conscious person, the desire for a garden salad can be of higher intensity than for French fries. In an undisciplined glutton, on the other hand, the vāsana function has a different shape altogether with the intensity of the desire for fries being much higher than for salad. These vāsanas will be active affecting the decisions and experience of the health conscious person and the glutton when they are in a cafeteria having lunch together. However, they will not determine their behavior when the two are instead engaged in, let us say, a game of chess.

The function V(x,t) represents all the vāsanas potentially affecting the jīva at time t, both latent and active. Therefore, the vāsana function is same whether the jīvas in the above example are deciding on what to have for lunch or what moves to make on the chessboard. But how it affects the wishing, willing, and experiencing of the jīva depends on the worldly events at play.

Two Characteristics of Vāsana Function

A vāsana function has two important characteristics: its *shape* and its *magnitude*. To illustrate their meaning, two vāsana functions, V_1 and V_2 are shown in Figure 8.3 below.

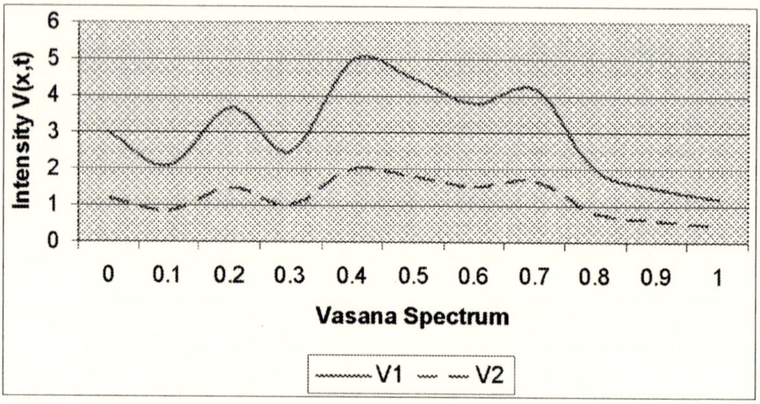

Fig. 8.3 Two Similar Vasana Functions

The two functions are similar in shape, but differ in magnitude. In fact the intensity under V_2 at any point is 40% that of V_1. Two vāsana functions $V_1(x,t)$ and $V_2(x,t)$ are to be considered "similar" in shape if $V_1(x,t) = a.\ V_2(x,t)$ for all x, for some $a > 0$.

The *magnitude* I(t) of a vāsana function V(x,t) is defined by the area under the curve and is given by

$$I(t) = \int_0^1 V(x,t)dx$$

We define the "normalized vāsana function", V'(x,t), by

$$V'(x,t) = V(x,t)/I(t)$$

With this definition it is observed that $\int V'(x,t)\ dx = 1$ and also that V' and V are of similar shape. In other words, the process of normalization transforms V into another function V' of similar shape but with magnitude adjusted to 1. It is also observed that V'(x,t) has characteristics of a probability density function over x, a feature which will be of use later.

Since

$$V(x,t) = I(t).\ V'(x,t) \text{ for all } x \in (0,1)\ldots\ldots (8.1)$$

we have effectively factored the function V into its shape, V'(x,t), and magnitude I(t).

In Figure 8.3, V_1 and V_2 have identical normalized vāsana function V' but magnitude of V_2 is 40% that of V_1.

Interpretation Of Shape, V' and Magnitude I(t)

The vāsana function V as a whole represents the intensity of all potential and active vāsanas affecting a jīva at time t. Vāsanas influence all types of worldly transactions that the jīva engages in: It influences *what* a jīva wishes, wills and experiences, as well as how strong or intense its desires, actions and experiences are.

V', which has the same shape as V, can be viewed as a function showing *the relative values cherished by the jīva*. It is a profile of the value system driving the jīva's life. For example, a vāsana function with V'(1,t) =2 and V'(0,t) = ½, represents a jīva whose pure *sāttvic* vāsana is four times as strong as its lowly, gross body related, vāsanas. As such it could describe a spiritually evolved jīva who is ready to make the physical sacrifices necessary to engage in austerities. A predominantly extroverted "alpha type" personality, on the other hand, will have a vāsana function peaking somewhere in the middle *rajasic* part of the spectrum.

A jīva's personality is defined by what it wishes and how it acts and reacts. We may therefore well say that a *"Jīva is what jīva does"*, borrowing a line made famous by the character Forrest Gump in the Hollywood movie of same title. Since it is the vāsanas that impel a jīva to wish, will and react, the function V'(x,t) is a quantitative abstraction of the jīva's personality at time t. No two jīvas are totally identical in personality and therefore, the vāsana function V', like the genes of the physical body, is unique to each individual. The genes change little over the life of the gross body, but the vāsanas can and do change within a single life time.

The Magnitude or Sentiency Factor I(t): Overlaid on the relative values is the other characteristic of the jīva, namely I(t), which may be called the "sentiency factor". Vāsanas, like all forces of nature, are unmanifest (*avyakta*) by themselves and recognized only through their effects. They need an alert, energetic mind-intellect in order to be manifested. More alert and energized the mind and intellect, more intense the vāsanas manifested. I(t), which is the area under the curve V(x,t), represents the total intensity summed over all vāsanas. I(t) is therefore a measure of the overall "vibrancy" or level of alertness of the mind. For example, I(t)= 0 in case of a jīva in deep sleep. Mind is still there and so are the vāsanas, but in deep sleep the mind is not vibrant as it is when awake or in dream[30]. In general, low values of I(t) indicate a non-vigilant mind, more asleep than awake.

Thus interpreted, Eq. (8.1) states that V(x,t), the intensity of the vāsana x of a jīva at time t, is a product of two factors: I(t), the overall sentiency of the mind, and V'(x,t), the Relative Values at that time.

An Alternate View

Implicit in the above discussion is the primary importance given to V(x,t). That is, we are implying that V(x,t) defines the basic spiritual personality of a jīva with I(t) and V'(x,t) being two aspects of it. Alternatively it is possible to view I(t) and V'(x,t) as the two basic characteristics of a jīva and consider V(x,t) as a product, or the combined effect, of these two primary characteristics. The two views are mathematically equivalent, though the latter view is more consistent with scriptures that speak of sentiency of the mind, *cetana,* and vāsanas as two distinct aspects.

"Ascent Of Man" - The Kuṇḍalini Theory

It will be recognized that the vāsana spectrum shown in Fig. 8.1 has features analogous to the concepts well known in *Kuṇḍalini Yoga*. Spiritual awakening is said to take place in a jīva as the *Kuṇḍalini* energy rises up along the *suṣuṁnā nāḍi* from "*mūlādhāra*"- the first *cakra* - to the other *cakras* above, ending with the final seventh *cakra*,

30 Mind is not the brain; nevertheless we note that electroencephalographic measurements of the human brain taken during deep sleep, relaxed meditation, and dream / awake states correspond with this view. The frequency of the electrical waves during these states are respectively in the range of 0.5-4 Hz (delta waves), 4-8 Hz (theta waves), and 8-30 Hz (alpha and beta waves), though some overlap does occur [103].

the "*Sahasrāra*"[31]. Fig. 8.4 and Table 8.1, adapted from [102], provide a summary of the seven *cakra*s and their spiritual significance.

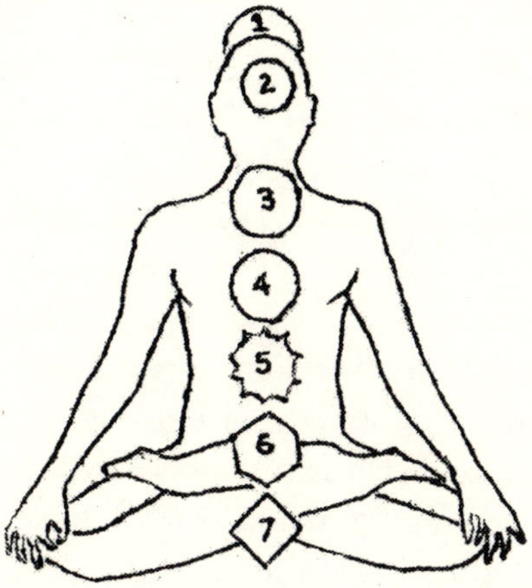

1. **The Crown Chakra**
2. **The Third Eye Chakra**
3. **The Throat Chakra**
4. **The Heart Chakra**
5. **The Solar Plexus Chakra**
6. **The Sacral Chakra**
7. **The Root Chakra**

Fig. 8.4: The Seven Cakras of Kuṇḍalini Yoga

Each *cakra* is associated with a set of values and sense of self that are spiritually more progressive and refined as shown in Table 8.1.[32]

TABLE 8.1: THE ASCENDING PATH TO PERFECTION

Cakras	Vāsanas	Orientation to self
1. *Mūlādhāra*	Survival	Self-preservation
2. *Svādhiṣṭāna*	Sensual Pursuits	Self-Gratification
3. *Maṇipura*	Power, self-esteem, Responsibility	Self-Definition
4. *Anahata*	Relationships, Love, Devotion	Self-Acceptance
5. *Viśuddha*	Self-discipline, Speaking truth	Self-Expression
6. *Ājñā*	intuition, Imagination, Intellect	Self-Reflection
7. *Sahasrāra*	Awareness, Spiritual Search	Self-Knowledge

31 *Nāḍis* are similar to the nervous system but at the subtle body level. *Cakras* are key interconnecting centers of the system. The *Suṣumnā nāḍi* corresponds to the spinal cord at the gross body level.

32 The numbering of the *cakras* in Table 8.1 is reversed from that in Fig. 8.4. Thus the first cakra *Mūlādhāra* in Table 8.1 corresponds to the seventh "base/root chakra" of Fig. 8.4 while the Sahasrāra in Table 8.1 is same as the "crown chakra" of Fig. 8.4.

The Kuṇḍalini symbolizes the ascending spiritual path that a jīva, aspiring liberation, has to take. The vāsanas in Table 8.1 beginning with Self-Preservation and ending with Self-Knowledge, encompass the spectrum of basic forces motivating living beings. They can be called as the *elemental vāsanas*. There is a gradual progression from *tamas* to *sattva* in the order of the vāsanas: *tamas* predominates in the first two vāsanas, *rajas* in the next three, and *sattva* in the last two.

Pañcadaśi, a well known text in Advaita Vedānta, also speaks of seven stages of spiritual development: ignorance, obscuration, superimposition, indirect knowledge, direct knowledge, freedom from grief, and total bliss [104]. The same progression of qualities (*guṇas*) from *tamas* to *sattva* can be found in the seven stages also, with the last stage, total bliss, being that of "*tattva*" that is beyond all three *guṇas*.

Thus the representation of vāsanas proposed in Fig. 8.1 is consistent with the concepts found in Kuṇḍalini theory and generally in Vedānta. The vāsana spectrum ranging from 0 to1 is analogous to the psychic body stretching from *Mūlādhāra* to *Sahasrāra*. The energy levels surrounding the various *cakra*s are represented by the vāsana function, V, over the range (0,1). Spiritual awakening is the transfer of energy away from *Mūlādhāra* (i.e. the region near x = 0) and towards *Sahasrāra* (near x = 1).

Subtle Energy

So far we have not explained how exactly a variable x may represent a vāsana. Nor have we described the basis on which one can rank one vāsana higher than another. The explanation of this process involves the concept of "subtle energy".

Embodied jīvas are endowed with both gross (i.e. physical) and subtle (i.e. mental or psychic) energies. These are related to the vitality of its gross and subtle bodies respectively and are manifested in its physical, mental and intellectual activities. Our inner vitality as conscious living beings lies in the vibrancy, or energy, of our mind-intellect complex, the subtle body. Powered by this subtle energy, the mind vibrates to external and internal stimuli, creating desires, thoughts, actions and enjoyment.

In many physical systems, energy is proportional to the frequency, or rate of vibration. For example, it is a well known law of Physics that the energy E of a photon is $h.f$ where h is the Planck's constant and f is the frequency. It is interesting to speculate if a similar law does not hold for "subtle matter" of which the "*sūkṣma śarīra*" (subtle body or the mind-intellect complex of a jīva) is composed. John C. Eccles, the 1963 Nobel Prize winner in Medicine for his work on synaptic neurophysiology, has put forward the theory that there exist elementary subtle particles similar to photons called "psychons" which are the basic packets of subtle energy [105]. In Eccles's view, psychons render the mind-brain interaction possible.

The terms "vibrations" and "energy" are commonly used in discussions of mind in spirituality. As mentioned earlier in relation to the awakening of *Kuṇḍalini*, spiritual traditions talk of the flow of energy along the *nāḍis* and vibration of the various *cakra*s. *Cakras* are points where the *nāḍis* inter-connect. The *cakra*s are related to the vāsanas in a jīva as shown in Table 8.1, and V(x,t), the "intensity of a vāsana", can be thought of as the frequency, or rate of vibrations, of a *cakra* or vāsana, x[33].

The mental energy in a jīva is normally directed outwards as observed in the following well-known *mantra* from the Upaniṣads:

> *"parāñci khāni vyatṛṇāt svayambhūḥ, tasmāt parāṅ*
> *paśyati nāntarātman, kaścid dhīraḥ pratyagātman*
> *aikṣat, āvṛtta cakṣuḥ amṛtatvaṁ icchan".*

"The Self-Existent (Brahma) created the senses with outgoing tendencies; therefore, man beholds the external universe and not the internal Self (Ātman). But some wise men with eyes averted (with his senses turned away) from sensual objects, desirous of Immortality, sees the Ātman within"[106]. Spiritual unfoldment is the gradual re-direction of the normally out-gushing mental energy towards the inner-Self. In an evolved jīva, more and more of the energy is turned inwards and, in the *samādhi* state of a Realized jīva, nearly 100% of the energy is centered on the Self.

Nature of out-flowing mind: Teachers and scriptures point out that it is the out-flowing mind –namely, a mind directed outwards in attachment to the world of Objects, Emotions and Thoughts- which causes bondage and suffering to a jīva. On the contrary, a contemplative mind turned inwards is a tool for spiritual progress and for destroying bondage.

---

33 By allowing x to have any value in the range (0,1), we are assuming that *cakra*s are not just seven discrete points, but that they form a continuous spectrum. This makes the subsequent mathematical representation simpler.

The outward attachment of the mind results in different manifestations of the ego depending on the nature of transaction:

Transaction Type	Manifestation of Ego
Wishing	"I want" or "My wish"
Acting	"I do" ("*kartṛtvaṁ*")
Experiencing	"I enjoy" ("*bhoktṛtvaṁ*")

Stronger the jīva's sense of "I want", "I do", and "I enjoy" notions, stronger is its bondage and higher the potential for suffering.

Significance of x, the vāsana spectrum variable

An inspection of Figures 8.1 and 8.4 as well as Table 8.1 indicates that the progression of the vāsana variable x from 0 to 1, is associated with an increasingly introverted mind. Points in the spectrum close to x = 0 denote *tamasic* vāsanas that have to do with survival and preservation of the gross body. Else they may denote mechanical or autonomic activities as in the case of inert objects. In either case there is little or no contemplative mind. At the other extreme, points in the vicinity of x = 1 are associated with *sāttvic* vāsanas responsible for Self-Reflection and Self-Knowledge when the mind is turned inwards nearly 100%.

For vāsanas lying between the extremes of 0 and 1, a part of the mental energy is directed outward in attachment to O-E-T. That is to say, the ego-centric notions of "I want", "I do" and "I enjoy" are muted to an extent, but not totally absent. This is the case, for instance, in a jīva which, abandoning narrow selfish interests, identifies itself with the welfare of larger and larger groups.

The value x attributed to a vāsana indicates the fraction of the subtle energy directed inwards while jīvas are under the influence of that vāsana. That is, fraction of energy directed inwards is x and (1-x) is the fraction of mental energy directed outward to O-E-T. Typically a jīva exhibits some attachment while engaged in its worldly transactions, but it also can witness own emotions, thoughts, and actions while performing the transactions. To use the "twin-bird" analogy of *Muṇḍaka Upaniṣad*, such a jīva is partially in the eating mode and partially in the witnessing mode.

x as a Probability- An Alternative Interpretation: It may be argued that a jīva, at a given instant, cannot be simultaneously in the witnessing and attached modes. In deference to this objection, instead of being fraction of energy directed inwards, x can be interpreted as the *probability* that the jīva will be in the witnessing mode when under the influence of vāsana x. This probability is low for "lowly" *tamasic* vāsanas compared to "higher" *rajasic* or *sāttvic* vāsanas. In fact, as per our characterization of the vāsana spectrum, a vāsana is considered low *because* of the low probability of being in the witness mode when under its influence. For instance, facing a life threatening situation, the survival instincts (which are vāsanas at the lower end near x=0) dominate the behavior of a jīva, unless it be a supremely accomplished *yogī*. At such moments, the jīva is fearful and all its attention is on possible escape routes; the probability of being in the pure witnessing mode is small.

The end point (x = 1) of the spectrum is special in that 100% of mental energy is turned inwards, with no attachment to the world. As noted earlier, this upper end-point of the spectrum is associated with Self and is not really a vāsana. For all other vāsanas with x <1, there is potential for mental agitation due to some out-flow of mind.

The Energy Equations

We can relate subtle energy of a jīva to its Vāsana Function V(x,t) based on the principle that energy is proportional to the frequency of vibration. Recalling that V(x,t) is the frequency or rate of vibrations at x, the total subtle energy at time t, denoted by $E_T(t)$, associated with vāsana function V(x,t) is

$$E_T(t) = c. \int_0^1 V(x,t)dx$$

where c is the constant of proportionality between energy and frequency.

By definition, $I(t) = \int_0^1 V(x,t)dx$ and therefore we have

$$E_T(t) = c.I(t) \text{.......................Eq. (8.2).}$$[34]

34 Note on Units of Measurement: I(t) has same units as V(x,t), which, being of the nature of frequencies, is usually expressed as Hz (i.e. 1/sec). The constant c is in units of "energy.sec" where "energy" is some appropriate unit of mental energy. We will not generally spell out the units in the following discussions, except when necessary for clarity.

E_T is also seen as the sum of E_O and E_{In}, where

$$E_O(t) = c. \int(1\text{-}x)\ V(x,t)\ dx, \text{ and}$$
$$E_{In}(t) = c. \int x\ V(x,t)\ dx$$

are respectively the total extroverted and total introverted energy associated with V(x,t). [35]

Let V'(x,t) = V(x,t)/I(t) be the normalized vāsana function. Consider $M'_x(t)$ given by

$$M'_x(t) = \int x\ V'(x,t)\ dx \quad \text{Eq. (8.3)}$$

Since V'(x,t) can be regarded as a probability density function of a random variable x ranging over (0,1), $M'_x(t)$ is the statistical mean value of x, or the "average of the vāsanas" at time t. As such $M'_x(t)$ is a measure of the jīva's evolution at time t, expressed in terms of its vāsanas.

Using the above definitions, we have the three energy equations stated below

$$E_O(t) = c.I(t). \int(1\text{-}x)\ V'(x,t)\ dx = c\ .I(t).(1\text{-}\ M'_x(t))\text{.......Eq. (8.4)}$$
$$E_{In}(t) = c.I(t).\ M'_x(t), \quad \text{.......Eq. (8.5), } \textit{and}$$
$$E_T(t) = (E_O(t)+\ E_{In}(t)) \quad \text{...Eq. (8.6)}$$

The last relation shows that the total subtle energy E_T is split between the outward and inward flowing energies.

E_T (t), the total subtle energy defined by Eq. (8.2) or (8.6), represents how alert the mind is; i.e. the degree of jīva's awareness of itself and the world around it at time t. As we saw in Chapter 2, Pure Consciousness, reflecting on the jīva's mind-intellect equipment, creates awareness. Therefore awareness can vary depending on the "reflectivity" of the mind-intellect; e.g. there is no awareness during deep sleep when the mind-intellect, totally covered by *tamas,* loses reflectivity.

$E_O(t)$, the part of $E_T(t)$ flowing outwards, depends on the attachment the jīva has to O-E-T and is a measure of the mental agitation occasioned by such attachment. The energy level of the out-flowing mind shows how much "the jīva is in love" with the world. On the other hand, the inward turned mind (measured by $E_{In}(t)$) shows how much "love for the

35 The range of x in these integrals is (0,1).

world is in the jīva". The former is attachment which is predominantly *tamasic* and *rajasic* in nature and causes bondage and suffering. The latter is Pure Love, predominantly *sāttvic*, leads to detachment and happiness.

Ego and Self-Concept

The word ego has many shades of meaning as used in the English language. Depending on the context, it can mean sense of individuality, arrogance, the psychological person, etc. Ego can also be used to mean the image we have of ourselves, or our "self-concept". In this case ego consists of our view of own strengths and weaknesses, our character, and our likes and dislikes. It is this image that we identify ourselves with as "I". How strongly we identify with this image is a measure of our "ego". A jīva which has strong vāsanas tying it to the world, will have more of its mental energy flowing outwards and also stronger identification with its self-concept. In this sense, the ego can be considered as the **e**nergy-**g**oing-**o**ut, E_O.

The Goal Of Spiritual Practices

The goal of spiritual practices is to bring own mind under control, whence the Self will reveal itself. As Adi Sankara says *"sendriya mānasa niyamādevaṁ, drakṣyasi nija hṛdayastaṁ devaṁ"* [107]. By control of mind alone one sees the Lord seated in own heart. Salvation requires disciplined self-effort to control the vagrant mind.

Eqs. 8.2 through 8.6 succinctly incorporate the theory and purpose of spiritual practices. Consider two vāsana functions, V_1 and V_2, which are of same magnitude but differ in their shape. The total energy c.I is the same in the two cases, but the normalized vāsana functions V'_1 and V'_2 are not the same. As a consequence the mean value of V'_1 and V'_2 are also, in general, different. Let us say $M'_{x1} > M'_{x2}$. From Eq. 8.4 and 8.5, it follows that while the total energy c.I is same under both V_1 and V_2, the inward flowing component E_{In} under V_1 is higher than that of V_2. In other words, the jīva with vāsana function V_1 has more of its mental energy directed inwards compared to the jīva with vāsana function V_2. A higher value of M'_x signifies a more evolved jīva.

The goal of spiritual practices is to minimize the outflow of mind in order to achieve nearly 100% concentration of mental energy on the Self. That is, the goal is to reduce E_O, the **e**nergy-**g**oing-**o**ut, to as close to zero as possible. We add parenthetically that this should be done without reducing the sentiency factor I. That is, the mind should remain alert and alive, with no reduction in its overall energy level. The goal of spiritual practices can now be stated mathematically thus: *Spiritual progress requires the re-shaping of the vāsana function V in such a way that M'_x, the mean value of V', is increased as close to 1 as possible, but without reducing the magnitude,* I. This statement only reiterates what is well known: Spiritual progress is achieved only by modifying the underlying vāsanas affecting our being.

Squeezing The Vāsana Balloon

Changing V, without changing I, implies changing the normalized vāsana function V'. Since $\int_0^1 V'(x,t)dx$ must always equate to 1, when one segment of V' is decreased, another segment must be increased. Re-shaping the normalized vāsana function is therefore like squeezing a balloon. When one part of a balloon is compressed, another part must inflate. Figuratively speaking, spiritual progress involves compression of the left part, or lower *tamasic* and *rajasic* vāsanas, so as to inflate the "Vāsana Balloon" on the right side where the *sāttvic* vāsanas are (See Fig. 8.5 below.)

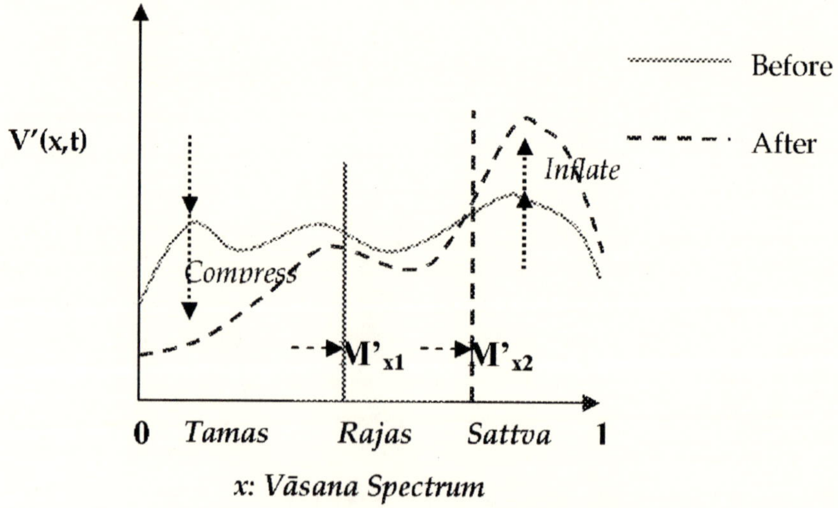

Fig. 8.5- Squeezing the Vāsana Balloon on the left to shift the mean M_x' to the right

The progression from *tamas* to *rajas* to *sattva* can be visualized as squeezing the balloon first at the left (*tamas*) which will increase the air pressure (that is, energy) in the middle (*rajas*) and right (*sattva*) parts. As the jīva gains more control over its mind, the squeeze is applied also to middle *rajasic* part to concentrate the energy in the *sattva* region. This must be continued until almost all energy is concentrated on the extreme right of the vāsana spectrum.

Is there a limit to how far to the right the vāsana balloon can be squeezed before it pops?

Limit To Spiritual Evolution

As lowly and middling vāsanas are reduced, the jīva becomes more and more *sāttvic* and the corresponding vāsanas (close to $x = 1$) intensify. If all subtle energy is confined to a very small segment of length δx close to 1, the normalized vāsana function $V'(x,t)$ will approach the form below:

$$V'(x,t) = 0 \quad \text{for } 0 \le x < 1-\delta x \text{ and}$$
$$= 1/\delta x \quad \text{for } 1-\delta x \le x \le 1 \; \ldots\ldots\ldots \text{ Eq. 8.7}$$

As δx approaches 0, vāsanas vanish everywhere except in the region very close to 1 where it assumes higher and higher intensity. The mean $M_{x'}$ of this vāsana function, it is easily verified, is $(1-\delta x/2)$.

If $\delta x = 0$, V' is zero everywhere, except for an infinite spike at $x = 1$. In this limiting case $M_{x'} = 1$. It refers to a jīva with actually no vāsanas at all; i.e. a jīva that has attained Realization or *nirvāṇa*. This limiting case will be discussed in greater detail soon.

For other unrealized, yet highly evolved, jīvas, δx is small. But there is a limit to how small it can be. To derive this limit, we first need to establish the connection between the two apparently different aspects of spirituality, namely, detachment and vāsanas.

The Relation Between Spiritual Detachment θ(t) And Normalized Vāsana Function V'(x,t)

Realization was defined in previous chapters as the state where $\theta = \pi/2$. In terms of the vāsanas, we are also defining it as the state where $M_{x'} = 1$. This suggests that $M'_x(t)$, the mean of the vāsana function varying between 0 and 1, should be related to spiritual detachment, $\theta(t)$.

To see what this relation might be, recall that x, the fraction of introverted energy at vāsana x, can also be interpreted as the conditional probability that the jīva will be in the witness mode given vāsana x. With this interpretation, $M'_x(t) = \int_0^1 xV'(x,t)dx$ is seen to be the unconditional probability that a jīva, with vāsana function V(x,t), will be in the witness mode, regardless of which vāsanas may be active. However, we argued in the earlier chapter on Sri Ramana's Principle that, in terms of θ(t), this latter probability is $\sin^2\theta(t)$. Hence we have the relation

$$\mathbf{\sin^2\theta(t) = M'_x(t)}, \text{ or}$$

$$\theta(t) = \sin^{-1}(\sqrt{M'_x(t)}) \ldots \text{ Eq. 8.8}$$

establishing the mathematical relationship between spiritual detachment and vāsanas. We also infer

$$\cos^2\theta(t) = \int_0^1(1 - x)\, V'(x,t)\, dx = (1 - M'_x(t)) \ldots\ldots \text{ Eq. 8.9}$$

This relationship enables us to draw upon the results developed in Chapter 6 regarding limits to spiritual detachment. For example, it was argued there that the maximum θ(t) can be is approximately $(\pi/2-(0.317*10^{-12}))$ radians. Since $M_x' = \sin^2\theta(t)$ and, for small δx it is also equal to (1- δx/2), we have $\delta x = 2.\ (1-\sin^2\theta(t))$. As θ(t) increases, δx decreases and therefore the minimum δx occurs at the maximum θ(t). Hence we have

$$\text{Min } \delta x \approx 2.\ (1-\sin^2(\pi/2-0.317*10^{-12})) = 2.\sin^2(0.317*10^{-12})$$

Using the approximation sinθ = θ for small angles, we deduce that

$$\text{Min } \delta x \approx 2.10^{-25}$$

For brevity, we denote the point $x = (1-2.10^{-25})$ in the vāsana spectrum by x*. It is the limit to which the vāsana balloon can be squeezed to the right. It is also the vāsana spectrum counterpart of the "*Brahmāji*'s Path" shown in Fig. 6.6. We can purify mind of vāsanas until the mean value M_x' reaches x*. Further purification, which takes M_x' from x* to 1 in one step, requires Īśvara's Grace. This is when the vāsana balloon pops.

Swami Chinmayananda, in his commentary on the Sixth Chapter, "Yoga of Meditation", of Bhagavad Gītā, defines the "halt-moment" in meditation as the "*last possible frontier up to which human effort can raise the mind*". "*There it ends itself*", continues Swamiji, "*just as a balloon, as it goes higher and higher, blasts itself in the rarified atmosphere of the higher altitudes, dropping itself down and merging the balloon space with the space in the altitude. Similarly, the mind too, at the pinnacle of its meditation, shatters itself, drops down leaving the Ego, and merges with the Supreme* [108]."

In Fig. 8.5, the vāsana balloon can be squeezed to the right until all energy is confined to (x^*,1) after which point the balloon cannot be squeezed any further by the jīva's efforts but must pop on its own.

Continuity of the Vāsana Spectrum

The discontinuity in the x-axis between x^* and 1 suggests that the vāsana spectrum may be discrete. In this case vāsanas may not be points on the x-axis, but rather discrete, non-overlapping, line segments. For example, the vāsana at the extreme right will be the line segment from ($1-x^*$) up to and including 1 (and not just the point $x=1$). The discrete-set view does not nullify the approach or the results above, except that we will need to consider sum over discrete values of x instead of integration over x. For sake of simplicity, we continue to work with the assumption that vāsanas, x, and time, *t*, are continuous variables.

One Small Step in Spiritual Evolution, One Giant Leap into Infinite Bliss

The *Brahmalok* is considered the final evolutionary state of a jīva before attaining Realization. In other words, there are no intermediate steps of development between the *Brahmalok* and Realization. These two states are represented by two points exceedingly close in the vāsana spectrum with the *quantitative*, or numerical, separation between x^* and 1 being only of the order of 10^{-25}. Yet, the *qualitative* separation between these two states is enormous. In fact it is the difference between the finite and the Infinite. It is the difference between the joy of *Brahmalok* and Absolute Bliss so emphatically and beautifully recounted in the previously cited *Brahmānandavalli* portion of the *Taittirīya Upaniṣad.*

The jīva must make this minute transition from x^* to 1, which nevertheless spans an infinite chasm, in one quantum leap. As Goswami says: "*This realizing the truth about the self -that the self is all- is a truly discontinuous jump- a gigantic quantum leap……. When we surrender to the Will of the One so totally that our will becomes the will of the One and vice versa, then do we quantum leap into complete freedom*" [109]. This final tiny yet gargantuan step in the jīva's spiritual evolution is possible only by Īśvara's Grace.

Can a numerically small step make an infinite qualitative difference? The mathematical reason is simple enough: V' in Eq. 8.7 assumes the form in Fig. 8.6 below when $\delta x = 0$. Here V'(x,t) is zero for all x<1 and *infinity at 1.*

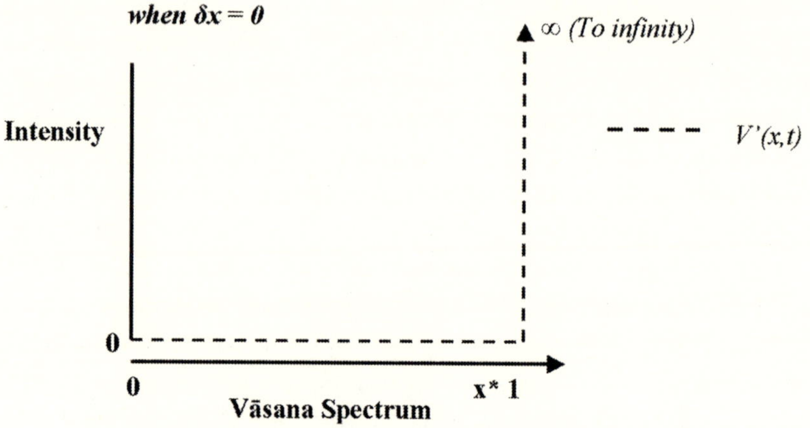

Fig. 8.6: ***Limiting Form of V'(x,t) in Eq. 8.7 when*** $\delta x = 0$

The limiting normalized vāsana function in Fig. 8.6 is that of a liberated being that has "gone beyond" the O-E-T. All energy is directed inwards and the jīva is fully established in the Self. It is instructive to study the non-normalized vāsana function of such a liberated being.

The (non-normalized) vāsana function of the Realized being, namely V(x,t) = I(t).V'(x,t), depends on I(t). Mathematically, four cases can be distinguished at this stage depending on the value of I(t).

Case 1: 0 < I(t)< ∞; Liberated Jīva as per Dvaitic Tradition: It can be verified that V(x,t) and V'(x,t) are identical in this case. Since I(t) > 0, it is inferred that there is still a vibrant individual mind, but with no vāsanas whatsoever to bind the jīva to O-E-T. Additionally, that mind is focused on the Self with infinite intensity. The presence of mind indicates that duality has not ended for the jīva, though the world has. This is the case, for example, of a jīva in *Vaikuṇṭh, Kailās,* or heaven by any other name, where the individual is totally focused on Totality, yet there is still a mind separating the jīva and the *saguṇa Brahman*, or Īśvara. This state corresponds to the dualistic (*dvaita*) concept of salvation.

Case 2: I(t)=0; Liberation as per Advaitic Tradition: V(x,t) =

0 for all x<1 as before indicating *nirvāṇa* and the end of the world for the jīva. With I(t)=0, there is however no more individual mind. Here, V(1,t) = 0.∞ is undefined, meaning this jīva cannot be said to be either focused or not focused on Self. This is the case if the jīva, merging its identity with Brahman the Self, has ended all seen-seer duality. Having ceased its own individuality and merged with Brahman, one cannot talk any more of individual I(t), or impute any value to it. This case corresponds to the Advaitic (non-dualistic) vision of salvation.

Throughout its life prior to Realization, a jīva has a mind. That is, I(t) > 0, except during brief, finite periods of deep sleep etc when the mind is covered by *tamas*. If this is so, how and when does I(t) become irrevocably zero, as required in Case 2? *Dvaitin*s may hold that this in fact is *not* possible. Indeed this objection may be at the heart of their difficulties with Advaitic philosophy. For Advaitins, however, the merger of jīva with Brahman is not only possible but guaranteed by the declarations in scriptures and affirmed by the experience of many Masters.

"The Last Wish" of a Jīva and a Reconciliation of the Dvaita- Advaita Views

Can both views be right? It is possible. It is possible if we assume that I(t) also becomes zero with the Grace of Īśvara only, even as the jīva, shedding the last of its vāsanas behind, is transported from x* to 1, from finite to Infinite. Ever the merciful, Īśvara is said to grant the devotee's wishes. So, it may be very well the case that, for a jīva that has advanced to the highest rung of spiritual ladder, what happens next depends on its "last wish". If, upon being transported from x* (i.e. *Brahmalok*) to 1 (heaven) the jīva wishes to maintain the dual jīva - Īśvara relationship, it is allowed to retain its now fully purified mind on arrival at "1", the Lord's Abode. On the other hand, if the jīva's desire is to break free from even the last vestiges of mind and end all duality and its own individuality, I(t), sentiency of the individual mind vanishes to zero, Īśvara and jīva both disappear, and Brahman alone remains. A very recent book discusses in fascinating detail this "final choice" available to a jīva entering the portals of the heaven [110].

Case 3: Infinite I(t)- Īśvara: Can I(t) be ever infinite? By I(t) = ∞ we mean a mind with infinite energy. Such a characterization can not apply to any finite jīva, but only to Īśvara, who is also considered sometimes as the Total Mind. For Īśvara, who by definition is in Lord's Abode, a vāsana function portrayed in Fig. 8.6 should apply, but with infinite I(t). Note that in this case V(x,t) is undefined for $0 \leq x < 1$. This means that Īśvara, the Creator, Sustainer, and Destroyer of the world, cannot be said to be either attached or detached from the O-E-T. He is attached to the extent required for controlling the world. But, as often emphasized by Gurudev Swami Chinmayanandaji, it is a "relationless relationship". E_O/E_T is zero by virtue of the limiting form of V'(x,t). That is, of the infinite total energy possessed, the proportion of energy outgoing for managing the world is zero.

Case 4: I(t) Undefined- Brahman: It is often said that either no description fits Brahman or all descriptions fit it. Hence for Brahman, I(t) is best left undefined. Brahman cannot be said to be with mind or without mind. In this case V, V' etc are undefined too. Therefore, concepts such as vāsana function or time do not apply to Brahman. This also applies to the jīva which has merged with Brahman (as in Case 2 above.)

Other Cases

Before we conclude this section, let us consider more "ordinary" jīvas and the characteristics of their vāsana function. The mean of the normalized vāsana function in these cases will be at the most x*.

Case 5: Jīva in Dream/Awake State: V'(x,t) is > 0 at least for some x and I(t)> 0. $M_x' \leq x^*$. This is the most common case and there are no remarkable features to mention.

Case 6: Jīva in Deep Sleep: Here I(t)=0 but V'(x,t) > 0 at least for some x. The mind-intellect, completely under the spell of *tamas*, shows no sentiency; i.e. I(t)=0 for the duration of deep sleep. But the underlying vāsana function V', though latent, is still intact and will express itself once again when the jīva wakes up.

Case 7: Highly Evolved Jīva: I(t) > 0, V'(x,t) is skewed towards 1 so that the mean, M_x', is near x*. In the limit, this is the case of *jīvanmukta*. *Jīvanmukta* can be active in the world in spite of lack of any but the purest *sāttvic* vāsana, but they only act in the best interest of the world. This is to be discussed in more detail when we consider how vāsanas affect a jīva's transactions with the world.

VĀSANAS AND LIFE'S TRANSACTIONS

Vāsanas drive the thoughts and actions every moment of our life. They affect what we wish, what we do, and how we experience life. However, vāsanas are actually only *tendencies* which predispose a jīva to act in certain ways, without *enforcing* such action. Further, multiple, conflicting vāsanas can be active at a time, making it necessary for the jīva to choose among them. The jīva makes its choice using free will[36]. In the presence of multiple vāsanas and free will, the transactions of a jīva (namely what it wishes, wills, and experiences in its contacts with the world) are unpredictable. They can be modeled only in probabilistic terms as shown in the following paragraphs.

Wishing/Desiring

Vāsanas are said to reside in the "*ānandamaya kośa*", the innermost of the "five sheaths", or the "causal body". The desires that arise in our mind are a manifestation of the vāsanas. The vāsanas are numerous, but at any given time many remain latent. The vāsanas that do manifest as desire are either in response to some external stimuli or are spontaneous, internally inspired. For example, desire for coffee can become active spontaneously anytime during wakeful hours or in response to the smell and sound of coffee perking in the next room. Desires of the former kind can be considered as "unforced" thoughts, and desires prompted by external stimuli as "forced" thoughts.

Desires are but one particular type of thoughts. When the mind is in a relaxed mode, i.e. when there are no significant external stimuli to force the thoughts in a particular direction, the thoughts that do appear in the mind reveal the nature of the underlying vāsanas: The more intense a vāsana, the more likely it will spawn a train of thoughts related to itself. According to some schools of psychology, even dreams are expressions of the vāsana complexes in the subconscious mind.

Recalling that V'(x,t), the normalized vāsana function, has the characteristics of a probability density function, we can consider each independent, unforced, train of thoughts arising in the mind as a sample randomly drawn from V'. The more frequent a thought, the more intense are the vāsanas underlying that thought. If this conjecture is valid, it has relevance to the problem of estimating the vāsana function.

---

36 It is Īśvara's Will that is relevant here, as discussed in several contexts earlier in the book.

It is conceivable that psychometric tests could be developed to discern the type of unforced thoughts occurring in a subject's mind and to trace the thought back to one or more elemental vāsana types.

Willing/Acting

It is said in our scriptures a jīva has always the option "to do, not to do, or do otherwise". This is in recognition of the fact that in most situations, a jīva has multiple choices from which to select a course of action. The choice made is dependent on how the jīva subjectively evaluates each option.

The vāsana function is a key ingredient in this subjective evaluation. In order to choose among the options, the jīva must judge as well as it can the likely consequences of each action and how well it likes or dislikes the consequences. Depending on the nature of the problem, a decision can entail a combination of material, emotional, and intellectual outcomes. It could involve, for instance, financial gains and losses, physical pain or comfort, honor and reputation of the family etc., rendering the choice very complicated.

Comparing Apples and Oranges

In theory, this poses a difficult analytical problem: How does one evaluate the choices when it involves a wide variety of disparate outcomes? For example, how does one trade off physical comfort with financial gains? It requires the proverbial comparison of apples and oranges, a logically meaningless task. For this reason, decision making is often confusing, demanding considerable soul-searching and, in very difficult situations, subjecting one to mental torment similar to that which Arjuna experienced in the battlefield. Tough though it may be, the fact is that, confronted with choices, jīvas do make decisions and act. Thus, asked to choose between an apple and an orange, most of us make that choice without much difficulty, notwithstanding the conceptual problems a theoretician has with the question. Jīvas accomplish this seemingly baffling task based on their likes and dislikes (as represented by their vāsanas). Let us see how.

We will use the apples and oranges example itself to illustrate the process. Suppose you and your friend, while in the midst of a long discussion, decide to take a snack break. There is only one apple and an orange on the fruit platter to choose from. Your friend, who you know is not too keen on apples, graciously offers you the first choice and asks you to pick whichever fruit you like. Now, your own taste buds also prefer an orange over an apple, but you are also aware that apple is in fact better for your health. Thus if you choose the orange, the expected consequences are a) the dissatisfaction of forcing your friend to eat a fruit he does not fancy b) the satisfaction of pleasing your taste buds and c) the dissatisfaction from not doing the right thing for your health. The consequences of choosing the apple are just the opposite. You must quickly weigh subjectively the different outcomes and make the decision.

The intensity of your various vāsanas at the time will affect the relative weights you give to the different outcomes. If your vāsanas to satisfy gross body demands are very strong (i.e. the Vāsana function around $x=0$ are of high intensity) you have a greater chance of choosing the orange. On the other hand if your health consciousness and/or feelings of loyalty to friends and family are strong then the choice more likely would be an apple.

This illustrates how in real life we do compare apples and oranges using, consciously or subconsciously, the relative values provided by our vāsanas; in this case, how much more you value pleasing a friend over pleasing your palate determines your choice. It is in this sense that we call the shape of the vāsana function as giving the "relative values" of the jīva. The example also reveals a basic trait of the human mind: *the common currency to which a jīva ultimately reduces the worth of all worldly outcomes is the extent to which they please its mind*[37]. While what happens out there in the world is vastly varied, a jīva evaluates everything the world has to offer simply in terms of its likes and dislikes as encoded in its vāsana function. This insight enables us to develop a mathematical model of a jīva's subjective evaluation of alternative choices that life often presents to it.

Desires vs. Vāsanas: The above example serves to illustrate another useful point: desire versus vāsanas. In the example above we can talk of desire for apple and oranges, but not of vāsana for either of these. In the decision making situation described, apple, the object, is seen to activate vāsanas related to Survival (i.e. health), Love (i.e. friendship and loyalty), and Sensual Pursuits (i.e. tasty food). These are among the basic, elemental vāsanas listed in Table 8.1. We note that the list does not, and need not, include specifically a vāsana for apple. In a

---

37 It is appropriate to recall here Sage Yājñavalkya's counsel to his wife Maitreyi: "*ātmanastu kāmāya sarvaṁ priyaṁ bhavati*" meaning "anything is dear only for the sake of love for own self" [111].

very different decision making context, say when deciding to buy apple rather than orange in the grocery mart, the same apple may cause other vāsanas to be activated. It is enough if we make sure that a list such as in Table 8.1 contains all elemental vāsanas. In other words, the continuum x: (0,1) need to include the elemental vāsanas only.

HOW A JĪVA OBTAINS HAPPINESS FROM OBJECTS

Perturbation Of The Vāsana Function

How exactly does an object please the mind and what happens to a jīva that feels pleased or displeased? Gurudev Swami Chinmayanandaji often explained the transient happiness we derive from worldly objects thus: The enjoyment of the object, say ice cream, reduces temporarily the usual agitation created in the mind by the attachment to that object. Having enjoyed the ice-cream, our mind is no more agitated by desire for the same. The reduced agitation, in turn, brings more peace of mind. It is this added peace of mind that we experience as happiness, though we erroneously attribute that happiness to the object. Usually the reduction in mind's agitation lasts but for a finite time and hence the happiness derived from worldly experiences is also finite. Acharya Vidyaranya, as previously mentioned, also offers this explanation in *Pañcadaśi* to prove his thesis that even bliss from material object is only a reflection of the Brahman-Bliss: "*Viṣayānando Brahmānandāmśarūpabhāk*" [112]. The opposite happens when we are frustrated in our desire. There is increased agitation of the mind (taking the form of anger, hurt etc.) reducing the peace of mind which is experienced as unhappiness. This effect is also finite.

Generally objects are a case of "mixed blessings"; that is, upon gaining an object one or more vāsanas are satisfied, some are denied, and yet a few others are left unaffected. The intensity of a vāsana is reduced if it has been satisfied momentarily by the object. On the other hand, the intensity of the vāsana is increased upon its denial. In the "apples vs. orange" example considered above, the expected (temporary) effect of choosing an orange is to reduce the intensity of vāsana for satisfying bodily needs while increasing the intensity of vāsanas associated with physical health and friendship (see Fig 8.7.)

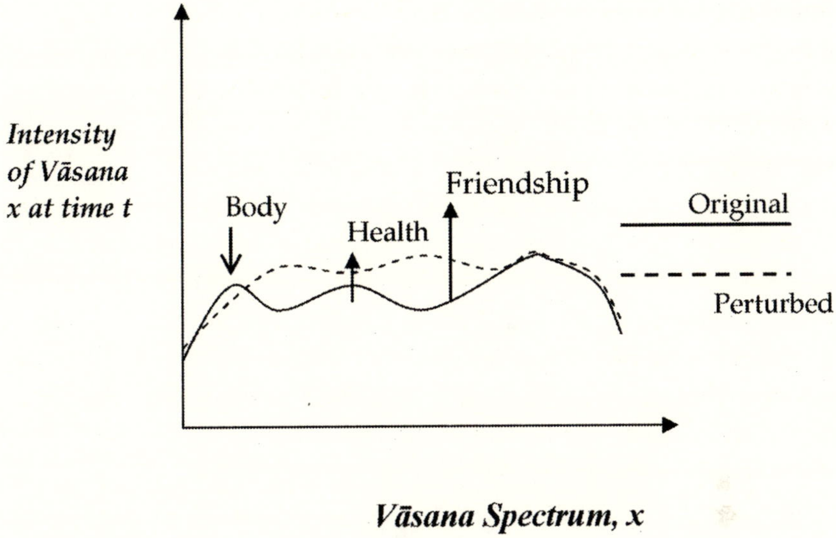

Fig 8.7: Perturbations in Vāsana Function on choosing Orange over Apple

The Perturbation Function W(x,t)

The above dynamics can be stated in precise mathematical terms. Assume for this discussion that the object in question is deemed overall desirable by the jīva, meaning the sum effect of the positive and negative consequences of attaining the object is to reduce temporarily the agitation (i.e. outflow) of mind. Cast in terms of the vāsana function, the effect of the object is to temporarily *reduce the energy out-flow* (1-x).V(x,t) at the values of x corresponding to the vāsanas satisfied, *increase* the outflow at vāsanas x which are denied, and leave it *unchanged* at vāsanas unaffected by the object.

Let {W(x,t). (1-x). V(x,t)} represent the energy out flow at x subsequent to obtaining the object; W(x,t) is less than 1 if x is satisfied, greater than 1 if x is denied, and equal to 1, if vāsana x is unaffected. W(x,t) is the factor by which the outflow is "perturbed" at x and is always non-negative. For all purposes, W(x,t) represents the object itself as it appears to the jīva at time t, with all its attractions and shortfalls. The total energy outflow upon gaining the object, denoted by $E_{OBJECT}(t)$, is given by

$$E_{OBJECT}(t) = c. \int W(x,t)(1-x)\ V(x,t)\ dx$$

$E_{OBJECT}(t)$ will be less than $E_{O,}$ if, as we have assumed, gaining the object is considered desirable overall by the jīva[38]. That is, the overall effect is to reduce the total outflow of mind, E_O. This is the first effect.

A second effect noted above is for the reduced agitation to induce a more peaceful mind. To explain this effect, we note that contact with the object does not change I(t), the sentiency of mind, even though it reduces E_O. By virtue of Eq. 8.6, this requires E_{In}, the inward flow of mind's energy, to increase correspondingly to compensate for the reduced Eo. The higher level of mental energy focused on the Self brings with it a temporary, limited Bliss, or peace. This is the second effect[39]. The process described is consistent with the earlier quoted *Pañcadaśi* principle that happiness from objects is also Brahman-Bliss alone.

Objects which are unpleasant overall will have the opposite effect of reducing E_{In}, meaning a less peaceful mind.

General Decision Problem

The previous apples-and-oranges example can be extended to a more general decision making situation. Suppose there are 'n' decision choices available to a jīva at a particular time t_0. Let the options be labeled 1, 2,....k,...n. Each possible option is expected to have a series of consequences perturbing the vāsana function in different ways. Let $W_k(x,t)$ be the predicted effect of Option k on vāsana x at time t (with $t \geq t_0$). By this we mean the *expectation* the jīva has regarding Option k, since it is based on such expectations that the jīva makes it decisions. The jīva has to consider not only how its choice will affect it now, but also in future. It is usually a subjective evaluation based on the jīva's

38 The limits of integration in many of the equations is not specified but should be understood as x=0 and x=1.

39 Two observations are in order at this point. 1) The increase in E_{In} can be considered to occur with or without changes to V(x,t) itself. For example, we can postulate an offsetting increase or decrease in in-flowing mind such that V(x,t) itself remains unchanged at every x. In this case W(x,t) cannot exceed (1/(1-x)). The inflowing subtle energy after perturbation is V(x,t){1-(1-x)W(x,t)} and is higher at every vāsana satisfied and lower at vāsanas frustrated. Overall E_{In} increases. Other models which involve changes to V(x,t) (but without changing I(t)) could be proposed, but the discussions in this paper are largely invariant to these assumptions. 2) We recognize there are objects, e.g. drugs, that change the sentiency of mind, I(t), but not V'(x,t). They may reduce suffering temporarily by making the mind dull, but Vedānta, in common with many other spiritual traditions, does not accept reliance on these objects as valid spiritual practice.

past experiences, present hopes, and concerns about the future. The expectations are seldom objectively quantified, except in some formal corporate decision making situations. Consequences of an action in the far future are often given less weight compared to its more immediate consequences. $W_k(x,t)$, we assume, already incorporates the effects of such discounting.

The peace of mind and happiness a jīva experiences are related to the agitation in its mind, and agitation is related to the outflow of energy. By choosing Option k, the expected outflow of energy at time t due to vāsana x is $c.(1-x)\ V(x,t_0)W_k(x,t)$. Note that we are using the vāsana function at $t= t_0$, which is the time of decision making.

The total consequence of choosing Option k, denoted by E_k, can be obtained by summing over all x and $t \geq t_0$ and is

$$E_k = c.I(t_0)\ \int(1-x)V'(x,t_0)\{\ \int_{t\geq t0} W_k(x,t)dt\ \}\ dx$$

The quantity represented by the inside integral $\int_{t\geq t0} W_k(x,t)dt$ is the total future anticipated consequences of action k with respect to vāsana x. If we denote this quantity by $W_k(x)$, then E_k is

$$E_k = c.I(t_0)\ \int(1-x)V'(x,t_0)W_k(x)\ dx \ \ldots\ldots \text{Eq. } 8.10$$

E_k represents the jīva's overall subjective assessment regarding Option k. Eq. 8.10 shows that the assessment is based on the vāsana function at t_0, the time of making the decision, and all future predicted consequences of Option k. In making its choice among the *n* options, it is this subjective assessment that the jīva uses to compare its likes and dislikes for the various options.

It is not implied that a jīva actually performs mathematical computations of the type in Eq. (8.10) every time it makes a decision. To so impute is no more valid than to suggest that the moon solves a set of differential equations representing the gravitational forces of the earth and the sun in order to decide what its next position in the orbit ought to be. Eq. (8.10) is meant to be simply a mathematical representation of the subjective process occurring within the jīva consciously and/or subconsciously.

The Role of Will Power in Decision Making

$V'(x,t_0)W_k(x)$ is the anticipated state of the (normalized) vāsana function upon choice of Option k. From Eqs. (8.4) and (8.10), E_k is seen to be the total anticipated out-flowing subtle energy under the perturbed vāsana function. As illustrated in Fig. 8.7, unfavorable consequences bump the vāsana function up and favorable consequences push it down. E_k is a summation of the positive and negative expectations the jīva has for Option k. A high value of E_k, which signifies a large out-flow of mental energy and a more agitated mind, is less desirable. Lower the value of E_k, the more favored is the Option k.

This however does not imply that the jīva necessarily chooses the Option with the lowest E_k. Unlike the moon whose behavior can be predicted with much accuracy, there is a great deal of uncertainty surrounding a jīva's action. For example a jīva may very well end up choosing an option which it dislikes over one which it likes. All that we can assert is that *the probability of choice of Option k, p_k, is higher if the assessment E_k is lower*, and vice versa. Expressed mathematically, we are saying that p_k varies as $(1/ E_k)$. The actual choice is unpredictable and is an evidence of the free will at play. Here, we recall the conclusion of the earlier chapter that, while there is free will in situations involving decision making, it belongs to Īśvara and not to jīvas.

Eq. 8.10, together with the observation that the probability p_k of choosing the k-th option varies with $(1/E_k)$, shows how the vāsanas affect a jīva's actions and choices in life.

Concept of Total or "samaṣṭi" Vāsana

There are many situations where choices are made based on the "collective will" of a number of individuals. For example, each individual in a group may register its choice based on own vāsanas, the group choice being then the one chosen by the most. Or, the choice may be made on behalf of the group by one individual based on his/her intimate knowledge of the vāsanas of every member of the group. The latter case is often held as a model for the life of a *jīvanmukta* who, though himself devoid of any worldly vāsanas, acts in the best interest of the world. If $V_i(x,t)$ is the vāsana function of the i-th individual in a group, then the sum $\sum_i Vi(x,t)$ is the "total" vāsana of the group. The vāsana function of the *jīvanmukta* is similar to the one in Fig. 8.6, with $V(x,t)= 0$ for x <

1. This means that, from a personal point of view, the jīva is indifferent to the worldly choices. Nevertheless, the enlightened being does make choices and acts purposefully in the world, as we know from the lives of the Masters like Buddha. It is said that the *jīvanmukta* makes its choice with knowledge of the total vāsanas of the beings around it. In terms of vāsana function, this jīva acts as if its vāsanas are $\sum_i Vi(x,t)$ for $x < 1$ while retaining its near infinite vāsana at $x = 1$.

Carried to the limit encompassing the vāsanas of total creation, this is exactly what our scriptures say of Īśvara. As pointed out in Chapter 2, the total causal body or vāsanas of the universe ("*samaṣṭi vāsana*") is termed as Īśvara. Ever established in Self and without vāsanas of own, Īśvara exercises His Will and acts with full knowledge of the vāsanas of the entire universe. That is, His Will is in accordance with the total vāsana and issues out as the actual actions of all things and beings. Thus, in the concept of "*samaṣṭi vāsana*", we have a mathematical interpretation of the Prakṛti-Īśvara paradigm.

Experiencing

Life of a jīva is an almost unbroken series of experiences, spurred by the events in the constantly changing world. These events may be the consequences of own actions or caused by the actions of other beings and objects. Thoughts occurring in the mind, based on vāsanas or memories, are the other, internal, source of the jīva's experiences.

Life's experiences come in two flavors: pleasant and unpleasant. Unpleasant experiences cause suffering while pleasant experiences bring happiness to the jīva; as a rule both last for a finite time only. There are also experiences which are neither pleasant nor unpleasant and to which the jīva is indifferent.

The doctrine of *Karma* asserts that the good and bad a jīva experiences at a given time is the result of all its past *karmas* (actions) in its present and previous lives. Even the events ostensibly caused by the act of other beings and objects, could have been precipitated by our own actions in some past life. No one is exempt from the laws of *karma* and one must necessarily endure the consequences of own actions. This does not mean that a jīva is condemned to a life of suffering. This is because, while pain is inevitable, suffering is optional. A main focus of the scriptures is to teach us the spiritual qualities, such as detachment, that help us avoid suffering. In particular, the scriptures, specifically the Bhagavad Gītā, lay great emphasis on the need for intelligent management of our expectations while transacting with the world.

Great Expectations = Great Sorrow

As discussed above, the choices we make depend on the expectations we have for the different choices. Basing choices on their expected consequences is a very reasonable thing to do and an essential part of planning our actions properly. When scriptures talk about curbing expectations, they are *not* advising against using expectations as a basis for planning our present decisions and actions.

However, once the choice has been made and action taken, it is not wise or even rational to hold on rigidly to the prior expectations. Doing so can lead to suffering. This is because the actual consequences resulting from our action cannot be predicted and hence no rigid expectations are justified. As Sri Ramana says *"kartur ājñayā prāpyate phalaṁ"*, meaning the fruits of action are as ordered by Īśvara [113]. Therefore we are advised to accept whatever we receive with equanimity. When we hold on to expectations of any kind, we end up measuring the actual outcomes against the expectations and suffer when the expectations are not met.

The essence of this *Karma* doctrine can be represented using the concepts developed so far. To do this, we need to consider all past actions and events affecting the jīva at the present moment, *t*. Consider *k*, one such action or event, which took place sometime prior to *t*. Following the previous approach, let $W'_k(x,t)$ be the actual impact of k on vāsana x at time t, measured by the extent to which it perturbs the vāsana function V(x,t). As before, positive and negative consequences are represented by $W'_k(x,t) < 1$ and $W'_k(x,t) > 1$ respectively. Let $W_k(x,t)$ be the impact of the same action k *anticipated* by the jīva[40]. The difference $\{W'_k(x,t) - W_k(x,t)\}$ between the actual and the anticipated outcomes determines if the outcome is perceived as pleasant or unpleasant by the jīva. In what follows, we will denote this difference by $\in_k(x,t)$. $S_k(t)$, denoting the total impact of action k over all x on the out-flow of mind, is given by the expression

40 As before, it is the vāsanas at time t and the expectation the jīva has from Option k now at time t, which affect the present suffering.

$$S_k(t) = c.I(t) \int(1-x)V'(x,t)\{W'_k(x,t) - W_k(x,t)\}dx \; ..... \; \text{Eq. } 8.11$$

The factor (1-x) in Eq. 8.11 is introduced for same reason as before recognizing that it is the outward flow of mind that measures its agitations, both positive and negative. A high value of $S_k(t)$ means more agitation and suffering.

If $\in_k(x,t) < 0$, then the actual outcome is better than expected for this x, the integrand is negative, and $S_k(t)$ is decreased. This represents a desirable outcome for the jīva. On the other hand, if $\in_k(x,t) > 0$, then actual outcome is not as good as expected and $S_k(t)$ is increased. This represents an unfavorable outcome. $S_k(t)$, the integral over all x, is the sum of these positive and negative outcomes. The consequences of action k as a whole is experienced, at time t, as unpleasant if $S_k(t) > 0$ and pleasant if $S_k(t) < 0$.

$S_k(t)$ is therefore a measure of the "suffering" of the jīva due to a past action k, by which we understand that it is a measure of the agitation in the mind, due to favorable and unfavorable consequences. Since all past karmas potentially affect the jīva, S(t), the suffering at time t, is the sum of Eq. 8.11 over all *karmas* k up to present time *t*. This is expressed as

$$S(t) = c.\ I(t).\ \int(1-x)V'(x,t)\ \{\ \textstyle\sum_k \in_k(x,t)\}\ dx \; .... \; \text{Eq. } 8.12$$

The expression in Eq. 8.12 captures an essence of the *Karma* doctrine: $\{\sum_k \in_k(x,t)\}$, the sum over all k, is the net effect of all past *karmas* on vāsana x at time t. These *karmic* effects do not automatically add up to real suffering. As is clear from Eq. 8.12, *how much a jīva suffers now due to the effects of its past karmas depends on the state of its present spiritual evolution indicated by V'(x,t).* Therefore, while the effects of past *karmas* must necessarily be experienced, they need not lead to suffering. In other words, in life, *"pain may be inevitable, but suffering is optional"*.

The Nature Of $\{\sum_k \in_k(x,t)\}$

Eq. 8.12 shows why it may be impossible to develop a theory that will have the capability of predicting the course of suffering for a jīva. Such capability will require knowledge of the vāsana function at all times as well as, more improbably, knowledge of all past and future karmas and their actual and anticipated effects. This does not mean that Eq. 8.12 is meaningless symbolism; its usefulness is something other than for its predictive power. It captures, as we hope to show, the essential wisdom of Vedānta as regards the means to end worldly suffering.

First of all we note that $W'_k(x,t)$, the actual outcome of action k, is one that a Vedāntin will say is determined by Īśvara's Will and one that a scientist would call a random variable. Hence $\{\sum_k \epsilon_k(\mathbf{x,t})\}$ is sum of a large number of random variables of which the best we can hope to know in advance are only the statistical properties such as mean and variance. If the jīva is in the habit of overestimating the benefits and underestimating the costs associated with its actions, its expectations will be biased such that the mean, $\delta(\mathbf{t,x})$, of the random variable $\{\sum_k \epsilon_k(\mathbf{x,t})\}$ will be positive[41]. On the other hand a jīva with lower expectations will have a negative bias.

S(t) in Eq. (8.12) is a random variable depending on a multitude of individual circumstances and Īśvara's Will and cannot be easily analyzed in its general form. But it assumes a particularly simple and useful form if we assume that the mean bias is same for all x, that is, $\delta(\mathbf{t,x}) = \delta(\mathbf{t})$ for all x.[42] In this case, the expected (i.e. statistical average) value of S(t), denoted by $\hat{S}(t)$, is

$$\hat{S}(t) = c.\ I(t).\ \delta(\mathbf{t}).\ \int (1-x)V'(x,t)\ dx \qquad \text{.... Eq. (8.13)}$$

Eq. (8.13), though it is for a particular case of uniform bias, could be considered as a first approximation for the general case where $\delta(\mathbf{x,t})$ is not same for all x.

In Eq. (8.13), the constant c, I(t), and the integral are all non-negative quantities, but $\delta(\mathbf{t})$ can be positive or negative. If $\delta(\mathbf{t}) > 0$ then $\hat{S}(t)$ is positive, indicating a dissatisfied mind; if $\delta(\mathbf{t}) < 0$ then $\hat{S}(t)$ is also negative indicating a happy mind. In either case the average level of agitation in the mind (due to sorrow or the excitement of happiness) is given by $\hat{S}(t)$.

We should be careful to note that the happiness referred to here

---

41 Such overly optimistic expectations are associated with a lower value of W(x,t) so that $W'(x,t)-W(x,t)>0$.

42 If the bias $\delta(t,x)$ does differ over the range of x, then it could be argued that the differences ought to have been captured in the vāsana function itself.

is one that is derived from getting better than expected results from contacts with the world. Vedānta does not advocate a life-style in pursuit of such happiness; in fact it looks upon both happiness and sorrow resulting from worldly contacts as equally unworthy and problematic. Both are afflictions arising from ignorance and both must be avoided. The goal therefore is to reduce both positive and negative agitations of the mind; i.e. to maintain the absolute value of $\hat{S}(t)$ to as close to zero as possible.

In what follows we will in fact mean by $\hat{S}(t)$ its absolute value only. Using Eqs. 8.9 and 8.13, this absolute level of suffering at time t is seen to be

$$\hat{S}(t) = c.I(t).|\delta(t)|.\cos^2\theta(t) \quad \ldots. \text{ Eq. 8.14}$$

where $|\delta(t)|$ is the absolute value of $\delta(t)$.

This is a very useful result, one which is in accordance with Vedāntic principles. Eq. (8.14) readily lends itself to a discussion of the various means for alleviating suffering that is known to us through scriptures and experience.

Three Paths to Overcome Suffering

The three variable factors that make up $\hat{S}(t)$ in Eq. 8.14 indicate the three different approaches- a *tamasic*, a *rajasic*, and a *sāttvic* means- to minimize suffering. $\hat{S}(t)$ can be reduced by reducing $I(t)$, or $|\delta(t)|$ or $\cos^2\theta(t)$.

a) ***The "tamasic" way- Reduce I(t)***: I(t) is related to the total energy of the mind and measures the awareness and degree of mental alertness of the jīva. Reduction of this awareness, by taking a sleeping pill to fall asleep for example, is one way to reduce suffering, albeit temporarily. But this is a "*tamasic*" approach, one hardly recommended in any scripture. The mind is only made temporarily inactive, not basically altered. On waking up, it therefore resumes its prior agitated state. As Bhagawan Sri Ramana observes "*laya vināśane ubhaya rodhane, laya gataṁ punar bhavati nomṛtaṁ*", meaning a mind that is put in a state of "*laya*" (temporarily absorbed) will rise up again, but a mind destroyed will not [114]. The mind can be suspended using breath-control (*prāṇāyāma*), by falling asleep, or by other similar physical means, but in all such cases the results are temporary. Sri Ramana has also stated that even the "involution of the mind in the Self, but without its (mind's) destruction, is *kevala nirvikalpa samādhi*.... Even though one practices it for years together, if one has not rooted out the vāsanas, he will not attain salvation" [115].

b) ***The "rajasic" way- Reduce*** $|\delta(t)|$: $\delta(\mathbf{t})$ is the mean difference between the actual and expected outcomes. If the two coincide $\delta(\mathbf{t})$ will be zero, and, by virtue of Eq. 8.13, $\hat{S}(t)$, the suffering, will also be zero. This approach calls for management of expectations and requires a good deal of mental discipline. Hence we call it the "*rajasic*" way to reduce suffering. It is better than the "*tamasic*" way, but only if expectations are managed the intelligent way.

There are times when we suppress our expectations in a bout of pessimism and hopelessness and meekly resign to whatever life has to offer. This is not the right way to manage expectations. This is the negative approach to the problem, at best a temporary fix, and potentially more harmful than beneficial in the long-run. Following this road, there is the clear danger of becoming depressed and incapable of undertaking any activity. That way does not lie immortal happiness! Lord Krishna explains this in Bhagavad Gītā while also pointing out to the right way:

"viṣayā vinivartante nirāhārasya dehinaḥ
rasavarjaṁ rasopyasya paraṁ dhṛṣṭvā nivartate"

"The objects of the senses turn away from the abstinent man leaving the longing (behind); but his longing also leaves him on seeing the Supreme" [116].

Commenting on this verse, Gurudev Swami Chinmayanandaji notes that "*we can observe cases wherein an individual comes to maintain sense-withdrawal from the sense objects due to some physical incapacity or due to some special mental mood of temporary sorrow or misery. In all those cases, though the sense-organs come to feel an aversion to the respective objects, their inclination for these objects merely remains dormant for the time being... under favorable or sufficiently tempting circumstances, they may again raise their hoods to hiss and to poison... these mental impressions of sensuous lives, lived in the past by the ego, from the beginning of creation to date, will be totally erased or at least made ineffective –as roasted seeds- when the seeker transcends the ego and comes to experience the Self*".

The Muṇḍaka Upaniṣad (II.2.8) also alludes to the same total liberating effect of experiencing the Self when it exclaims

"bhidyate hṛdaya granthiḥ, chidyante sarvasamśayāḥ
kṣīyante cāsya karmāṇi, tasmin dṛṣṭe parāvare"

meaning "*When a person realizes Him in both the high and the low, the knots of the heart are cut asunder, all his doubts destroyed and his karmas exhausted*" [117].

Thus it is clear that suppression of expectations by brute force is not the means to bring suffering to an end. The right way to manage expectations while actively engaged in actions is the main theme of the *Karma Yoga* (Path of Action) of Bhagavad Gītā where the seeker is advised to practice renouncing the fruits of action, *"karma phala tyāga"* by surrendering to the Will of Īśvara. By matching our expectations to what Īśvara has in store for us, we are reducing the difference δ(t) to zero. Also, in doing so, we are turning our attention more and more to Īśvara or Self and less and less to the fruits of our action. This is when *karma yoga* becomes efficacious as a spiritual practice.

But how are we to match our expectation to Īśvara's Will when that Will is unpredictable? Are we supposed to somehow gain this predictive capability? That is not what is expected of the seeker. What is required of us is simply to have no specific expectation at all and accept gratefully whatever we receive as Īśvara's blessings, *"prasād"*. Possessing such an accepting mind-set (*"prasād-buddhi")*, there is no occasion for regret or joy, but there is only peace. Further, while performing the action, one is not distracted by anxiety for specific results, and instead the mind is free to focus entirely on doing the work correctly. Thus, endowed with an accepting mind, one is not only at peace while at work, but also more skilled in successfully executing the work. It is for this reason that Lord Krishna calls yoga as "dexterity in action" (*yogaḥ karmasu kauśalam*) [118]. There is no suppression of mind but only its sublimation. Spiritual detachment is strengthened from maintaining the attitude of "*prasād-buddhi*" during all actions.

The mathematical model and the Eq. 8.14 derived from it are consistent with the thrust of the above statements. Realization is defined as the state in which $\theta(t)$ equals $\pi/2$. But neither I(t) nor $|\delta(t)|$ has a direct relationship with $\theta(t)$ in the model. Therefore driving $|\delta(t)|$ or I(t) to zero does not necessarily imply that $\theta(t) = \pi/2$; that is, the *tamasic* and *rajasic* ways to avoid suffering do not equate to Realization. However the *Karma Yoga* can lead to salvation because, when correctly practiced, it decreases the lowly vāsanas, shifting the mean M_x' to right and thus increasing detachment $\theta(t)$.

c) ***The "sāttvic" way- Reduce $cos^2\theta(t)$***: Increasing detachment is the third and best way to reduce suffering. As detachment $\theta(t)$ increases, $\cos\theta(t)$ decreases and with that $\hat{S}(t)$ also. Increased detachment is possible mainly through the practice of *Jñāna* and *Bhakti yoga*s (Path of Knowledge and Path of Devotion), but also through *Karma Yoga*. In *Jñāna Yoga*, the seeker develops increased "*vairāgya*" (i.e. dispassion and detachment) based on "*viveka*" (i.e. discrimination of Real from the non-real.) With *Jñāna* (Knowledge), virtues such as devotion and surrender to Īśvara's Will (i.e. *prasād-buddhi)* naturally arise in the seeker. Devotion to God and universal, unconditional Love for all beings in creation are the hall mark of a jīva that has gained the Supreme Knowledge. In the Path of Devotion, a jīva gains *vairāgya*, *viveka* and *prasād-buddhi* through Love of God. All worldly vāsanas get extinguished in this Love as illustrated by the life of Meerabai. *Bhakti Yoga* leads to the same state of Knowledge that *Jñāna Yoga* does and *Jñāna Yoga* leads to same Universal Love that *Bhakti Yoga* aims for.

Absence Of Suffering Vs. Realization

Realization was defined as the ultimate state of detachment and purity of mind. This is the state where $\theta(t) = \pi/2$, implying, by virtue of Eq. 8.14, $\hat{S}(t) = 0$. Thus liberation implies elimination of suffering. However the converse is not necessarily true. Liberation, or *mokṣa*, is more than just an end to suffering. More significantly, it is the Bliss associated with Knowledge of Self and Universal Love. There is not only no suffering, but there is Infinite Bliss. Reducing I(t) and/or $|\delta(\mathbf{t})|$ can eliminate suffering, but without the Bliss of Realization. In *Pañcadaśi*'s seven steps of evolution mentioned earlier, it is worth noting that "Cessation of Suffering" is considered as the sixth step and "Perfect Satisfaction" the seventh and final one. Perfect Satisfaction requires perfect detachment, whether through *Karma*, *Bhakti*, or *Jñāna yoga*s.

The Paths of Action, Devotion, and Knowledge

Much has been written about these three primary paths, comparing the efficacy of one against another. Most spiritual scientists agree that the three paths lead to the same goal and on realizing the goal, one becomes equally well established in dynamic selfless action as a *karma yogī*, in devotion as a *bhakta* and in Wisdom as a *jñāni*. There cannot be consummation of one path without the attainment of the goal of the other two paths. As Mata Amritanandamayi Ma puts it

"*devotion without the proper understanding of the essentials of spirituality can only lead to attachment; it cannot give liberation ...(on the other hand) Knowledge without devotion is like eating stones*" [119].

Bhakti and *Jñāna* are thus the same and manifest in the seeker as universal, unconditional Love and understanding. *Karma yoga* of true selfless action is as natural as breathing for one endowed with this Love and Understanding.

The path towards Perfection lies in eliminating the vāsanas and achieving ever higher levels of detachment from the world while at the same time actively serving that world.

How Vāsana Function Gets Modified In Practice

The mathematical model presented in this chapter showed how vāsanas affect life's transactions and experiences. It did not address the equally important reverse process of how the vāsanas get modified by life's experiences. Eq. 8.14 provides one clue to this process: $\hat{S}(t)$ represents the fruit that life presents to the jīva at time *t*; the jīva, in order to make that fruit more palatable, must modify $\delta(\mathbf{t})$ and $\theta(t)$. This process is of essence for spiritual evolution, since it is life itself that provides both the motivation and resources needed for inner transformation.

There are several ways by which this inner transformation can happen, some of which are mentioned below.

a. *Vāsana Modification*: As a jīva acts in response to a vāsana, it is subjected to experiences that are either pleasant or unpleasant. Intelligent reaction to the ensuing "suffering" can bring about accepting mind (*prasād-buddhi)*, increasing detachment and reduction in that vāsana. On the other hand, unintelligent reaction to life's experiences may increase the attachment to the O-E-T (if the experience is pleasant) or lead to depression (if the experience is unpleasant). Thus, depending on the jīva's reaction, the net effect is to diminish or augment the vāsana. This perhaps is the most common pathway to vāsana modification but one which may lead to evolution or devolution.
b. *Force of Habit*: Once in a while we find ourselves making a choice which runs against the grain of our normal habitual preferences. Such an instance can portend lasting changes in the vāsana function, especially if the outcome of the choice is to our liking. Further, a break with routine strengthens the jīva's will power, allowing it greater future freedom from the thralldom of vāsanas.
c. *Reinforcing Effect*: As a jīva progresses spiritually, it can find its next step in growth a bit easier based on the discipline and knowledge it has already gained. That is, a positive "feed- back loop" may exist because of which the very progress achieved up until a point of time acts as a catalyst for further progress.
d. *More Realistic Expectations*: Strictly speaking this does not change the vāsana function, but the *prasād-buddhi* that one develops can lead to a quieter mind and *Bhakti*, and a quieter mind to contemplation of Reality or *Jñāna*.
e. *Vāsana Reshaping through Knowledge*: Knowledge is a very powerful force and one that is arguably the most effective. The role of Guru (teacher) and *satsang* (company of the good) are emphasized in Vedānta because they are the best means to acquire correct knowledge. The contemplation on the scriptural declarations followed by sincere practice (*śravaṇaṁ, mananaṁ, and nidhidhyāsaṁ*) reshapes the vāsana function leading

towards higher evolution. By the same token, unfortunately, false, worldly knowledge can have a devolutionary effect.

An informative discussion of the various processes by which the vāsanas are modified can be found in Sw. Tejomayanandaji's commentary on *Yoga Vasiṣṭa* [120].

Modeling Inner Transformation- An Unsolved Problem

The mathematical framework developed so far will need to be augmented with additional concepts if it is to adequately represent the above processes of inner transformation. Goswami's "quantum memory" concept referred to in Chapter 4 may prove useful here. The current work of behavioral neuroscientists in modeling how we make changes to our behavior based on positive and negative experiences could also be relevant [121]. Other models borrowed from the material world may prove helpful to a degree in this effort. For example, in the physical realm, the acceleration of an object depends on its mass and the magnitude of the accelerating forces acting on it. Lesser the mass and stronger the force, higher is the increase in speed. Similarly, we may postulate that the spiritual progress of a jīva depends on two factors: ego and will power (corresponding to mass and acceleration respectively). Less the ego (mass) and stronger the will power (accelerating force), quicker is the progress towards Realization. As the saint respectfully known as The Mother of Aurobindo Ashram, phrases it:

"*I shall tell you what there is in aspiration and what in prayer and why both of them are beautiful...Some dislike prayer; if they entered deep into their heart they would find pride- worse than that, vanity. And then there are those who have no aspiration, they try and they cannot aspire; it is because they do not have the flame of will, it is because they do not have the flame of humility. Both are needed. There must be a very great humility and very great will to change one's Karma* [122]."

Four spiritual disciplines, collectively known as *sādhanā catuṣṭayaṁ (Viveka, vairāgya, samādhiṣaṭka saṁpatti, mumukṣutvaṁ),* have been prescribed in the scriptures. Their consistent practice can reduce the ego as well as strengthen the will power [123].

Does the Spiritual Path Get Easier or Harder?

The energy-going-out, E_o, is a measure of the ego and, by virtue of Eqs. (8.4) and (8.9), it is $c.I(t).\cos^2\theta(t)$ showing that the ego gets lighter as detachment increases. Regarding will power, however, we have not been able to find a variable in our mathematical model to represent the will power possessed by a jīva at a given time. But it was noted that the will power *required* for further spiritual progress is related to $(1/\sin^2\theta(t))$. Therefore the will power required is also seen to decrease as detachment increases and ego gets lighter. On this basis, one may conjecture that progress in the spiritual path gets easier as a jīva advances along the path and gradually reduces its ego. This view seems to be supported by the life of a realized Master like Sri Ramakrishna who stayed in *samādhi* effortlessly; i.e. without any overt exercise of will power. If this conjecture is correct, then the trajectory of a jīva entering serious spiritual *sādhana* can be conceptually similar to the launch of a rocket. As the rocket fires (i.e. *B-M-I of the jīva practices spiritual sādhanas*), the thrust (*will power*) developed imparts increased velocity (*spiritual detachment)* to the rocket. At the same time, firing of the engines depletes the fuel (*exhausts the vāsanas*) which reduces the mass (*ego*) to be propelled, thus making it possible to attain even greater acceleration with the same thrust. The result is a path of exponentially increasing velocity, much like the one shown in Fig 7.2. In the context of the rocket example, it is interesting to note that the word *Nirvāṇa* is sometimes translated as "burnt out of fuel"!

In their survey of literature on the measurable effects of Transcendental Meditation on its practitioners, Alexander et al [124] report that the "*...mastery of TM- Sidhi performances is both a distinctive indicator and facilitator of growth of higher states of consciousness.*" That is, the level of mastery attained is itself a factor facilitating further spiritual growth. On this basis it is reasonable to infer that the path of evolution gets easier as one attains higher levels of mastery in that path.

A contrary view is also possible based on life history of sages and saints. There are accounts from the life of J.Krishnamurthi which indicate that the final days and hours preceding realization may be the hardest [125]. The life of Buddha and Jesus, with allusions to the severe tormenting temptations they were subjected to just before enlightenment, suggest that the "razor's edge" may get sharper towards the end. If this is the more real scenario, then a more suitable model may be one from Relativity Theory which shows that mass increases as a body gathers speed. This makes further acceleration harder. When the speed approaches that of light, the mass is near infinite and requires near infinite energy to accelerate. Lacking infinite energy, a body with mass cannot attain speed of light. In the spiritual realm, however, a jīva can and does attain Realization, but only by giving up the very last vestiges of ego by the infinite Grace of *Īśvara*. As we saw earlier, the jīva can advance by own will power only up to *Brahmalok*; the transit from *Brahmalok* to Self is by God's grace.

It is not possible to judge which of the above two scenarios is more accurate lacking, at this time, even a definition of what precisely we mean by the terms "easy" or "hard". The answer may have to wait until we are able to model the process of inner transformation by which a jīva advances along the spiritual path.

CHAPTER 9

The Mystery of Time

The eleventh chapter of the Gītā describes in glorious poetry the magnificent vision of the Cosmic Form of the Creator that Lord Krishna reveals to Arjuna. In that vision, the Creator personifies the cosmos in its entirety, affording Arjuna a peek into its past, present, and future. Arjuna sees his enemies disappearing into the fearsome mouth of the Cosmic Being, portending their imminent destruction. Amazed and shaken by the awesome sight, Arjuna asks Lord Krishna who He really is, to which the Lord replies: "I am Time". Then, referring to the enemies confronting Arjuna in the battlefield, the Lord makes a curious statement, addressing Arjuna as "*savyasacin*", "the left handed one":

"*mayaivaite nihatāḥ pūrvameva, nimittamātraṁ bhava savyasācin*"

"These (your enemies) have already been killed by me, (so) you be merely an instrument, savyasacin" [126].

This raises an obvious question: If the enemies have already been killed, what is it that Arjuna is supposed to be an instrument of? Lord Krishna apparently anticipates this question and in the next verse answers by saying *"I have slain (them), you kill"*. Thus the Lord wants Arjuna to *become* an instrument for an act which in fact has *already* been performed by Him. On the face of it, the statement stands contrary to commonly held views on time and causality. But it turns out that the statement points to a truth which science has discovered only in the 20th century.

The cosmos is very dynamic with a multitude of events happening in every corner of the universe and within every little bit of microscopic matter, all the time. The imprint of Time is clearly visible to us as it relentlessly changes every facet of creation. In the previous chapters of this book we represented the changing world as a series of waves in the $\mathscr{M}$-space, the waves signifying the state of the world at successive points in time. We also assumed that jīvas move with, or, are moved by, the spreading waves and are thus pushed from experience to experience. Here, the jīvas move with time and they experience the world of time t, even as that world is coming into existence. This view is popular since it accords with our usual understanding of the world. We see the world as it is being transformed from moment to moment and therefore assume that the changes are actually happening as we see them. However, a radically different view is suggested by Vedānta and the findings of modern science.

Vedānta and modern science acknowledge that the jīvas see a changing world. But they also proclaim that there really is no such thing as time. This begs another obvious question: If there be no Time in reality, how is it that the jīvas experience it so vividly? We examine this "Mystery of Time" in this chapter from the point of view of Vedānta, Physics, and Neurosciences and show how a logical resolution of the riddle leads us to "a truth that is stranger than fiction". Strange though it might be, this vision of Reality is consistent with Vedāntic teachings, including in particular the above statement by Lord Krishna.

Co-Existence of Past, Present, and Future in the $\mathscr{M}$-Space

We introduced previously a two-dimensional model shown in Fig. 9.1 representing the world and its knower by the Polar coordinate system of (t,θ).

Time and Space are part of creation and they are in the *Mahat*. On the other hand, Īśvara, the Creator, is not in time or space. Creator is a timeless entity and concepts such as past, present, and future, do not apply to It. It is also changeless, since change implies time. Such being the case, it cannot be that, for Īśvara, the wave DH at time =1 arises first and then disappears from Its vision before the wave EF at time =2 is born. If this were so, the Creator, who sees one world now and a different one next, is also in time domain. Instead, the Creator sees all the waves from t=0 to t = ∞ at once, as in Fig 9.1. From the

Creator's point of view, all the waves exist together in the 𝒨-space. That is to say, the "past, present, and future" worlds co-exist along with all the experiences they have in store for all the jīvas. It is not that the past "was", the present "is" or the future "will be", but in fact the past, present and future all "is". There is only "is- ness" in the higher realms of reality associated with Īśvara and *Mahat.*

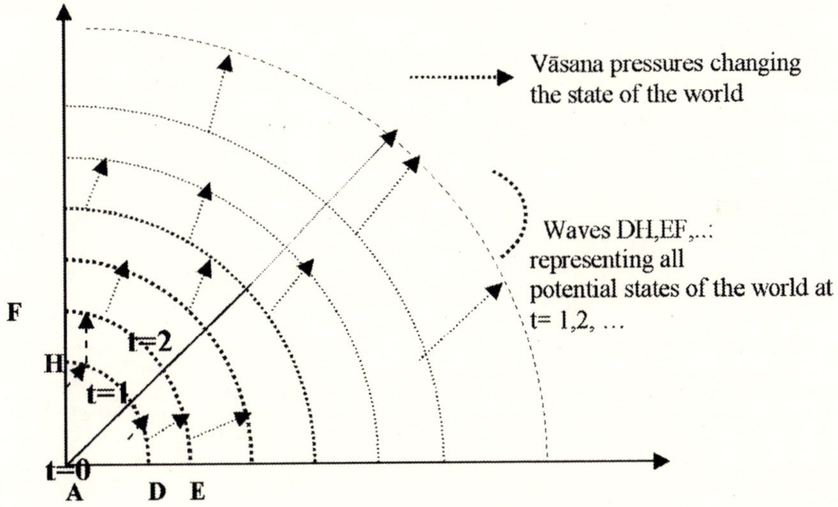

Fig. 9.1: The World and Its Knower

The waves in Fig. 9.1 have time tags attached to them, such as t=1, t=2 etc. Since there is no time concept associated with the 𝒨-space, the tags do not refer to time as we jīvas understand and experience it. We have been referring to *t* as "cosmic time" only to differentiate it from a jīva's "experienced time".

The view of the creation shown in Fig. 9.1 is not available to any creature, but only to the Creator, or to an Arjuna chosen to see it. Jīvas see only one wave at any time. Under the spell of *māyā*, they move from one wave to next in the 𝒨-space thus earning one life experience after another. Time is experienced by jīvas as a result of the flow of experiences. We will return to this topic later when we discuss how jīvas experience time.

The 𝒨-space of Fig. 9.1, with wave upon wave spreading outwards from the origin A, resembles a CD disc with the entire story of the cosmos recorded on its tracks. Other mystics and philosophers have held similar views; the concept of "ākāśic records" espoused by psychic Edgar Cayce (1877-1945) is an example[43]. But of immediate interest to us is the similarity of this idea to Einstein's Relativity Theory.

The "Block Universe" Model of Relativity Physics

Relativity Physics views the universe (as seen from "outside") in terms very similar to the Vedāntic view of *Mahat*. Einstein proposed, and later observations confirmed, that time and space are not independent of each other but form one integral whole, namely the "space-time continuum". Each point in this continuum refers to potential or actual "events". Fig 9.2 shows the universe in space-time coordinates as the

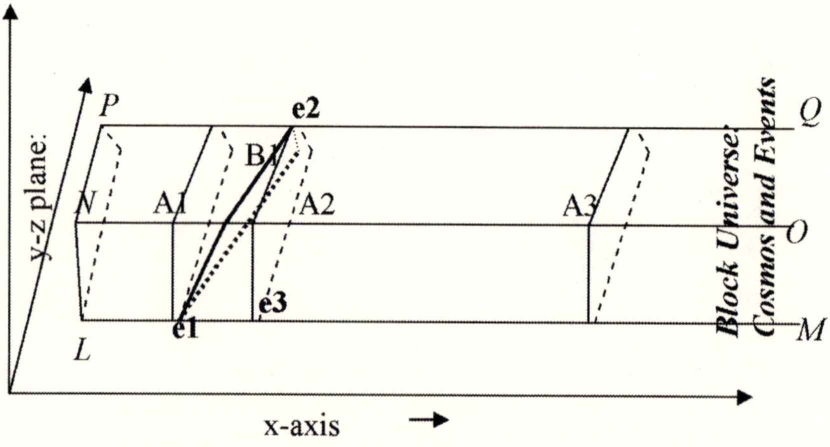

Fig. 9.2 The Block Universe and Space-Time Continuum

open rectangular box *LMNOPQ* open at one end. Resembling a loaf of bread, this space-time representation is sometimes called the "Block Universe". Time progresses from left to right generally along the x-axis. The cross-sections of the block labeled as A1, A2, and A3 (which are like three slices of the loaf of bread) show the universe at three different

43 The online encyclopedia Wikipedia offers the following information: "The **akashic records** (akasha is a Sanskrit word meaning "sky"or "space") is a term used to describe a compendium of mystical knowledge encoded in a non-physical plane of existence. These records are described to contain all knowledge of human experience and the history of the cosmos. They are metaphorically described as a library and other analogues commonly found in discourse on the subject include a 'universal computer' and the 'Mind of God'."

points in time for some observer A. e1, e2, and e3 are three points in the time-space continuum of which **e1** lies in the time-slice A1 while **e2** and **e3** both are on slice A2. This means that the observer A sees event **e1** first and then at a later time sees **e2** and **e3** simultaneously. However, another observer B, who is in uniform motion relative to A, will in effect slice the space-time block at a different angle. Therefore, for this observer, both **e1** and **e2** may be in the same time-slice B1, and **e3** on a subsequent slice B2 (not shown in the Figure). Thus B will see **e1** and **e2** happening at the same time, and **e3** by itself later. Though contradicting each other regarding the timing of event **e2**, both A and B are right in what they experience.

The example illustrates a basic assertion of the Special Relativity Theory. There is no one correct way to slice the bread. The time slices by A and B both are valid from their own perspective. There is no unique set of time slices, implying that what exists is only the un-sliced loaf as a whole. Referring to Fig. 9.2, we say that the space-time continuum exists as a whole with no special significance attached to the different "time slices" one may make of it. Therefore, all events -past, present, and future- coexist in the Block Universe though observers *in* the universe see them sequentially. Past, present, and future have no meaning in this modern conception of the cosmos.

These revelations of Relativity Theory are contrary to our common sense notions of time and space, but many thinkers have come to accept it as the truth in view of experimental evidence supporting the theory. As Einstein himself once observed, *"To us convinced physicists, the distinctions between past, present, and future are illusory, however persistent"* [127]. The famous astronomer Sir Arthur Eddington concurred:*"Events do not happen: they are just there, and we come across them.... (as) the observer on his voyage of exploration."*. Louise de Broglie, another famous physicist stated the same view thus: *"Each observer, as time passes, discovers, so to speak, new slices of space-time which appear to him as successive aspects of the material world, though in reality the ensemble of events constituting space-time exist prior to his knowledge of them...the aggregate of past, present and future phenomena are in some sense given a priori"* [128].

Albert Einstein

The "future" is not necessarily known a priori to any observer who is part of the universe, but only to someone who has the view, as in Fig. 9.1 or Fig. 9.2, of the universe from *outside* the space-time continuum. Observers in the universe do not have the timeless view possible from outside and thus are subject to time. Time is an artifact (or illusion, in Einstein's words) experienced by observers moving through space-time continuum.

Clearly, the space-time continuum picture of the modern day physics shares many similarities with the $\mathscr{M}$-Space, or *Mahat*, of Vedānta. However, there is a major difference between the two. In the Vedāntic model, the emphasis is on the world as experienced by the jīvas. Thus we find one of the two polar coordinates in Fig. 9.1 specifically designated for the experiencer. In Physics, on the other hand, the observer is more of an afterthought, brought into the picture rather reluctantly only when needed to explain the physical world better. The space-time continuum description treats the observer more like a physical sensing device and less as a conscious entity that may have presence in dimensions other than the space-time continuum. Neuroscientists, who must deal with the world perceived by the sensory organs and the brain, often find themselves positioned somewhere in between the Physicist and the Vedāntin. We will see later how at least one neuroscientist has tried to bridge the gap.

Cosmic Time, Physical Time, and Experienced Time

The distance between two consecutive waves in Fig. 9.1 was termed as a unit "cosmic time" since this is the interval between the cosmos "now" and the cosmos "next". The term "cosmic time" is somewhat arbitrary since, as we saw in an earlier chapter, the interval between two waves is more like the Minkowski measure of distance in space-time continuum. There is no concept of pure time when viewed from a point outside the Field of Experiences of Fig. 9.1 or outside the Space-Time Continuum of Fig. 9.2. But time *is* experienced by sentient beings within the Space-Time Continuum or the Field of Experiences. The time measured by an observer within the physical realm of space-time continuum depends on its motion in space and may be called "physical time". It can be measured by a physical clock stationary relative to the observer. The time experienced by a jīva is yet another concept, different from both cosmic time and physical time. It depends on the jīva's spiritual detachment. This "experienced time" is a mental or psychological construct and cannot be measured by a physical clock either.

We may illustrate the three different time concepts with the example of twin siblings used in teaching Relativity Physics. John and Jay are twin brothers who are together at time *t1* celebrating their 19th birthday. The same day Jay leaves for a distant galaxy traveling at a very high speed. Immediately after reaching the galaxy, Jay turns around and returns back to earth at *t2*. Because of his high relative motion in space, physical time runs slower for Jay - let us say 60% slower- than for John. Five years have passed on earth when Jay returns just in time for the twins to celebrate their birthdays together again. But now there is a big difference: it is the 24th birthday for John and 21st for Jay. All this is shown in Fig. 9.3 by plotting the locations of J1 (for John) and J2 (for Jay) at the two birthday party events. At time *t1*, J1 and J2 are at the points P1 and P3 respectively, and at time *t2* they are at P2 and P4. Though J1 and J2 will be co-located in space-time continuum at the two birthday events, they are in different locations in the $\mathscr{M}$-space in view of their different spiritual detachment, thus underscoring the fact that the two spaces are not the same.

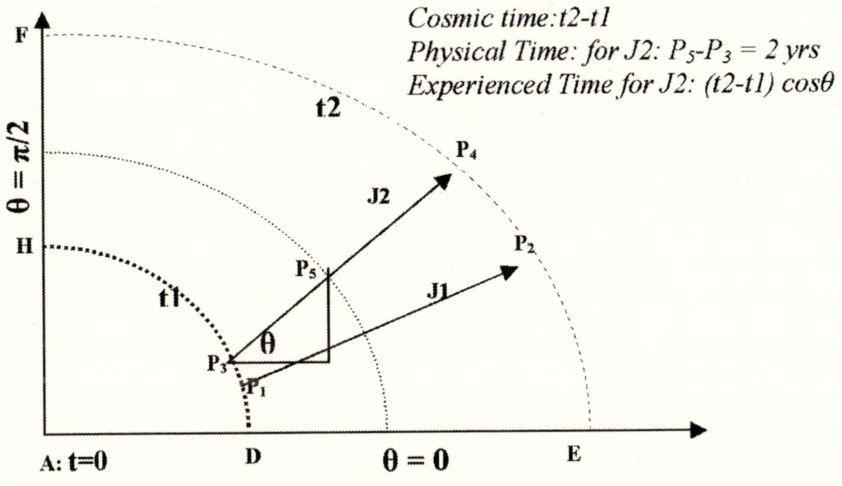

Fig. 9.3: Cosmic, Physical, and Experienced Time

Cosmic time between the two birthday events is the interval (t2-t1) between the two waves DH and EF. As emphasized earlier, we call this interval as time only for sake of convenience. The physical time corresponding to this cosmic time is different for the two brothers. For J1, bound to earth, physical time elapsed is 5 years whereas for J2 it is 2 years. This difference is due to the effects of relative motion in space-time continuum. The cosmic interval (t2-t1) is itself neither 5 nor 2 years. We cannot measure it in time. It is just that the interval P_2-P_1 in the J1's trajectory translates into 5 years, while the interval P_4-P_3 in J2's trajectory translates into 2 years. We may show this disparity by locating J2 at a point P_5 which is 2/5 the distance from P_3 as P_4 is from P_3. It is as if J2 has moved from P_3 to P_5 during the interval (t2-t1) when J1 moves from P_1 to P_2. This representation compromises the "outside" view of the cosmos, but may be more suitable to describe a jīva's "inside" personal view of the world it encounters.

The time we *experience* is a function of our mind and it is more psychological than physical. Clearly, it is not the same as the time registered by the watch we wear. In deep sleep, for example, we are not with the world nor are we aware of time, but the watch keeps ticking. As we have seen in earlier pages, the degree to which a jīva is identified with the world, (as given by the jīva's spiritual detachment) determines what its experienced time is. In Fig 9.3, physical time is 2 years for J2, but his experienced time, defined as the projection of the cosmic time on the horizontal axis, is (t2-t1).cosθ yrs. The experienced time for J1 can also be similarly expressed as (t2-t1).cosθ_1 years, assuming θ_1 is its spiritual detachment during the period t1 to t2.

We now turn to address two questions of major significance raised by this view cosmos. 1) How is that sentient observers (jīvas) experience time when the there is no such thing as time in creation *per se*? 2) If past, present, and future co-exist, does it not deny the free will for the jīvas to change the future by how they act now?

Perception of Time

We saw Sri Ramana's statement in Chapter 5 that the concept of time presupposes a state, one's recognition of it, and also the changes to the state. The interval between two states is called time. It follows from this definition that, for time to be experienced, there must be changes and also there must be recognition of the changes by some cognizant being. Where there is no change, there is no sense of time. From the perspective of jīvas, the world of Objects-Emotions-Thoughts, is always in a state of flux. Jīvas experience the states of the world and perceive the interval between the experiences as time with its connotations of past, present, and future.

In Fig. 9.1, the successive states of the world are shown by series of waves. A jīva's encounters with the successive states of the world can be shown, as in Fig. 9.4 below, as a point on each wave. As the jīva moves from one wave to the next, it experiences the changing states of the world, and the experience of changes results in the perception of time.

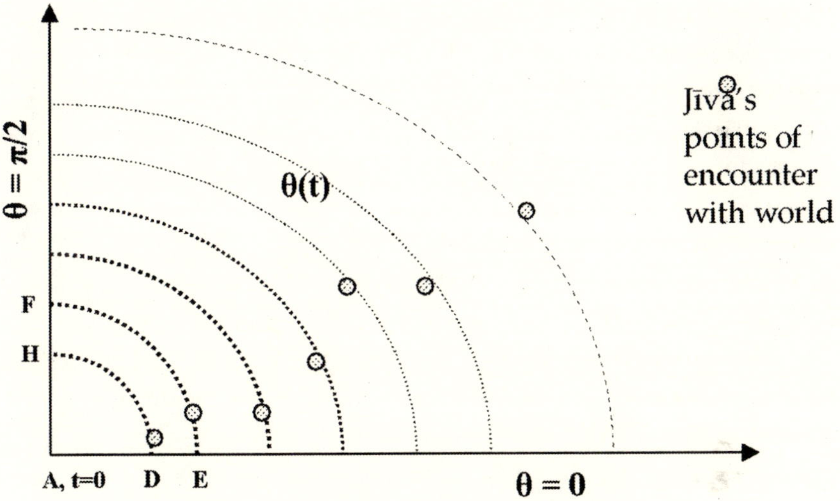

Fig. 9.4: Jīva's Encounters with the World

What keeps a jīva bound to the plane of the waves, one may ask, propelling it from one wave to the next? In other words, what keeps a jīva bound to time and to the changing world? From the point of view of science, worldly life is all there is and hence the question does not even arise. For a Vedāntin, on the other hand, it is a very relevant question. It is *māyā* that keeps the jīva bound to world by its power of delusion. It is the same *māyā* that Īśvara, the Creator, wields to project the world on the Cosmic Mind. The difference is that, *māyā* is under the control of Īśvara, whereas jīvas are controlled by *māyā*.

What exactly moves when we say a jīva moves from wave to wave? The answer Vedānta gives, as well as what some neuroscientists now suggest, challenge some of the deep-rooted beliefs we have about ourselves and the world we live in.

A jīva, as explained in Chapter 2, has three bodies: a *gross* (physical) body, a *subtle* body constituted of mind and intellect, and a *causal* body constituted of its vāsanas. All three bodies are part of the creation and therefore in the 𝒜-space. None of these bodies can be what moves from wave to wave in Fig.9.4 to produce the life's experiences for the jīva. These bodies are not sentient by themselves and therefore they cannot be the primary instrument of our experiences. Scriptures suggest that the sentient jīva is born when the Ātman or Self "identifies" with the individual body-mind-intellect complex; that is, sentiency in an otherwise insentient body-mind-intellect complex is produced by its association with the Self, which is Pure Consciousness. This theory was explained with the help of Fig. 2.4 in Chapter 2, suggesting that Consciousness reflecting off the intellect (*buddhi*) produces the "beam of intelligence" in the light of which a jīva recognizes objects-emotions-thoughts. According to Adi Sankara "*buddhi*" is the determining faculty in us and an object is recognized when the *buddhi* determines, in the light of the reflected consciousness, what that object is[44].

When a jīva "encounters a wave" it cognizes and experiences the state of the world represented by that wave in the beam of reflected consciousness. All the waves, and the state of the world they imply for the jīvas, as we saw in our discussion of Figs. 9.1 and 9.2, exist eternally in the 𝒜-space, as though waiting to be illumined. A stream of experiences is produced when the beam of reflected consciousness

44 Sri Ramana taught a slightly different interpretation of the theory. He says that *"the vāsanas or latent tendencies of the mind of the individual, acting as the reflecting medium, catch the all-pervading, infinite light of Consciousness arising from the heart and present, in the form of a reflection, the phenomenon called the mind. Seeing only this reflection, the ajñāni is deluded into the belief that he is a finite being, the jīva. If the mind becomes introverted through enquiry into the source of ahaṁ-vritti, the vāsanas become extinct and in the absence of the reflecting medium, the phenomenon of reflection, namely the mind, also disappears being absorbed into the light of the one Reality, the Heart. This is the sum and substance of all that an aspirant needs to know."*

Sri Ramana thus holds that 1) the all-pervading Pure Consciousness is in the Heart of every jīva, and 2) the vāsanas of the jīva (-which is also in the Heart since the locale of *Prajna* is identified as the Heart in Māṇḍukya Upaniṣad-) reflect this Pure Consciousness in the form of mind (which includes mind-intellect-ego and all thoughts or *vrittis*.)

illumines wave after wave to "read" the state of the world encoded in each wave. This stream of experiences is life and the sequential character of experiences is the source of the experience of time. The waves are like tracks of music recorded on a CD and the reflected consciousness of the jīva is like the laser "read head" moving over the recorded tracks and making life come alive.

The Grand View and the Science to Support It

Each jīva has a unique view of the world, its experience at any time being unlike that of any other jīva. A happy moment for one jīva can be a painful one for another. The grand picture that emerges is one of a multitude of jīvas- from plants and animals to humans and *deva*s or demigods- moving from wave to wave, each experiencing what is in store for itself. It is a picture that sharply differs from what we generally believe: That we reshape the world moment by moment by what we do and what we do is according to our will. What we find instead is that the jīvas only experience what already exist and can do nothing "now" that has not been "already" done.

Science is also veering towards similar views in its effort to explain how there can be the dynamic experience of time and changes in a timeless, static universe. The explanation, as the following quotations show, usually invokes consciousness [129].

Physics itself recognizes no special moment called 'now'—the moment that acts as the focus of 'becoming' and divides the 'past' from the 'future'. In four-dimensional space-time nothing changes, there is no flow of time, everything simply is . . . It is only in consciousness that we come across the particular time known as 'now' . . . It is only in the context of mental time that it makes sense to say that all of physical space-time is. (Russell Stannard,Physicist, Open University of UK, 1987)

'The objective world simply is, it does not happen. Only to the gaze of my consciousness crawling upward along the life-line [world line] of my body does a section of this world come to life as a fleeting image.' (Hermann Weyl, Physicist, Princeton University, NJ, 1922)

". . . particles do not even move, being represented by "static" curves drawn in space–time. Thus what we perceive as moving 3D objects are really successive cross-sections of immobile 4D objects past which our field of observation is sweeping". (Roger Penrose, Mathematician, 1994)

A Neuroscientist's View of Reality

Consciousness figures prominently in the above statements, though scientists have yet no consensus as to what it is. There is also a subtle hint in the statements that Consciousness is not part of the 4-dimensional space-time observed. In Vedānta, Consciousness is verily the Brahman, the supreme reality, as made clear by the declaration *"prajñānaṁ brahmā"*. All of creation arise, live, and dissolve in Consciousness. But as we discussed in Chapter 4, neuroscience has only a number of hypotheses to offer at this time and no consensus has emerged as to what consciousness is.

This is certainly discouraging to the materialists who would see consciousness only in terms of the physical brain and its activities. But there are other scientists who approach the study of consciousness with a more open mind. The views of Dr. Smythies referred to earlier are illumining and very relevant to our discussions. In his paper on "Time, Space, and Consciousness", Smythies makes three key points:

1) What we perceive is only a representation of the external world constructed by the brain and not the external world itself. There is a "physical world" out there and a corresponding, but separate, "phenomenal" world inside. To quote the author "*Phenomenal objects, together with the space in which they are located, are constructs of the central nervous system and in no sense are they direct views of the external objects that they represent. .... the results of a large number of experiments in psychophysics.... demonstrate beyond any doubt that, in vision, we do not perceive the world as it actually is, but as the brain computes it most probably to be*".

2) The phenomenal space, or the space in which the phenomenal objects are located, is different from the 4-dimensional space-time of physics. Smythies refers to the 11 dimensional space and "branes" proposed by string theorists and suggests that the "phenomenal space and physical space are simply different spaces, different parallel universes whose contents are causally related." That is, the phenomenal space lies on a separate multi-dimensional "brane" independent of the physical space-time. Smythies does not define or explain consciousness, but suggests

that "consciousness is in this brane and not in the brain". That is, consciousness is associated with the mental or phenomenal world and not with the brain which is part of the physical world.

3) The physical and phenomenal worlds, though in separate dimensions, are causally related and therefore affect one another. The physical space-time is static with co-existent past, present, and future. But the phenomenal world is dynamic since there is perception of changes. Smythies suggests that the sense of time is generated by the relative motion of the phenomenal and physical spaces. The "now" is the point of contact between the two spaces.

This is similar to the Vedāntic model in Fig. 9.4 where the "now" is the point of contact between jīva, the experiencer, and world, the experienced. This is remarkable given that the starting point for Fig.9.4 was the Vedāntic teachings, whereas Smythies bases his views on Physics and modern Neuroscience. It is noteworthy too that a neuroscientist should propose, based on clinical evidence, that consciousness is in a space altogether separate from the physical brain.

There are differences, however. Smythies suggests that consciousness is in the phenomenal space or "brane". Vedānta denies absolute reality to the physical and phenomenal world, Consciousness being the only Reality. Therefore Consciousness cannot be in the brane of phenomenal space; rather the brane, as well as the physical space is in *Mahat*, the Cosmic Mind, which itself is in Consciousness. Secondly, there is a question about the nature of the "brane" and the individual observer's phenomenal space. Vedānta says that there is only one Consciousness but with many individual reflections. Smythies seems to suggest that there is one brane in which there are many individual "consciousness modules". A final significant difference is in regards to the spiritual dimension of our existence. Smythies, keeping the discussion within the traditional confines of science, does not talk about spirituality. However, if reality is the timeless, changeless universe scientists now say it is, and if individual experience of change and time is (to use Einstein's words) only an illusion, then should not awakening from this illusion to that timeless reality be a goal of all individuals?

This in fact is the goal of spirituality. For example, the well known Upaniṣadic *mantra "mṛtyor mā amṛtaṁ gamaya"*

is a fervent prayer to lead us from death (meaning time and changes) to immortality (timelessness and changelessness). In the final sections of this chapter we turn our attention to this spiritual goal.

Free Will and the Spiritual Evolution of Jīvas

In the cosmic scenarios shown in Figs. 9.1 and 9.2, future events co-exist with the past and present events. Hence what a jīva will meet at the "next" moment is beyond its power to change by doing something different "now". The jīva's actions are events in the Cosmic Mind and they exist "eternally", like all other events. Therefore a jīva does only what has "already" been done. This basically denies any role for personal free will in our life. If a jīva has personal free will, it can exercise that will to engage now in actions that would change the world at the next moment. Since this possibility is negated, one must also negate, or greatly restrict, the free will attributable to jīvas. This is an implication of the timelessness of the universe suggested by both ancient Vedānta and 20th century science. It is a conclusion which is supported by scriptures, logic, and neuroscience, as we saw in Chapter 3 during our discussion of the Prakṛti-Īśvara paradigm.

While the jīva has no control over what experience it will meet with in the future world, we saw in Chapter 7 that it has the choice as to how to confront that experience. It can: 1) Identify with the experience and "eat" (i.e. suffer or enjoy) the results, or 2) Identify with the Self and merely be a "witness" to the experience. We also saw that the vāsanas and spiritual detachment of the jīva determine which of these two options the jīva is likely to choose.

All these concepts and theories put together suggest a simple, yet totally unfamiliar, view of jīvas and the time-bound world they experience.

Be the Instrument That Plays the Cosmic Record

The alternate view of time and cosmos suggested by Vedānta and modern science presents a picture of worldly life that is unlike anything we generally take to be the truth. A good analogy to describe that picture is an audio CD and the way it is played back. The hundreds of spiraling tracks burned on the disc contain music. When the CD is played (that is, when the laser beam reads the information coded on the tracks and converts it to audible sound), the music comes to life. We hear the beginning notes followed by the subsequent notes until the final notes are sounded. We hear the beat of the music and sense the movement in the melody. Altogether, when the CD is played back, we experience progression of time. The CD player is the instrument which brings the recorded music to life. If we were to just hold the CD in our hand and look at it, we will not hear the melody nor feel the beat of music in it. Nevertheless, the various melodies are imprinted on it in their proper time sequence and exist "eternally" on it.

The Cosmic Mind, $\mathscr{M}$, is like the CD. The waves in the $\mathscr{M}$-space are records of the state of the world from beginning of creation till its end, and include the past, present, and future lives of every jīva. There is no time associated with $\mathscr{M}$-space itself from the point of view of the creator. The notion of time is produced in a jīva when its light of (reflected) consciousness illumines wave after wave to "read" the particular experience recorded in it. In this analogy, the sentient jīvas are like the CD player; they are the instruments that illumine the recorded experience. Thus seen, the statement by Lord Krishna is no longer enigmatic. Lord Krishna has "already" caused Arjuna's body-mind-intellect to kill the enemies; this event and experience are recorded on the cosmic mind. Arjuna, -the sentient jīva which is about to encounter this event-, is being asked "now" by the Lord to be aware that he is merely the instrument that will soon play that record. The teachings of Gītā on the right manner in which to live in the world and engage in action–namely, without a sense of doer ship, with detachment, as a witness, with no expectations, and surrendering to the Lord's Will- all follow logically, loyally, simply, and elegantly from this timeless view of the cosmos[45].

Instead of knowing itself to be the mere instrument (*nimitta mātraṁ*)

---

45 As a jīva experiences a "pre-recorded" universe, its vāsanas can change from, say, a *tamasic-rajasic* mix to a more *sāttvic* one as the jīva progresses spiritually. One might ask if the changing vāsanas of the jīva will not also induce changes in the world from what it is in the "pre-recorded" version and thus invalidate the concept of a timeless universe. This is not necessarily the case if it is recalled that the vāsanas affect only the probability of the different outcomes and not the actual outcome. The actual outcome depends on Īśvara's Will.

that illumines experiences, an ignorant jīva thinks it is the doer and enjoyer and suffers the good and bad consequences of the experience. It is the power of *Māyā* that keeps the jīva moving forward on this illusory journey until it attains Realization, the Enlightening Knowledge.

PART III

Vedānta's Answers to Life's Persistent Questions

CHAPTER 10

Riddles of Life

Life is full of riddles that have persisted over the millennia no matter how hard humans have tried to answer them. Why is there a world at all? What is the purpose of life? What is the ultimate fate of the world? Is that fate pre-destined or is there a free will that can alter it? Who am I? Is there a God and if so how is He or She involved in the affairs of the world? Why is there evil and suffering? Is the world temporary or will it be around forever? Can lasting improvement be wrought on an ever-changing world? If not, why labor to make the world a better place? The list goes on.

We have glimpsed in the previous pages Vedānta's answer to many of these questions. The questions are baffling, it turns out, because of our several misconceptions about what the world is and who we are. The overall vision offered by Vedānta dispels these misconceptions but only by turning many of our commonly held views upside down. A simple analogy- a child's play- may help in putting the Vedāntic vision in a comprehensible format.

A Child's Play

Vedānta's description of Brahman and the phenomenal world brings to this writer's mind decades old memory of watching his young nephew playing with his toys. The child had a shoe box full of assorted toys of tiny people, cars etc. Often after breakfast, he will go to a small room where he kept the toys and start playing with them all alone. I noticed to my amusement how my nephew had invested each person in his toy collection with definite human qualities so that they were like real people to him. There were good guys and there were bad guys and very predictably the play will involve verbal exchanges and fights between them. Picking up a bad guy, the child will walk him towards one of the good guys while making threatening statements like "You get out of here else I will clobber you", or "Give me all the chocolates you have in your pocket". "I will not! I am not scared of you", the good guy will reply. Then just as the bad guy gets ready to attack the good guy, the child may pick up a car and run over the bad guy scolding "You are a naughty boy and this is your punishment!" At other times, he may console the good guy by giving some treats from his own pocket. Many variations of these scenes will be concocted by the imaginative mind of the child and the play will go on for an hour or more until all bad guys have been appropriately dealt with and good guys rewarded. At the end, all toys, good and bad, will be carefully picked up and put back lovingly in the same shoe box they had come out of earlier.

The actions, rewards, and punishments in the play are as willed by the child. There may be mock anger, appreciative comments, pretended fear etc in the game but underneath all of this there is only the joy of play for the child. There is no harsh feeling that the child bears towards any of the toys, but only love. The child wants all toys to be safely back in the shoe box, their home, at the end of the day.

The world is said to be Īśvara's *līla*, or the Lord's sport, a sport much like the child's play. The child plays when it is in a happy, contented mood. Īśvara, ever in Bliss, also creates this world out of that bliss, *ānanda*, only. Each jīva in the world, like the toys, is invested with good and bad character. The child gives each toy a role in his play consistent with its character, the scene played out being decided by the child. Similarly, there are actions, rewards and punishments in the world just as in the child's play and they happen at the Lord's Will only. The child takes care of all the toys, good and bad, and he would be distraught if any of them goes missing or is damaged. Īśvara's love for the jīvas, irrespective of their good and bad character, is also universal and total. No jīva hopelessly wanders around in *samsār* without finding the way back to its spiritual home sooner or later.

The toys are insentient and they do not experience the play they are engaged in. To create his make-believe world of the play, the child has to lend the toys his own sentiency. He talks and acts for them. That is the case in Īśvara's play also. According to Vedānta, the Body-Mind-Intellect of a jīva is insentient; it gains sentiency only when Īśvara "enters" the jīva, allowing Consciousness to reflect off its Intellect. The jīva is born because of this association of the Self with the Non-Self and each jīva works with the character it is assigned in the Divine Play.

The analogy is good but not perfect. The toys are not all of the child's own making; they are usually designed and created by someone else using materials from some outside source. But, for Īśvara, the all pervasive, there is no "other" to help with the creation. He is at once the efficient, material, and instrumental cause for creation. Still, the child's play illustrates well the Vedānta's answers to life's riddles. Since the answers often run contrary to our commonly held beliefs about the world and ourselves, they may themselves sound like riddles, especially to newcomers to the philosophy. So, here are eight conundrums which answer "Life's Persistent Questions"[46].

Eight Conundrums

- The world cannot be improved but we must work to improve the world.
- Evil must be avoided but it is a necessary evil.
- We have choices but the choice is not ours.
- With love for everything but in love with nothing.
- There is nothing in this world to complain about, except that which complains about everything.
- I have nothing to do but I do it very well.
- I am a saint but I commit sins incessantly.
- There always were problems; there always will be problems; but there never is any problem.

The statements sound self-contradictory and need explanation. Resolution of the apparent contradiction leads to valuable insight into the Vedāntic view of life.

Conundrum # 1: The world cannot be improved but we must work to improve the world.

This seemingly self-contradictory statement underlies the hopelessness a human being feels as it deals with a notoriously imperfect world. The world seems to be in a perennial state of disrepair. Something or the other

46 "Life's Persistent Questions" is a phrase borrowed from Garrsion Keillor's long running, popular radio show *"A Prairie Home Companion"*.

is always in need of our immediate attention and action. As responsible denizens of this world, we are advised by our teachers, parents, as well as political and religious leaders to dedicate ourselves to the improvement of our family, society and world at large. Most of us in fact do this, either directly or indirectly. For a majority, while the immediate motive for work may be to make a living that feeds, clothes and shelters ourselves and our immediate family, we perform our work for institutions, either public or private, whose goal is make this a better world for everyone in the community. Thus even our work for wages is indirectly aimed at the betterment of the world. For some noble individuals amongst us, welfare of the world is in fact the primary objective. They sacrifice personal needs in pursuit of their lofty goals. History of all nations and of all times holds examples of such persons, including scientists, soldiers, philosophers, spiritual teachers, or statesmen. Thus, by and large, we have the improvement of the world as our goal.

However, both experience and theory strongly suggest that this world cannot be improved, at least not on a permanent basis. History tells us that our efforts to establish a harmonious world have not been, and may never be, an unqualified success. A relatively peaceful time may be achieved through consistent effort for a while, but is sooner or later broken by open war. Crime and corruption are ever present and widely prevalent, taking new forms with advancing technologies, in spite of the growth of highly organized law enforcement institutions to fight these evil all over the world. There is no reason to expect the future to be any different either, as long as human nature remains what it is. Natural phenomena like earthquakes, draughts, and epidemics are also likely to be with us forever. These disasters cannot be ever totally eliminated even though man is bringing to bear more and more of his technological prowess to reduce their catastrophic effects on human life.

Fundamental laws of science project a future for the universe that is even more forlorn. Modern science is nearly unanimous in its view that there will be no life form left on this earth, as the sun swells into a red giant before collapsing in five billion years. Regarding the fate of the universe as a whole, there is as yet no consensus in the scientific community. Different scenarios have been presented by cosmologists going by such dramatic names as "big crunch", "big freeze", "heat death" and "big bounce". Life as we know will be impossible under all these scenarios even if for different reasons. "The universe is going to have a long, slow end. It will first begin with ignorance. And if we are right, it will end with death", says physicist Dr. Starkman [130]. In the big crunch scenario, the universe collapses to the same state it was just before the Big Bang, namely a mere speck of nearly infinite density. In the "big freeze", the universe expands for ever becoming more and more cold and snuffing out all life. In the "heat death" scenario predicted by the second law of thermodynamics, the universe is too disorderly to support life. In the "big bounce" theory, the big crunch is followed by a big bang in which a new universe is created. In this scenario, the death of the universe is the precursor to the birth of the next, thus perpetuating a perennial cycle of cosmic birth and death.

Many religious faiths and their scriptures also echo similar thoughts in what is perhaps an unusual convergence of scientific and religious opinions. For example, the above "big bounce" scenario is very similar to the Vedāntic views of creation and dissolution of the cosmos. Other religions foresee the end of the world in fire, flood etc. The underlying spiritual principle in all these religious views is that the seen world is not the ultimate reality and hence it is necessarily perishable. Therefore, the faithful should not expect everlasting happiness from the world. That happiness must be found somewhere else.

Thus, according to both science and scriptures, the world is ultimately a losing proposition. Is it not meaningless then to spend our precious human lives in improving the world? It is futile, after all to try to fix something which cannot be really fixed. In Kerala where I grew up, they tell the enigmatic story of the "Mad Man of Narayanath". The story has it that every day this mad man would roll a big boulder painstakingly up a hill. Reaching the top after much effort, he will give a push to the boulder and clap his hands in glee while watching it hurtle downhill. Then he will climb down and push the boulder back up the hill to start the crazy ritual all over again. Thus he labors for hours day after day. While this sounds like sheer madness, human effort spent in improving the world must also be equally laughable if that world is only destined to go downhill and perish.

What then is the purpose of all human effort? This is the question posed by the first conundrum.

Resolution: The truth is that we must act to improve the world, but we do this not to improve the world, but to improve ourselves spiritually.

I walk early in the morning along a popular beach. There were likely lots of adults and children here yesterday, but right now I am practically alone. As I walk down, I see the ruins of a sand castle built by children the previous evening. The children must have taken much delight in building it, giving hours and hours of their effort. But all that has disappeared overnight as the castle was washed away by the rising tide. Yet the children will return this evening and build more castles. They will have great fun. They will learn the art of constructive work.

This is the crux of the *karma yoga*- acting without expectations for the result. We can have fun and learn while in this world if we do not take that world as the be all and end all of our existence. This is the way to Perfection and Eternal Bliss.

An alternate statement of same conundrum could read *The World Cannot be Saved, but Every Being of the World Will be Saved.* Fortunately, world, being insentient, is not in need of salvation either. Salvation makes sense for sentient jīvas and it is assured for every jīva.

Conundrum #2: Evil Must Be Avoided but It Is a Necessary Evil

Let us ponder for a minute:

What good can a physician do in a community that knows no disease?

What is charity good for in a country where no one is poor?

What good can goodness do in a world without evil?

If one contemplates these questions, an answer to one of the most bedeviling questions of life will present itself: Why evil?

Evil has always been with us and, as far as we can tell, it will always be with us in this world. It cannot be simply wished away. At the same time, evil is evil and everyone is rightly advised to scrupulously avoid it at all times. So why is evil there if everyone is barred from it? There should be no evil, goes the familiar argument, in a world created and controlled by a merciful God who personifies and promotes goodness. Why does God permit evil?

In truth, this is an unfair criticism of God. It is like finding fault with Shakespeare for having murderous and greedy villains in his plays, instead of only virtuous heroes and heroines. Such accusation, if ever made, will be readily dismissed as being frivolous because we know that there can be no real interesting story to tell without a mix of villains and heroes. It is the play of the opposing forces such as love and hate, or valor and cowardice, which provide the fit material for an absorbing story. To cite another example from art, a painter cannot create a picture using only one shade of a single color. The black and white tones together bring out the picture. Without contrasting colors, no picture can emerge from the canvas.

Duality is necessary for any creation, be it a play or a painting created by a mortal, or the universe projected by Īśvara. The world is seen by Vedāntins as a cosmic play of the Lord, a play that opposes Good and Evil. The Lord, it would seem, thrills in performing an infinite number of variations on this eternal theme. Mythologies as well as recorded human history portray story after story of the confrontation between Good and Evil with the victory going ultimately to the good (or at least the less evil) side. "*satyameva jayate*", declares the Muṇḍaka Upaniṣad. Truth alone is Triumphant. Virtue alone is Victorious. God is Goodness and hence it is only logical that Good should win over Evil in God's cosmic plays.

So why is there evil in God's world?

Resolution: There is evil in the world so that goodness may manifest and assert itself in all its Glory.

Without evil, God's goodness cannot become manifest. Edmund Burke is credited with making the famous statement *'The only thing necessary for the triumph of evil is for good men to do nothing.*" The tragedy in the world is not that there is evil, but that goodness does not readily assert itself in the face of that evil. Adolf Hitler was no doubt an evil individual, but what brought on the tragedy of the Holocaust was the submissiveness of the good people around the globe who offered no opposition to this evil for a number of years. The eventual World War II and the victory of the (relatively good) Allied forces is just another episode in the eternal cosmic play featuring Good vs. Evil.

The divine play is enacted not only around us in the world outside; it also goes on within us all the time and is the very fabric of our evolving spiritual life. The evil manifested in the world outside ultimately has its source inside each of us in the form of anger, greed, and unworthy thoughts of all kinds. We, using the goodness in us, must learn to subdue this evil without giving it a chance to express itself. The jīva which has completely vanquished the evil within itself "goes beyond".

But what about the world as a whole? *Will Goodness ever root evil out of the world for good? If so, what kind of a world will it be without any evil?*

We can only speculate. May be the world will end, like all fairy tales, when evil is no more. When the valiant Prince has fought off and vanquished all evil monsters, marries the beautiful Princess he has liberated from captivity, and "lives happily ever after", the fairy tale is at its end. With the story book closed, there is neither the valiant Prince nor the evil monsters; the child goes to peaceful slumber in the arms of her loving mother. With no evil left in the world, the cosmic play comes to a happy ending, and the world dissolves back into the undisturbed Bliss of the Cosmic Mind. As Mother of Aurobindo Ashram summarized it "*It is said that if the world, if the creation realized its perfect identity with the Divine, there would no longer be any creation.*"

Conundrum # 3: We have choices but the choice is not ours

It is evident that there are choices in life. Typically at any given time we have more than one course of action open to us. For example, those of us who go to office for work, have the choice every morning to either go to work or take the day off. We can choose to do any one of the available courses of action or may choose not to do any of them. "To do, not to do, or do it otherwise" (*kartum, akartum, anyathā kartum*) is how some texts express this freedom of choice available in life.

Given such real choices, we cannot say that the world moves towards a pre-destined future, irrespective of the choices made by individuals. There is simply no support for such a fatalistic notion in Vedānta. The question of Free Will, therefore, is not whether the individual has choices by which it can change the world for itself and others around. It certainly has. The pertinent question to ask is: When an individual makes a "personal" choice, is it really the individual who makes this choice consciously or is it some other entity doing this through him? We have discussed this question at great length in this book and need not repeat the arguments here. Based on both science and scriptures we concluded that the decisions responsible for individual choices are not made at the will of the individual but at the will of Īśvara. We act merely as instruments of that Divine Will. The *jñāni* knows this and enjoys the unfolding world as a witness; the ignorant jīva does not know this truth and suffers thinking he is the doer.

Resolution of Conundrum #3: There is Free Will, but it belongs to Īśvara and not the Jīva.

At this point, another question is raised by some schools of philosophers: Īśvara is Omniscient and therefore cannot but know in advance what choices lie ahead and which choice actually will be made. As such, is not the future of the world really pre-destined?

Not necessarily. Īśvara may know it, but the jīva does not know what choices will be available or what choice will be made. The jīva thinks that there are real choices to be made that will affect the future of the world. Therefore, the fate of the world is not pre-destined, from the jīva's point of view. The alternate view of Time presented in Chapter 9 brought into sharp focus this difference between jīva's and Īśvara's points of view. According to that discussion, pre-destiny is not a meaningful concept from Īśvara's standpoint either. This is because Īśvara is beyond time. Past, present and future all exist contemporaneously in the *Mahat*, the Cosmic Mind of Īśvara. The phrase "knowing in advance" does not have any meaning in such a timeless context.

Conundrum #4- With Love for Everything, but In Love with Nothing

The Man of Perfection is portrayed as one who revels in the welfare of all beings. A jīva's suffering in the world decreases as it grows spiritually and cultivates "unconditional love" towards other beings. As this unconditional love expands without limit and becomes universal enough to embrace all beings, the jīva attains the Bliss of Perfection. Such a *mahātmā* has necessarily love for everything in the world.

At the same time, the Man of Perfection is also portrayed as one totally detached from everything in the world, including own body, mind and intellect. This detachment, as we have seen, is the single most basic parameter characterizing spiritual evolution. Armed with supreme detachment, the *Yogī* regards "gold and dirt" equally [131]. Bhagavan Adi Sankara goes one step further when he suggests that the dispassionate one regards all sense-objects with same aversion as one would have towards the droppings of a crow! [132]. Surely, such a one cannot be *in love* with anything of this world.

This leads to an apparent contradiction: How can one *have love for everything* in this world and at the same time *not be in love with anything?*

Resolution: To be in love with something is to be attached to it and results in suffering. On the other hand, Love for all beings expresses as pure joy and is the apex of spiritual perfection.

When I am *in love* with something or some being, my happiness is also dependent on that thing or being. I must therefore demand and receive favors from that source in order to feel complete and happy. Hence this is not love, but attachment, which is the opposite of detachment. As we have seen, it is the cause of suffering.

When I *have love for* something or some being, my happiness is in no way dependent on that thing or being. On the other hand, I am capable of providing for the welfare and happiness of that being, out of the care and compassion I possess towards it and I get joy in acting out of my love.

Thus it is possible to have love for something and yet not be in love with the same. When Lord Krishna declares that "They are in Me, I am not in them" the Lord is indicating this strange "relationless relationship" between Creator and created [133]. The Creator is not in love with the creation and is not dependent in any way on the creation for own perfection or happiness. On the other hand, He has love for His creation, affording all things and beings His compassionate universal, unconditional love.

Conundrum # 5- There Is Nothing In This World To Complain About, Except That Which Complains About Everything

No thing or no being of this world can be faulted. After all, they all act as per the laws of Prakṛti and the Will of Īśvara. The problems we perceive with the world are a result of our ignorant, vāsana ridden mind. Instead of complaining about the world which is not under our control, the real remedy is to rid the mind of its impurities and strive for independence from the world. The world is not improved by just expressing displeasure about it. Feeling displeasure merely makes us miserable without benefiting anyone or anything in the world.

Resolution: The only thing we can complain about in this world is our constantly complaining mind.

Vedānta is unique in the overwhelming emphasis it puts on controlling the capricious mind. Rishi Patanjali begins his famous treatise, *Yoga Sūtra*, with the call for "*citta vṛtti nirodhana*" or control of activities of mind [134]. Without that, practicing any or all of the other eight limbs of Yoga is fruitless.

"*nahyastyavidyā manasotirikta*", says Adi Sankara in Vivekachūḍāmaṇi [135] meaning, ignorance of the true nature of Reality is the root cause of all suffering and this ignorance is nothing other than the mind itself. Thus it is said that "*mana eva manuṣyāṇām kāraṇaṁ bandha mokṣayoḥ*" or "*mind alone is the cause of bondage and liberation of men*" [136]. The spiritual seeker has to work on own mind to gradually get rid of the ignorance.

For one who has thus mastered and quieted the otherwise incessantly complaining mind, both mind and world become friends and there is nothing left to complain about.

Conundrum # 6 - I have nothing to do but I do it very well

An active man is constantly besieged by the thought of all the work that awaits him. Being a victim of the sense of agency *(kartṛtva bhāva)* he is under constant pressure and compulsion to perform action.

The Man of Perfection, on the other hand, has really no work that he must do. As Bhagavan Sri Ramana asks "*naṣṭamānasotkṛṣṭayoginaḥ, kṛtyamasti kiṁ svastithiṁ yataḥ*" [137]. For the Perfect yogī who has transcended his mind and is firmly established in his Self, there is really nothing left to be done. Such a Yogī has accomplished everything that needs to be accomplished. There is nothing more that he needs to do, nor is there anything more to be gained by him in his life. Having gone beyond the cycle of births and deaths, and burned all his vāsanas, there is no work waiting for him in a future life either.

Yet the Yogī does not retire into a life of inactivity. True, not being *rajasic*, he does not seek work or initiate grandiose schemes of his own; in Gītā's words he is a "*sarvārambha parityāgī*" or one who has renounced all initiatives [138]. But he is not *tamasic* either and hence applies himself happily and energetically to any work that presents itself to him. He performs his actions with great efficiency since he is not hamstrung by an oppressing sense of ego, agency, or selfish agenda; he works out of love for the welfare of all beings. The resulting dexterity in action, the Gītā avers, is natural to such a karma yogī.

This is exactly how Īśvara- sometimes addressed as the Lord of Yogīs- also functions in dealing with his creation. The Lord says

"na me pārthāsti kartavyaṁ triṣu lokeṣu kiñcana
nānavāptam avāptavyam varta eva ca karmaṇi".

"There is nothing for me to do in the three worlds, Arjuna, since there is nothing to be attained that has not already been attained; yet I remain engaged in action always." [139].

Resolution: For one established in Self, there is no other goals left in life and hence no further work to be undertaken. But whatever work needs to be done for the service of the world is performed with great skill and success.

Conundrum # 7- I am a Saint; I commit sins incessantly

A verse found in many devotional hymns reads thus:

"aparādha sahasrāṇi kriyanteharniśaṁ mayā,
dāsoyaṁ iti māṁ matva kṣamasva parameśvara!"

The devotee confesses in this verse to committing thousands of sins day and night but, as a servant of the Lord, pleads for His forgiveness. I am not sure which great soul authored this verse, but surely he or she was deeply devoted to the Lord. Now, can someone who is a sincere devotee of the Lord possibly commit "thousands of sin day and night"? The statement is thus at least an exaggeration if not an outright contradiction. Or, is there an element of practical truth here?

Vedānta says that the real nature of all jīvas is the pure, saintly, blemish-less Self. The jīva is merely an instrument of Īśvara in all its actions, and for this reason it is only a servant of the Lord. Viewed thus we all are, or ought to be, saints provided we have the right knowledge.

The tragedy is that the jīva does not have this knowledge. It is ignorant of own identity. As a result, it is engaged in many activities, some good and some evil, but almost always with the sense of doer ship. In the beginning, the jīva is not even aware of its ignorance.

Then, by the grace of Īśvara, in some birth the jīva becomes aware of its ignorant state, possibly through a teacher or scriptures, and is set on a course of spiritual quest. The jīva becomes more and more sensitive to its imperfections and rightly begins to attribute its sufferings not to the world but to its separation from the Self. To such a spiritually refined jīva, any moment which it spends identifying with the Non-Self is a moment lived in sin. In repentance, it can turn only to that Self pleading forgiveness.

Resolution: The real sin is the ignorance which envelops the jīva "day and night" because of which it identifies with the Non-Self and forgets its real nature as Brahman. This sin carries its own immediate punishment, namely the suffering that comes with the contact of the world. The forgiveness that the devotee seeks from Īśvara is release from ignorance.

Conundrum # 8: There always were problems; there always will be problems; but there never is any problem.

This is indeed comical, if only it did not have a tinge of sadness to it! We become worried now thinking about the problems the future may hold and wallow in regret thinking about mishandling the problems of the past. But if we were to focus on the very instant "now"- the present live, breathing, moment- we will find that there is no problem, only peace.

Resolution: Mind totally focused on the present moment is the witnessing consciousness; it is pure, immaculate, free of all dualities, full of peace and joy. "Past" and "future" are fictions of the mind. A mind turned outwards in contemplating past and future is full of dualities and all the fear and regret that go with such dualities. This is the logic behind the Buddhist practice of living in the present moment.

The Cosmic Play of Īśvara and The Meaning of Life

We can now address one by one the basic questions of life posed at the beginning of this chapter. If the answers provided below look too short or off-hand considering the profundity of the questions, it is only because we have discussed extensively most of it already in the preceding pages of the book.

What is this world, what is life and who am I? The world is best seen as a play taking place in Īśvara's Cosmic Mind. The objects and beings of the world constitute respectively the props and actors of the play. The character of the actors and props is defined by the respective *vāsanas* bestowed on them by *Prakṛti.* The character of the actors is consistent with many possible plots for the play. The actual play is scripted and directed by *Īśvara*.

Jīvas, the actors, perform only as willed by Īśvara, the director. The body-mind-intellect of the jīva is therefore an instrument of Īśvara. However, this does not make the jīva a mindless robot. Unlike a robot, the jīva has the sentiency to experience itself and the world. It is aware of the world and is also aware of its awareness, giving rise to the notion of "I". The awareness of the jīva takes place in the light of Pure Consciousness reflecting off its mind-intellect. The jīva lives under the false notion of independent individuality only when it has forgotten its true nature and, identifying with its body-mind-intellect, assumes it is the doer.

Why the World? Brahman is of the nature of *sat, cit, and ānanda*. Of these, *ānanda* is the creative aspect responsible for the projection of the world and its creatures. As the creator, Brahman is known as Īśvara. Īśvara does not create the world for happiness, but out of happiness, *ānanda*.

What is the purpose of my life? That depends on who we are. For God or a God-realized jīva, the world is but an entertaining sport; for a jīva yet to realize God, the same life serves as a classroom which will surely teach it the path to God-Realization through life's experiences.

What is the Fate of the World? This world will be "dissolved", that is absorbed back into the source it came from. *What is the fate of the jīvas?* Every jīva is a "child of immortality", *amṛtasya putrāḥ*, as the Upaniṣad addresses them. It is so called because a jīva is in reality that Brahman alone. As such every jīva is destined to shred the shroud of ignorance in which it is wrapped now and realize the Truth sooner or later.

Why evil? Evil is present so that goodness may shine and thus continue the cosmic play portraying Good over Evil to the amusement of *jñānis* and the edification of the worldly jīvas.

For what purpose is our action? The ultimate purpose of any of our actions is for own spiritual growth. Changes to the world caused by our actions are incidental, impermanent, and secondary. *Is our action driven by our free will?* It is driven by Prakṛti's laws and Īśvara's Will. *Is there a God and if so how is He involved in the affairs of the world?* As per Īśvara-Prakṛti Paradigm, without Īśvara's Will the world will remain just a possibility, and not an actuality. The fact that we experience a world, and not just the possibility of a world, shows that there must be a Will actively involved in the manifestation of that world. This Will belongs to God, Īśvara. In this aspect Īśvara the Creator, is said to be immanent in His creation. In His transcendent aspect, Īśvara is verily the Brahman which, in association with *Māyā*, the creative power, projects the world and the Prakṛti's Laws on the Cosmic Mind, *Mahat*. In this aspect, Īśvara is not of the world, but the world is of Him.

How do we know that the truth is as given above by Vedānta? This is a valid question. The theory spelled out by Vedānta is logically consistent and does answer basic questions of life, but one cannot assert on that basis alone that it must be the truth. We depend on scriptures as authority (*pramāṇa*) in postulating Brahman as the ultimate and only Reality and Existence-Consciousness-Bliss, *sat-cit-ānanda*, as its nature. By definition, the ultimate truth is something that cannot be proved but which must be "self-evident". If it can be proved, the proof used must contain a more fundamental truth. Consciousness fulfills this requirement as the ultimate truth since it does not need anything else to prove it and, further, nothing can be proved without it. The rest of the principles such as Īśvara, Prakṛti, jīvas etc are logically related to Brahman and they explain the world with a minimum number of concepts. Therefore, Vedānta as a whole is seen as a) being logically consistent; b) using concepts parsimoniously; c) explaining the created world and its creatures in a credible way; d) not being at odds with modern science; and finally, e) promoting a view of the world and a mode of living that brings welfare to all beings.

The last point mentioned, namely the ability of the Vedāntic vision to bring peace within and welfare to all, is of paramount significance. Truth, it is often said, must be necessarily simple and beautiful. We may in the same vein also insist that Truth, to be qualified as truth, must be a blessing for the entire creation and not a curse of any kind to any being. The truth espoused by Vedāntins, which emphasizes Universal Love as the *summum bonum* of worldly existence, does indeed qualify as Truth in this sense. It is "*satyaṁ, śivaṁ, sundaraṁ*", - Truth, Auspiciousness, and Beauty- all three rolled into One.

In the next chapter we discuss the "many splendored" thing that Love is.

CHAPTER 11

The Love That Cures All Ills

"The highest prayer in this world is service, the greatest devotion is loving the people around us; and the noblest character trait is divine compassion for all living creatures"
-Gurudev Swami Chinmayananda

"Where there is Love, no rule is required; where there is no Love, no rule is required. This is a law I have discovered"
- Guruji Swami Tejomayananda

"A human being is part of the whole, called by us "Universe", a part limited in time and space. He experiences himself, his thoughts and feelings as something separated from the rest – a kind of optical delusion of his consciousness. This delusion is a kind of prison for us, restricting us to our personal desires and to affection for a few persons nearest to us. Our task must be to free ourselves from this prison by widening our circle of compassion to embrace all living creatures and the whole of nature in its beauty"
- Albert Einstein

It is easy to fill hundreds of pages with quotes like these extolling the virtue and beauty of love. Love is one of those precious few things all religions readily agree on; they see Love as a, if not the, defining trait of spiritual evolution. The Love the great masters talk about is the "universal, unconditional love" we discussed at some length in previous chapters. We now explore this foundation of spirituality from different perspectives by making some obvious, and some not so obvious, statements that express the nature of Love.

Love is the Religion that God Practices: Religions demand strict observance of various rituals and practices by their followers. They do so in the name of their God, promising heaven for those faithfully adhering to the injunctions and hell for those who do not. But what religious practice does God follow? Does God go to church every Sunday or perform the daily *havan*? If not, what qualifies God as the ruler of the heaven?

The religious practices are meant for the mortals and not the God. After all God does not need anything from anyone else and nor is there any higher power to seek anything from. But there is one thing that mortals are required to practice that God also practices in abundance. That is Love. God is of the nature of Love and hence practicing Love is natural to God. It involves no deliberate effort, unlike in the case of ordinary jīvas. Endowed with infinite love for all creatures and possessing infinite knowledge, God is known in all religions for just compassion. The same view prevails in Vedāntic teaching also, even though its concept of God, Īśvara, is not necessarily anthropomorphic. In our previous discussions, Īśvara, the *saguṇa Brahman*, is characterized as the abode of Love and Knowledge.

In the Hindu tradition, a renunciate, *sannyāsi,* whose goal is the realization of oneness with the Brahman, is also relieved from most of the religious obligations. Such a spiritually detached soul does not seek anything from this world or heaven, instead must devote all its effort to purify the mind whereby its capacity to love all beings can grow.

Love is its own reward: Love is the fundamental law of spirituality. That law, which we called as the "Law of Love", states that as a jīva progresses more and more towards the ideal of unconditional love for all beings, it suffers less and less in this world. Thus spiritual love is its own reward; it is synonymous with peace and joy. In spiritual evolution, Love is the way and the goal - the abode of Īśvara- is also Love.

Love is the basis of all morality: All religions see in Love a moral imperative. Other moral virtues, such as truth, non-injury, charity, and cheerfulness, follow from Love. On the contrary, without Love, other virtues cannot be practiced. Stated another way, absent Love, all actions are potentially immoral. With love, no other spiritual practice is needed;

without love all religiosity is but a pretense. *"Owe nothing to anyone, except to love one another. The one who loves has fulfilled the other law. For the law says, "do not commit adultery, do not murder, do not steal, do not covet," and any other commandment, is summed up in this very word: "you shall love your neighbor as yourself...... Love is the fulfillment of the law."* [140]

Love of humanity is Love of the Lord: Gurudev Swami Chinmayanandaji constantly reminded his students that "Service to the country is service to the Lord of Lords and devotion to the people is devotion to the Supreme Self". Vedānta teaches us that the world and its beings are manifestations of the Divinity. No service can be rendered to that Divinity without being of service to the world. As the saying goes "*jana seva janārdana seva*", meaning *service to people is service to the Lord.* The true seeker is a servant of the Lord and hence is ever at the service of the world. It does not matter if the world returns the favor to the seeker with material rewards for his/her service or not. The true reward for such service, as we have seen, is spiritual progress which is better than any material reward. Material rewards cannot be carried over to the next birth, but spiritual rewards can be. To be true, the love and service of the seeker must be all encompassing and universal. Doors to the heaven remain closed for one whose love excludes any being.

The E-F Principle

There are many simple phrases that teachers have used to summarize Vedānta. The great statement "*tat tvam asi*" or "You are That" and Adi Sankara's "*Brahma satyaṁ, jagat mithyā*" are well known. "Shut up and get out" was how Gurudev Swami Chinmayananda once summarized Vedānta to a rather startled questioner. Another way to remember the essence of Vedānta's spiritual advice is by what we may call the "E-F Principle". The diagram below may resemble the several figures employed earlier in the mathematical representation of spiritual detachment. But here, the symbols have a different meaning. The letters E and F stand for "Empty" and "Fill", somewhat like in the gas gauge in a car. But empty what and fill what?

Empty the mind of *thoughts that lead to worldly attachment.*

Fill the heart with *Love that is universal and firmly based on Knowledge.*

Empty the mind of thoughts and fill the heart with Love.

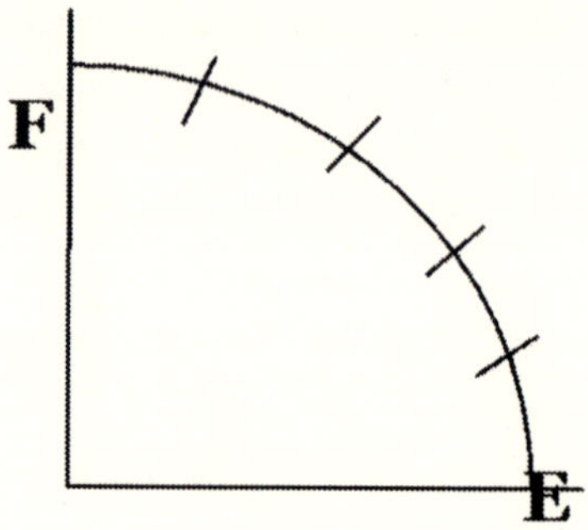

The E-F Gauge

This indeed is essence of the various *sādhanas* prescribed in the scriptures. Emptying the mind of thoughts is the way to detachment, but it needs to be simultaneous with filling the heart with Love.

But, is it possible to free the mind of all thoughts? If so, is it possible to carry on transactions of life without thoughts? These and similar questions have been extensively commented upon and are particularly relevant to the art of meditation. Scriptures and teachers do assert that one can reach a state of "*nirvikalpa samādhi*" where all thoughts have ceased but without losing awareness of the Blissful Self. Reaching that ultimate state is a gradual process of learning to control the mind. Ironically it requires the help of the very mind we are trying to control and finally conquer. Normally our thoughts flow outwards to worldly objects. Such thoughts bind us to the world if we allow ourselves to be caught up in the thoughts, the consequence being suffering. The spiritual practices of *viveka* and *vairāgya* help us gradually replace thoughts of the world with thoughts about our true nature as the witnessing Self of these thoughts. As Swami Chinmayanandaji often remarked, by this practice the quantity of thoughts are decreased while the quality of thoughts are increased; that is, thoughts become more and more directed inwards. Continued practice results in increasing ability in us to rise above the mind and be a witness to the mind. Life's activities go on uninterrupted, while remaining attached to true Self.

This process has been compared by many teachers to the art of surfing on the ocean waves. To be caught up with the waves is to invite danger. But to ride the waves without being drawn into them is to enjoy the bliss of the ocean. The thoughts which arise in the mind are like waves in Consciousness, the witnessing Self. Sogyal Rinpoche, a Tibetan

Buddhist scholar, describes the process of surfing the mind thus: "So whatever thoughts and emotions arise, allow them to rise and settle, likes waves in the ocean. Whatever you find yourself thinking, let that thought rise and settle, without any constraint. Don't grasp at it, feed it, or indulge it; don't cling to it and don't try to solidify it. Neither follow the thoughts nor invite them; be like the ocean looking at its own waves, or the sky gazing down on the clouds that pass through it."[141].

Viveka and *vairāgya*, if correctly practiced, will lead simultaneously to decreased attachment to the world (Non-Self) and increased attachment to the Self. Getting rid of thoughts from the mind without Love in the heart is not spiritual detachment and, if followed, would lead to an unhappy, zombie-like existence. This sort of detachment is called "*śmaśāna vairāgya*", that is, "detachment of the burial ground", to indicate that it is often the result of dejection and disaffection with the world after some traumatic experience. True spiritual detachment from the world implies attachment to the Self with its connotations of Love and Knowledge. There is no room for unhappiness there. Therefore a yogī who has transcended the mind and gained the vision of Self has his heart filled with universal love; that yogī is a blessing to the world and is himself in Bliss.

Śreyas and Preyas

Love is thus the essence of spirituality; but that love is also necessary even at the materialistic level for the every-day-world to go on. "Love makes the world go around" is a popular adage. An infant cannot survive without mother's love. A community or nation cannot function without self-less work, charity, and philanthropy of some members at least some of the time. The birth of many nations has been marked by the sacrifice of its many heroes. Such self-less dedication will not be possible unless there is an element of love to support it.

If this were an ideal world where all jīvas possessed universal, unconditional Love, then that love alone would have been sufficient to keep the world working smoothly. But the world we live in is far from that ideal. The love that we do find in the material world is not the spiritually perfect "unconditional, universal" love. It is not unconditional as there is some degree of selfishness behind most of our actions. Even rarer it is to find universal love; as a rule, our love is restricted to our family or some other group of people we closely identify with, to the exclusion of others. Love for what we identify with is often reinforced with hostility for others. That is the sad truth.

The only way to secure a semblance of peace and harmony in such a world is to impose a regime of law and order, inducements and penalties, cops and judges. The voluminous penal codes and extensive network of courts of law required to keep order in the society attest to our failure to cultivate Love. Even with all the laws in the book, there is no lack of crime and corruption in all corners of the world. This is not a surprise since, as Guruji Swami Tejomayanandaji says "Where there is Love, no law is required; where there is no Love, no law is required", meaning absent love, no law can really work.

Vedānta is rich in its practical understanding of human behavior. Kathopaniṣad suggests that motivation for human activities fall in one of two broad categories, *preyas* and *śreyas.*

"*The good (śreyas) is one thing; the pleasant (preyas) is another. These two having different purposes, bind a man. Of these two, it is well for him who takes hold of the good; he who chooses the pleasant misses his end. The good and the pleasant approach a man; the wise man considers and distinguishes the two. Wisely does he prefer the good to the pleasant, but a fool chooses the pleasant for its worldly good.*"[142]

Actions under the influence of *preyas* are undertaken to satisfy one's desires and are sometimes also called as *kāmya karma*s or desire-prompted actions. On the other hand *śreyas* prompts actions undertaken for the sake of the welfare of the family, nation etc and are selfless actions or *niṣkāma karma*. Generally speaking, *kāmya karma* is seen as a path of spiritual devolution leading in the long run to discontent. In contrast, *niṣkāma karma* can contribute to spiritual evolution and happiness all around, provided they are performed out of love. We should distinguish this from actions performed for reasons such as fear of punishment, sheer economic necessity, or social pressure. These actions, which fall into the category of "*kartavya karma*", or obligatory duties, may also do good to the larger community but do not have the same spiritual merit as selfless actions performed out of Love.

Modern Economies

Besides a multitude of laws, there is one other powerful tool man has been forced to invent: Money, the grease that keeps the wheels of modern economy turning. "Moneytheism" is an aptly coined word to signify the stature of money in modern economies approaching godhood in its power and prevalence.

What is an economy and what ultimately is the measure of success of an economic system? I am not a professional economist, but I think it is not incorrect to say that an economic system is there to ensure that the society produces, and makes available in a timely manner, all the goods and services *needed* by its members. Further, to be efficient, it must do this with minimum waste of human and natural resources. The key to the success of an economic system lies in its ability to motivate people to perform economically necessary functions in an efficient and timely manner.

Communism was one of the two major economic systems of the past century, and it failed by ignoring consumer desires and the material benefits of *kāmya karma*. Its experiments with "cooperatives" to tap into the potential of *kartavya karma* also failed when people were in effect forced to work for state-owned enterprises run by corrupt party bureaucrats. In sharp contrast, the other major economic philosophy of our times, namely capitalism, has succeeded spectacularly by whipping up endless desires in individuals and leveraging the power of *kāmya karma* to raise human activity to very high levels.

However, the sweet success of capitalism is merely a sugar coating on the bitter pill inside. General happiness among the populace simply does not track the GDP of a nation. Take the US economy for example. Amidst a general prosperity that is unprecedented in history, there is also a high degree of constant insecurity and anxiety affecting people of all professions and segments of society. The financial crisis of 2008 was a grim reminder of the flaws inherent in the system. Crises are only to be expected when short-term profits and bottom line considerations dictate human relations instead of long-term trust and love. Another paradox is that, in spite of the tremendous productivity gain brought on by automation, people are working longer hours today than they did a few decades ago. A reason is that all capable people are required to be gainfully employed in a society where every man is to himself. But high levels of employment along with high productivity is possible only when the society produces, and people are persuaded to consume, an ever increasing array of goods and services, whether they really *need* it or not.

The result is the ugly spectacle of over consumption that we see today in many parts of the world. A significant percentage of what is produced and consumed is wasteful as it is unnecessary for meeting any real need of humans, or, like narcotic drugs, even outright harmful to them. The impact of over consumption on the environment and ecology is a well documented fact. It is sad that so many people should be working so hard to produce so much waste and poison and admire it as a successful economy with full employment, technological progress, and high standard of living!

Is the new millennium likely to see the emergence of a new economic system that is more stable and sensible? As societies become aware of the painful problems associated with present day economic systems, it is possible that they will look for new ways to run their economy without the gut-wrenching roller coaster cycles of boom and bust or ecological destruction. We can only speculate what shape the new system will take, but can argue, as we do below, that a system which taps more into the potential power of altruism, that is *niṣkāma karma* based on Love, may be an answer.

Money is synonymous with security and power. Money can buy almost any good or service and thus gives a much-needed sense of security to those who possess it. Money is also a source of power and influence for those who have it in abundance. In all countries and at all times, it is usually people of wealth who rule the land and conversely it is people who rule that amass wealth. The inducement to acquire money is therefore very strong. But this strong motivation is both a blessing and a threat. It is a positive blessing to the extent money makes people engage in productive work. It poses a threat when some people are motivated to amass wealth by any means, fair or unfair, and use the power of wealth to dominate the society. Greed to acquire more money and fear of losing money already acquired are the underlying psychological currents in a money-driven society. Depending on which sentiment predominates, the economy lurches from boom to bust. There is seldom stability and without stability there is insecurity at all levels of the society. As Lord Krishna asks

"*aśāntasya kutaḥ sukhaṁ*?"

"*Where is happiness for one not in peace?*" Indeed can there be real happiness in society lacking security and peace?

Money is quite efficient in getting work out of people, but the problem is that it appeals to the baser instincts of greed and fear in the human being. As such money oriented pursuits are seldom spiritually ennobling. Sri Ramakrishna was never tired of expressing his aversion to money and avoided even touching money [143].

But is there any real alternative to money which is efficient as an inducement to productive work but at the same time spiritually rewarding?

What Money Can Do, Love Can Do Better

Universal, unconditional love is a *potential* alternative to money as an engine to power an economy. It is a potential that in fact is realized to some extent today, but whose wider application will have to await a sea change in the spiritual awareness of the average citizen and government.

The power of love to harness work is most readily seen in the functioning of an ideal family. The love that the parents bear toward their children is sufficient motivation for them to work day and night. They work so that the children, and not just themselves, are well provided for. They endure many discomforts and hardships with a fortitude made possible by their dedication to the family. There is little or no money exchanged for services within the family but everything is done out of love and a sense of duty.

Besides ideal nuclear families, there are numerous other institutions where love and duty energize members to work with selfless dedication. In most countries around the world, especially developed countries, volunteers contribute significantly to a nation's economy. Non-profit and non-governmental organizations play a vital role in espousing and advancing legal, social, religious, health, educational, and environmental causes. The work of these organizations is typically sustained by the efforts of a large corps of unpaid or underpaid volunteers. They bring to the table a wide variety of professional and technical skills. Their rank can include doctors and lawyers, accountants and managers, nurses and social workers whose work normally would command high salaries. A Johns Hopkins study estimates the output of the non-profit sector in the United States at US$1.1 trillion (or nearly ten percent of the national income) in 2002. The study also puts the number of volunteers in this sector at 10.6 million full-time equivalent workers. The dollar value of their service, assuming a nominal $50,000 per year, would be more than half a trillion dollars.

Huge as it is, even this monetary picture does not tell the full story of the value and valor behind volunteerism. Volunteers work for worthy, humane causes that profit seeking enterprises and governmental institutions turn away from. They work often in very difficult physical conditions in the midst of famine, natural disasters, and war. There is little to gain by way of material reward; on the other hand, there is every chance of risking comfort, money, life and limb in the course of the service.

What can make such altruism possible if not the love these workers have for their cause? That love may not be universal, but it has to be unconditional in order to sustain work with little or no reward. This is in stark contrast to what typically goes on in a money-driven enterprise. The work put in by the employees is for wages in fulfillment of a contract; there is no love lost in the employer- employee relationship. These workers are in fact receiving miserly spiritual rewards, since as Gītā says [144]

"*kṛpaṇāḥ phala hetavaḥ*"

Where money is the goal, what ensues is tortured labor that enslaves. Where selfless love is the motive, the result is a work of joy that liberates.

Love is Not a Zero-Sum Game

Thus, love is not only a possible alternative to money as an engine to drive economic activities, but a superior one at that. One basic undeniable fact about money is that it is a limited commodity; it has no value if it were unlimited. Money-based transactions are therefore "zero-sum games" in the sense that somebody's gain is necessarily at the expense of another person's loss. Therefore, when money is the sole measure of rewards in a transaction, there is competition among the parties to the transaction, each vying to maximize its reward or minimize its loss. Competition can lead to mistrust and to unfair, unethical practices. At the end, the outcome of the competition can leave everyone feeling hurt and dissatisfied.

Love, on the contrary, is not a zero-sum game; it is in this respect just the opposite of money. By giving love, the love one has does not diminish; rather it grows. Therefore cooperation is natural when people are engaged in a common selfless effort "*yajña*" out of love; they do not and need not act in competition and at cross-purposes. The outcome is much more likely to be beneficial materially and spiritually to all involved.

Money and love differ in other ways too. Money is not a goal in itself even though many of us work for it all our lives. Usefulness of money lies in its ability to acquire material goods, services, power and prestige. Love, on the other hand, is its own reward. Love practiced for acquiring something else is not unconditional love.

Work done for money can be drudgery, demeaning and devoid of the joy of creativity. True creativity such as seen in the works of poets, artists, and scientists, is possible only if there is love for the work. In fact love can transform any work into an act of joy. A young mother attends joyfully to the needs of her baby however menial the chores might be.

Love Based Economies?

Thus, in theory at least, love can replace money as the fuel to power an economy. All human activities- whether they are in trade, agriculture, administration, technology or arts- can be potentially accomplished through the power of love. The work efficiency and productivity in such an economy can be as high as in a money-driven economy. Gītā's teaching

"*yogaḥ karmasu kauśalaṁ*"

implies that work done with love is naturally efficient. Absent the greed, fear and destructive competition associated with money, there is no risk of panic-driven market crashes or greed-driven boom markets. The threat of environmental and ecologic disasters posed by over consumption can also be more easily averted when greed and competition are not factors. Democracy and human rights, which today often take a back seat to economic considerations, will naturally flourish in a love-based economy. But the greatest benefit of all of such a system is the justice, peace and happiness that one can rightly expect to flow out of an economy working on a "*yajña*" spirit.

All this seem at least theoretically possible, though this ideal condition has never been even approximated in recorded human history. Does that mean it is not ever achievable anytime in future? The answer depends on how optimistic one is about the evolution of human beings in the centuries ahead. Given our past, it is easy to be pessimistic and write off such a rosy future as a mere fantasy or as a dead-on-arrival concept. But then there also visionaries like Sri Aurobindo who sees the forces of natural evolution leading to a more spiritually enlightened, and less materialistic, society in the future [145]. In between these opposites lies perhaps the more wise and pragmatic view: Let us not waste our energy speculating whether mankind as a whole will become more benevolent or not. Instead, it should be possible for societies to support and strengthen the reach and extent of the existing volunteer organizations so that their contribution to the economy is not ten percent, but thirty or forty. Personally each of us can get involved in volunteer work to help our own spiritual evolution, while also helping the world at large. There is, even now, numerous organizations engaged in good social work that need more help from selfless, dedicated volunteers. Lack of workers holds back these organizations from achieving their full potential.

A solution to this human resource problem is to educate individuals, both young and old, in spiritual principles by which they may clearly see the benefits of selfless work to oneself and the society. The importance of spiritual education cannot be over emphasized and it is a topic which we will address next in the concluding chapter of this book.

CHAPTER 12

The Path Ahead-
Research and Education in Spirituality

It is hoped that the discussions in this book have demonstrated that

- Spirituality can be studied and taught as a science in its own right, with minimum appeal to religious conventions;
- A mathematical approach has the potential to make our understanding of spirituality more precise and deep, thus helping to communicate the scientific principles behind spirituality with confidence and clarity
- Spirituality and modern science are not only not in conflict, but are complementary and mutually supportive; and
- Educating people, especially the youth, in spiritual principles is of paramount importance in countering the numerous negative forces that threaten mankind with crises and calamities.

The theory of vāsanas and the concept of spiritual detachment, it has been shown, are central to a mathematical description of spiritual evolution. The implications of the theory are by and large consistent with the teachings of Vedānta and this can be taken as a validation of our overall modeling approach. The Law of Love, which is an immediate and primary result of the theory, is echoed by all religions. Interestingly, the concept of time has a pivotal role in our theory of spirituality as it does in Physics. Many scientists and philosophers have previously commented on similarities between Vedānta and modern physics. Therefore, the many parallel features that have been shown to exist in the theory of spirituality advanced in this book and in Einstein's theory of time and space should not come as a total surprise. However, we must hasten to add that the validity of Vedāntic truths does not in any way depend on the veracity of today's scientific theories. The fact that our theory uses Vedāntic principles also should not restrict its relevance in any way, since these principles are universal, with no religious or cultural context.

Research In Spirituality

Notwithstanding its possible accomplishments, the theory of spirituality presented here before the reader is not the final, definitive, word on the subject, but only a first step in opening a potentially new field for exploration, discussion and research. Research in spirituality will be necessarily a multi-disciplinary effort and it can in the long-term make a positive impact on the world. There is opportunity here for students of philosophy, psychology, religion, mathematics and science to collaborate. The work will involve not only building new edifices defining spirituality as a science, but also dismantling the old historical scaffoldings binding spirituality to unnecessary religious dogma.

Ideally, as in other branches of science, the implications of the mathematical theory need to be verified through observations. The Law of Love, for example, states that an individual's measure of contentment in daily life increases with his or her unconditional love and understanding for other beings. The statement makes intuitive sense, yet it is nevertheless a hypothesis that can benefit from scientific verification through carefully designed studies. This will most likely require developing psychological measures and neurobiological correlates for the underlying spiritual concepts such as detachment, universal love, contentment in daily life, and vāsanas. The field of Psychometrics, with its array of techniques for measuring various human psychological traits, will be valuable in such research. Functional MRI and such other modern brain imaging techniques have already been applied by researchers studying spirituality and could be useful to verify the various results of the mathematical models. A second result implied by the theory that could be potentially tested is the observation that as a jīva evolves higher in the spiritual path, the personal will power required to stay in the witness mode decreases.

Further work is required in some key areas in order to complete the mathematical theory. The model presented in Chapters 5-8 represents the "feed-forward" process in Fig. 2.6 of how detachment determines the probability of identifying with the Self or Non-Self at any given moment. However, we do not have yet a mathematical basis to describe the "feed-back" process which determines how an individual's vāsanas and detachment are modulated by spiritual practice. It is reasonable to assume that it is the elements of suffering and knowledge inherent in life experiences that are important here, but we do not have at this time a model to represent the cause-effect relationships involved. Also, as discussed in the chapter on Sri Ramana's Principle of Personal Will, the will power of a jīva figures prominently in its spiritual development. But we lack a sound basis to even define this spiritual will power of a jīva.

Developing techniques to estimate the vāsana function will mark a major breakthrough in understanding human spirituality and will bring this field closer to other branches of objective science. Psychological tests currently in use for measuring a wide variety of human traits offer the best prospects here, but a lot more work needs to be done before this potential can be realized.

The nature of cosmic time is another area in need of further study and clarification. We have treated cosmic time as continuous for the sake of simplicity, but this does not seem to be a necessary condition for the overall theory to hold. In a similar vein, the vāsana spectrum, x, could also be considered as discrete rather than continuous. The mathematics of the discrete case is probably straightforward, but has not been addressed in this work. The discrete cosmic time case, in which changes to the cosmos occur at discrete points in time, has interesting implications. Appendix 3 has some speculations on this question.

The discussions in this book have occasionally suggested other problems that may interest the mathematically inclined reader. Some examples are:

1) For the illustrative case shown in Fig. 6.10, it was found that $\tau(t^*) = G(t^*)$. For what general class of progress functions does this result hold and what is its significance?
2) It was shown using the example in Fig. 6.11 that the depth of meditation is more important than its duration or length. How general is this statement?
3) The Eq.7.2 proposing a probabilistic equivalent for the spiritual

evolution of a jīva suggests that the jīva, at any given moment, is like a quantum entity which can be in one of two states: Self with probability $\sin^2\theta(t)$ and Non-Self with probability $\cos^2\theta(t)$. Is it possible to formulate a rigorous quantum mechanical equivalent to this probabilistic model? If so, what could be the spiritual significance of the model?

Education in Spirituality

The vital need for education in spirituality has been emphasized at many points in this book. Materialism, though by itself not an evil, can be a recipe for calamity unless it is properly balanced by a holistic spiritual outlook. Today, education in spirituality is imparted mainly through religious institutions. The quality of the education suffers in the process since religious messages get priority over spiritual truths. What is unifying and ennobling in the spiritual teachings tends to be overlooked in favor of ideas that promote respective religious agenda. The sad result is that, instead of uniting mankind under a common spiritual banner, the present day religious education often perpetuates barriers that artificially divide people from people and at times even sets one group of people against another.

This must change and can be changed. It can be changed if it is appreciated that spirituality is a science rather than the appendage of any religion, and therefore it can be taught as a science with little reference to any particular religion. This is the other message that this book endeavors to convey. It should be possible to put together a robust program for youth in schools and college that teaches the basics of spirituality. It would teach the students the essentially identical spiritual nature of all human beings and impress on them the fact that the proper nurture of our spiritual personality is necessary for true happiness, peace and harmony. A mathematical approach, such as in this book, is useful in communicating clearly the underlying principles, but is not an absolute necessity. The course will necessarily include relevant material from sociology, psychology and cognitive sciences and draw upon the accumulating scientific evidence on the efficacy of meditation and other spiritual practices. Exposure to emerging concepts in Physics and Biology will make the students comfortable that spirituality and science are indeed in agreement. A survey of human history to illustrate the dangers of material prosperity without social conscience, and religion without spirituality, would also be pertinent. An objective review of world religions will be a very useful part of the course but it should be directed towards respect for all religions and understanding how they can help in spiritual development.

It will be a golden day indeed if and when universities and schools develop such a scientifically robust curriculum in spirituality and begin teaching the facts about that most basic of all human traits- namely, spirituality- to their students.

APPENDICES

Appendices

Appendix 1: *A Law of Conservation of Information?*

The decrease over time in the orderliness and information content of the material world dictated by the Second Law of Thermodynamics occurs even as jīvas living in that world gain in spiritual knowledge. It is as though there is a Law of Conservation of Information at the cosmic level where the diminishing order in the material world is compensated by the increasing spiritual knowledge. Jīvas generally evolve from low to higher forms of life. The higher life forms are more spiritually evolved and also usually demand more order (information) from the material world. The experiences of life are the stepping stones in this spiritual ascent; it is as if jīvas convert their experiences in the material world into spiritual growth. In gaining worldly experiences, they contribute, as do all life forms, to increasing disorder of the external, material world; in gaining spiritual knowledge, they increase the order in the internal, spiritual realm.

The second law of thermodynamics is a statistical law in the sense that the decrease in order over time is a statistical expectation. There is the possibility that during some interval of time the degree of order could actually increase despite the odds against it. However, in the long run, disorder will catch-up with the universe. In the same way, the spiritual progress of a jīva is also an expectation over the long run. In the short term, a jīva may regress spiritually depending on how it handles life's experiences. The spiritual practices prescribed in Vedānta and world religions are intended to provide the know-how for a jīva to meet experiences intelligently so that it may progress in its spiritual path rather than fall behind. But lacking this know-how, or lacking the necessary will power, the jīva may behave in such a way that it actually sinks deeper into ignorance from its encounters with the world. Unintelligent ways of living reinforce the vāsanas, instead of exhausting them. Such occasional regression is a short term feature, progress being the norm for the long-term. The negative feedback implied in the doctrine of *karma* is one main reason why this is so: bad *karma*s will sooner or later produce negative experience, forcing the jīva to mend its ways.

Appendix 2: *The Logic Behind One, and Only One, Consciousness*

"We are all zombies" is what Dennett finds himself saying to express his view that there is nothing really special about the human beings to set them apart from artificially intelligent robots. But this only begs the question: Can a zombie *know* it is a zombie to make such an assertion? A zombie cannot have any personal knowledge of truth. So, if it does "know" it is a zombie, then it is not really a zombie! If it does not know, but still makes this assertion on its own authority, then the statement is clearly unreliable. The statement will have some validity only if it was prompted from "outside" by some entity (e.g. a robot may make such a statement, having been so instructed by an outside programmer.) Now, can this outside entity itself be a zombie? If it is, we have the same credibility problem with the statement- if that outside entity cannot know itself, much less is the chance that it can know if something else is a zombie or not. We thus conclude that there must be at least one non-zombie for a statement "*We are all zombies*" to have validity. In other words, Dennett's statement is self-contradictory.

Therefore there is at a least one non-Z, where by Z we mean a Zombie, or an insentient thing, and by non-Z we denote the opposite, a conscious being. Also, one non-Z is sufficient for every Z to say (but not know) "I am Z" or "I am non-Z", if this sole non-Z has access to "program" every Z. With one non-Z, all statements by Z's are possible, whether they are true or not. Hence the Advaitic view (that there is only one non-Z) is sufficient. The dualistic assumption of multiple non-Z's is at least superfluous; it is also non-verifiable by jīvas since the Z or non-Z nature of one jīva cannot be ascertained by another jīva.

Appendix 3: *Duration Of Brahmāji's Brief Deviation From State Of Perfect Awareness and the Planck's Constant*

In our representation of the changing cosmos shown in Fig. 5.3 etc, the changes occur at regular intervals- say every λ units of cosmic time. Taking a discrete view of creation, we assume that the changes occur during a brief burst lasting h units of time. After each such change, the cosmos is at "rest" for the remaining (λ-h) units of time in each interval. We can visualize these rhythmic changes as though they occur to the steady beat of a drum. λ is the time interval between two consecutive beats of the drum. Each beat itself is a brief pulse lasting h units, a fraction of the interval λ. The cosmos changes from its present state to the next during this brief pulse lasting h units of time; it is followed by a much longer period of (λ-h) units of time when the cosmos is at rest. Successive cosmic changes can be shown now as a train of pulses occurring at the rate of 1 every λ units of time (Fig. A.1). The duration, h, (or "width") of each pulse is a small fraction of λ.

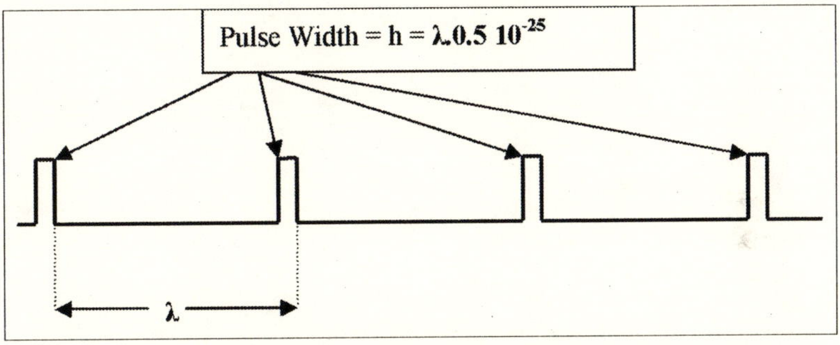

Fig A.1: Sequence of Pulses Showing Successive Cosmic Changes

Now, the fraction h/ λ can be related with some justification to the minute fraction of time when *Brahmāji*'s attention is devoted to the business of creation. This fraction, as seen in Chapter 6, is 0.5. 10^{-25}; on this basis the pulse width h is λ. 0.5. 10^{-25} time units. What we need now is an estimate of λ.

The interval λ is extremely small since the cosmos keeps changing at an incredibly fast pace. We can get an idea of its size from the very high frequencies associated with some of the extremely energetic particles in the universe. The wave length of one of the highest energy radiations known, the so-called "Pure Energy" or Gamma Rays, is 1 x 10^{-9} cm. The time it takes to travel one wave length is (wavelength in cm) /c where c= speed of light = $0.3x10^{11}$ cm/sec. For Gamma rays, this time is about $3x10^{-20}$ sec. Therefore λ is at least as small as $3x10^{-20}$ sec. and the pulse width h is at least as small as $1.5x\ 10^{-45}$ sec.

Interestingly enough, this quantity turns out to be very close to the *Planck's time* (smallest measure of time as per modern physics), namely 10^{-44} seconds. The close correspondence is indeed curious but, given the speculative nature of the reasoning behind it, could be a mere coincidence. The idea is presented here only to suggest possibilities for further study, should they be warranted.

Finally we note that the separation between two consecutive waves in the $\mathscr{M}$-space, denoted by λ, is more like a metric of the space-time, rather than pure time as we assumed above. We could as well assume λ to be wavelength measured in cm rather than time measured in seconds. This would lead to a similar conclusion about *Planck's length.*

References

1. Tejomayananda, Swami. *"Hindu Culture- An Introduction"*, Chinmaya Mission Trust, Mumbai, 1993.
2. Boole, M. *"Indian Thought and Western Science in the Nineteenth Century"*, 1901. As quoted by Jonardon Ganeri in *"Indian Logic: A Reader"*; Curzon Publishing, Richmond, UK, 2001.
3. Chidambaram, Raju. *"Science, Spirituality, and Religion"*, Bhavan's Journal, Bharatiya Vidya Bhavan, Mumbai, Sep 30, 2009.
4. Schrödinger, Erwin. *"What is Life"*, pp 93, Cambridge University Press, 1963.
5. Hourihan, Paul Ph.D. *"Why Vedānta"*, www.VedānticShoresPress.com.
6. Alexander, C., Boyer, R.W., and Alexander, V. *"Higher States of Consciousness in the Vedic Psychology of Maharishi Mahesh Yogi: A Theoretical Introduction and Research Review"* Modern Science and Vedic Science, Vol. 1, No. 1, 1987.
7. Underwood, Lynn and Teresi, Jean. *"The Daily Spiritual Experience Scale: Theoretical Description, Reliability and Exploratory Factor Analysis"*, Annals of Behavioral Medicine, Vol. 24, Number 1, 2002.
8. Chinmayananda, Swami. *"Talks on Sankara's Vivekachoodamani"*, v.125, Central Chinmaya Mission Trust, Bombay, 1976.
9. Boyer, Robert. *"Bridge to Unity"*, Institute for Advanced Research, Malibu, CA, 2008.
10. Chinmayananda, Swami. *"The Holy Geeta"*, Ch. XII, v.5, Central Chinmaya Mission, Mumbai, 1985.
11. Watts, Alan. *"The Supreme Identity"*, Vintage Books, NY, 1972.
12. Chinmayananda, Swami. *"Hymn to Sri Dakshinamoorthy of Adi Sankara"*, Central Chinmaya Mission Trust, Bombay, 1981
13. Chinmayananda, Swami. *"Vedānta- the Science of Life" Vols. I-III.*, Chinmaya Mission Trust, Mumbai, 1979.
14. Hourihan, Paul, Ph.D. *"Children of Immortal Bliss: A New Perspective*

on our True Identity based on the Ancient Vedānta Philosophy of India", Vedāntic Shore Press, Redding, CA 2008.

15. Chinmayananda, Swami. " *Discourses On Taittariya Upaniṣad"*, Ch III, v.1, Chinmaya Mission Trust, Bombay, 2nd Edition, 1992.

16. Chinmayananda, Swami. *"Atma Bodh"*, v.6, Chinmaya Publications Trust, Madras, 1979.

17. Chaitanya, Svarupa. *"Tattva Bodha of Sankaracharya"*, Central Chinmaya Mission Trust, Bombay, 1986.

18. Swahananda, Swami. *"Pancadasi of Sri Vidyaranya Swami"* Chapter 15, v. 17-19, Sri Ramakrishna Math, Madras, 1967.

19. *The Holy Geeta, op.cit,* Chapter XVIII, v.61.

20. Chinmayananda, Swami. *"Discourses on Mandukya Upaniṣad with Gaudapada's Karika"*, v. 6, Central Chinmaya Mission Trust, Bombay, 1953.

21. Jung, C. as quoted in Joseph Campbell's *"The Mythic Image"*, pp. 362, Princeton University Press, Princeton, NJ 1974.

22. Tejomayananda, Swami. *"Sri Kapila Gītā"* Ch. II, v. 5, Central Chinmaya Mission Trust, Mumbai, 1996.

23. Tejomayananda, Swami. *"Yoga Vaasishtha Saara Sangrahah"*, Ch.3, v.7, Central Chinmaya Mission Trust, 1998.

24. *Talks on Sankara's Vivekachoodamani, op.cit,* v. 218.

25. *The Holy Geeta, op.cit,* Ch XIII, v.22.

26. Tejomayananda, Swami. *Sri Kapil Gītā, op.cit,* Ch II, v 6 and 7.

27. *The Holy Geeta, op.cit,* Ch II, v. 14.

28. *Ibid.* Ch IX, v.7.

29. Krauss, Lawrence and Scherrer, Robert. *"The End of Cosmology?"* Scientific American, March 2008.

30. *The Holy Geeta, op.cit,* Ch IX, v.21.

31. *Atma Bodh, op.cit,* v. 3.

32. *The Holy Geeta, op.cit,* Ch XIII, v.12.

33. Chinmayananda, Swami. *"Discourses on Mundakopaniṣad"* Ch I, Sec I, v. 4 and 5, Central Chinmaya Mission Trust, Bombay, Reprint 1988.

34. *The Holy Geeta, op.cit,* Ch VI, v.29.

35. Chinmayananda, Swami. " *Commentary on Aparokshanubhuti"* v. 128, Central Chinmaya Mission Trust, Mumbai, 1985.

36. Chidambaram, Raju. *"Vedānta of Decision Making"*, Chinmaya Management Review, Bangalore Vol. 4, No. 1, Dec 2000.

37. Chidambaram, Raju. *"Unraveling Uncertainty"* in *"India's Intellectual Traditions and Contributions to the World"*, ed. Bal Ram Singh et al, World Assn. for Vedic Studies, 2009.

38. Koza, John. et al *"Evolving Invention"*, Scientific American, Feb 2003.

39. Sri Mata Amritanandamayi Devi. "*For My Children*", pp 79-80, Mata Amritanandamayi Mission Trust, Amritapuri P.O., Kerala 1986.
40. Nikhilananda, Swami. "*Ramakrishna: Prophet of the New India*", NY, 1948. (as quoted by Alan Watts in "*The Supreme Identity*", pp. 125, *op. cit.*)
41. *The Holy Geeta, op.cit,* Ch III, v. 27.
42. Sir John Maddox "*The Unexpected Science to Come*", pp 62-67, Scientific American, Dec 1999.
43. Libet, Benjamin. "*The Experimental Evidence for a Subjective Referral of a Sensory Experience Backwards in Time,*" *Philosophy of Science* 48, 182-97, 1981.
44. Mudaliar Devaraja. "*Gems From Bhagavan*", pp 35, Sri Ramanasramam, Tiruvannamalai, 1965.
45. Wolfson, Richard. "*Einstein's Relativity and the Quantum Revolution*", pp 59-63, The Teaching Company, Chantilly, VA, 2000.
46. Chalmers, David. "*Facing Up to the Problem of Consciousness*", Journal of Consciousness Studies, 2 (3), pp 200-219, 1995.
47. Zeman, Adam. "*Consciousness- A user's guide*", pp 286- 290, Yale University Press, New Haven and London, 2002.
48. *ibid.* pp. 290.
49. *ibid.* pp. 291.
50. *ibid.* pp. 295.
51. *ibid.* pp. 296.
52. Dennett, Daniel C. "*Consciousness Explained*", Little, Brown & Company, 1991.
53. Noe, Alva. "*Out of Our Heads: Why You Are Not Your Brain and Other Lessons From the Biology of Consciousness*", Hill and Wang 2009. (As quoted in Scientific American, March 2009.)
54. Eccles J.C. "*How the Self Controls its Brain*", Springer-Verlag, New York, 1994.
55. Smythies, J. "*Time, Space, Consciousness*", Journal of Consciousness Studies, Vol.10, No. 3, 2003.
56. Goswami, Amit. "*Physics of the Soul*", Hampton Road Publishing, Charlottesville, VA, 2001.
57. Deshmukh, Vinod. "*The Astonishing Brain and the Holistic Consciousness- Neuroscience and Vedānta Perspectives*", NOVA Health and Human Development Series, NY (to be published).
58. *Talks on Sri Sankara's Vivekachudamani, op.cit,* v.399.
59. *The Holy Geeta, op.cit,* Ch. IX, v.1.
60. *"Discourses on Mundaka Upaniṣad", op.cit,* Ch I, Sec 1, v.3.
61. Hagelin, J. S. "*Restructuring Physics From its Foundation in Light of*

Maharishi's Vedic Science", Modern Science and Vedic Science, Vol. 3, No. 1, (1989).

62. Srivastava, J.N. "*Life Comes From Life*", Savijñānam, Vol. 1, Bhakti Vedānta Institute, Kolkata, India, Nov 2002.

63. Budnik, Paul. "*What is and What Will Be*", Mountain Path, Lulu Press, CA, 2006.

64. *The Holy Geeta, op.cit,* Ch III, v.33.

65. "*Talks With Sri Ramana*", Sri Ramana Ashram, pp 454, Inner Directions Publishing, CA 2000.

66. Mohan, S. Ram. "*Concepts of Time in Indian Heritage*" in "India's Intellectual Traditions and Contributions to the World", *op.cit,* 294-319.

67. Tejomayananda, Swami. "*Adi Sankara's Drg Drsya Viveka*", v. 1, Central Chinmaya Mission Trust, Mumbai, 1994.

68. *Talks on Sri Sankara's Vivekachoodamani, op.cit.*, v. 36, 43.

69. *Ibid.* v. 497.

70. "*Yoga Vaasishtha Saara Sangrahah*", *op.cit,* pp 81.

71. Vivekananda, Swami. "*The Limitations of Time and Space*" reproduced in "*Time and Beyond*", Mananam Series, Vol. XV, No. 2, Chinmaya Mission West Publications, 1993.

72. Chinmayananda, Swami. "*The Universal Person- Purusha Suktam*", v. 3, 4th edition, Central Chinmaya Mission Trust, Mumbai, 1999.

73. *The Holy Geeta, op.cit,* Ch IX, v. 9 and 10.

74. *ibid.* Ch XV, v.6.

75. "*Mundaka Upaniṣad*", *op.cit,* Ch. 3, Sec 1, v. 1 & 2.

76. Tejomayananda, Swami. "*Upadesha Saar of Bhagawan Ramana Maharshi*", v. 24, Central Chinmaya Mission Trust, Bombay, 1987.

77. *Mundaka Upaniṣad, op.cit,* Ch 3, Sec 1, v. 3.

78. Chinmayananda, Swami. "*Discourses on Kathopanishad*", Ch. II, Sec 4, v.12, Central Chinmaya Mission Trust, Bombay, 1963.

79. *The Holy Geeta, op.cit,* Ch IX v. 20 & 21.

80. Chinmayananda, Swami. "*Discourses On Taittariya Upanishad*", *op.cit,* Ch II, Brahmanandavalli, page 133.

81. *The Holy Geeta, op.cit* Ch VI, v.40-42

82. Sivananda, Swami. "*The State of Samadhi*" reproduced in "*Time and Beyond*" *op.cit.*

83. "*Talks With Ramana Maharshi*" *op.cit,* pp 178.

84. Rajan, N.N. "*Once You Experience the Self, You Are Held by It*", The Maharshi, Vol. 18, No. 5, Arunachala Ashrama, Jamaica Estates, NY.

85. *The Holy Geeta, op.cit,* Ch VIII, v.17.

86. Capra, Fritjof. *"The Tao of Physics"*, Shambhala Publications, Inc, Boston, MA, 1975.
87. Greene, Brian. *"The Elegant Universe"*, pp 49-50, Vintage Books, NY 2000.
88. *"Mundaka Upanishad"*, *op.cit,* Ch 2, Sec 2, v.2.
89. The Bible, Acts 17:28.
90. *"Talks With Ramana Maharshi", op.cit,* page144.
91. *Talks on Sri Sankara's Vivekachoodamani, op.cit,* v.477 .
92. *The Holy Geeta, op.cit,* Ch VIII, v.16.
93. Glasberg, R. *"Mathematics and Spiritual Interpretation"*, Zygon, Vol. 38, No.2, Blackwell Publishing, June 2003.
94. Maor, Eli. *"e The Story of a Number"*, page 153, Princeton University Press, Princeton, NJ, 1994.
95. *The Holy Geeta, op.cit,* Ch II v.12.
96. Mudaliar, A. Devaraja. *"God and Destiny"*, The Maharshi, pp 4-5, Vol. 16, No. 1, Arunachala Ashrama, Jamaica Estates, NY, Jan/Feb 2006.
97. Chinmayananda, Swami. as quoted in *Tapovan Prasad*, page 64, January 2010.
98. Greene, Brian. " *The Fabric of the Cosmos*", pp 143-176, Alfred A. Knopf, NY 2004.
99. Nikhilananda, Swami. *"The Gospel of Sri Ramakrishna"*, Vols. I-III, Sri Ramakrishna Math, Mylapore, Madras, 1942 .
100. *The Holy Geeta, op.cit,* Ch.VI, v. 35.
101. *"Are Our Brain Wired for Enlightenment?"* Hinduism Today, Himalayan Academy, Hawaii, July-Sep 2009.
102. Campbell, Joseph. *"The Mythic Image"*, *op.cit,* (Table 8.1 is adapted from Ms.Livia Pravda's website www.reiki-for-holistic-health.com/chakra-diagram.html
103. Hamilton, W. *"Freedom of Mind"* http://www.astrosciences.info/FreedomMind.htm
104. *Pancadasi*, *op.cit,* Ch.7, v 33.
105. Pribram, Karl and Singh, T.D. *"Science is Spiritual"*, Savijñānam, pp 41. Vol. 1, *op.cit.* Nov 2002.
106. *"Kathopanishad"*, *op.cit,* Ch. II Sec 4, v. 1.
107. Chinmayananda, Swami. *"Sankaracharya's Bhaja Govindam"*, v. 31, Central Chinmaya Mission Trust, Bombay, Reprint 1991.
108. *The Holy Geeta Gita, op. cit,* Ch. VI, v. 28.
109. *Physics of the Soul, op.cit,* page 224.
110. Armstrong, Jeffrey. *"Spiritual Teachings of the Avatar- Ancient Wisdom for a New World"*, pp. 113-117, Atria Books, Simon & Schuster, New York, NY, June 2010.

111. *Brihadaranyaka Upanishad,* Ch 4, sec 5, v. 6, Sri Ramakrishna Math, Mylapore, Madras, 1951.

112. *Pancadasi, op.cit.*, Ch 15, v. 1.

113. *Upadesh Saar of Bhagawan Ramana Maharshi, op.cit.,* v.1.

114. *ibid.* v. 13 .

115. Frydman, Maurice. *"Aham and Aham Vritti",* pp 4-6, The Maharshi, Arunachala Asrama, Jamaica Estates, NY, July/Aug 2009.

116. *The Holy Geeta, op.cit* Ch II, v. 59.

117. Mundaka Upanishad, *op.cit*, Ch. II, Sec. 2, v.8.

118. *The Holy Geeta, op.cit.,* Ch. II v. 50 .

119. *"For My Children", op.cit.,* pp. 48-49.

120. *"Yoga Vasishta Sangrahah", op.cit.*, pp 30-32.

121. Dreyfus, Stuart. "*Neuroscience and Operations Research: A Two Way Street*", OR/MS Today, Institute for Operations Research and the Management Science, Marietta, GA, April 2010.

122. Mother, Aurobindo Ashram. *"Fate and Free Will"*, All India Magazine, page 55, Aurobindo Ashram, Pondicherry, Nov 2004.

123. *Talks on Sri Sankara's Vivekachoodamani, op.cit.*, v.17 -30.

124. *"Higher States of Consciousness in the Vedic Psychology of Maharishi Mahesh Yogi", op.cit*, pp. 119.

125. Lutyens, Mary. "*Krishnamurthi- The Years of Awakening*", pp 170-171, Avon Books, NY 1975.

126. *The Holy Geeta, op.cit*, Ch XI v. 33 .

127. *"The Fabric of the Cosmos", op.cit.*, pp 139.

128. Smythies, J. "*Time, Space, and Consciousness*" *op.cit.* page 53.

129. *ibid.,* page 54.

130. Starkman, Glenn. *Think*, Magazine of the Case Western Reserve University, Fall/Winter 2008.

131. *The Holy Geeta, op.cit*, Ch. VI, v. 8-9.

132. *"Adi Sankara's Aparokshanubhuti"*, *op.cit.*, v. 4.

133. *The Holy Geeta, op.cit*, Ch. VII, v. 12.

134. Satchidananda, Swami. "*The Yoga Sutras of Patanjali*", v. 2, Integral Yoga Publications,Yogaville,VA 1978.

135. *Talks on Sri Sankara's Vivekachoodamani, op.cit.*, v. 169.

136. *Amritabindu Upanishad.* v. 2. Chinmaya Mission, San Jose, CA

137. *"Upadesha Saar of Bhagawan Ramana Maharshi" op.cit.*, v. 15.

138. *The Holy Geeta, op.cit.,* Ch XII, v 16 .

139. *ibid.,* Ch. 3, v. 22.

140. Pagels, Elaine. "*The Gnostic Paul*", page 44, Trinity Press International, Harrisburg, PA 1992.

141. Rinpoche, Sogyal. "*Bringing the Mind Home*", Mananam Series "*Mind-Our Greatest Gift*", pp 95. Chinmaya Mission West, 1995.

142. *"Kathopanishad"*, *op.cit.*, Ch. I, Sec. 2, v. 2.

143. "*The Gospel of Sri Ramakrishna*", *op.cit.*

144. *The Holy Geeta, op.cit.,* Ch. II, v.49.

145. Sri Aurobindo. "*The Future Evolution of Man*", Aurobindo Ashram, Pondicherry, 1963.

Glossary of Sanskrit Terms (Alphabetically Listed)[47]

ā-gā-mi: Results of actions performed in present life which are to be experienced in a future birth- see also *sañcita* and *prārabdha*

a-dhyā-ro-pa: superimposition such as seen when a rope is mistaken to be a snake. The snake is said to be "superimposed" on the rope.

ā-nan-da: Bliss associated with Brahman

a-dvai-ta ve-dā-nta: The Non-dual system of philosophy which holds Brahman as the only reality, everything else being only its apparent manifestation. Jīvas, in their real nature, are identical with Brahman and not separate from It.

a-haṁ: I, which depending on context could mean the ego, Self etc

a-haṁ-kā-ra: Ego, the sense of "I".

a-ni-tya: Impermanent, transient

āt-man or ātmā*:* Self, the sentient factor in the individual and identical with Brahman

a-va-tā-r*:* An incarnation of Īśvara to teach and guide the jīvas

a-vi-dyā: Ignorance due to the veiling power of *Māyā*

a-vya-kta*:* Unmanifest, that which cannot be perceived by sensory organs, mind, or intellect

bha-ga-vad gī-tā: The teaching of Lord Krishna to Arjuna found in Mahābhārata, the epic Hindu poem; it is one of the three basic scriptural authorities on Vedānta.

bha-jan: singing in devotion to God.

bha-kti yo-ga: The path to Realization through devotion to God

bho-ga*:* Enjoying or experiencing the world of pain and pleasure. See also *Yoga*

47 Vedāntic terms can have alternative interpretations and multiple meanings. The meaning given here is the one generally used in the book.

bho-gī: A jīva who, identifying with the world, suffers its pains and pleasures. See also *Yogī*.

bho-ktṛ-tvaṁ: The sense of enjoyer ship; the notion "I am enjoying". See also "*Kartṛtvaṁ*".

bra-hmā-ji: One of the Hindu Trinity of Brahma – Viṣnu – Śiva; associated with the creative aspect of Īśvara.

bra-hma sū-tra: An exposition on Vedānta, which, along with the Upaniṣads and Bhagavad Gītā, provides the foundations of Vedānta

bra-hma-lo-k: The world of Brahma ji

bra-hma-n: The One and Only Reality which appears as the experienced world and the experiencing jīvas.

bu-ddhi: Intellect, the faculty that determines the nature of things perceived. See also *manas, citta, ahaṁkāra.*

ca-kṛa: Interconnecting centers in the system of "*nāḍis*".

ce-ta-na: Sentiency or alertness, of the mind in a jīva

ci-t: Consciousness

ci-tta: Faculty of subtle body associated with memory

dī-pā-va-li: The Hindu "Festival of Lights"

de-va: One of many Divine beings, or demigods, which preside over forces of nature, sensory organs, and organs of action

dvai-ta: System of philosophy which holds that jīva is separate from Īśvara and Brahman

dva-nda: dualities, or opposites, such as pain and pleasure, heat and cold, and honor and dishonor

gra-nthi: knots tying the jīva to the world, namely *avidyā, kāma, and karma*

gu-ṇa: the three basic constituents of *Prakṛti*, namely *tamas, rajas, and sattva*

ha-va-n: The Vedic ritual of worship where grains, clarified butter etc are offered in the sacred fire invoking the various *devas*.

hi-ra-ṇya-ga-rbha: Total mind, the macrocosmic counterpart of the *taijasa*

hṛ-t: the spiritual center or "heart" in jīva; residing where the Īśvara controls the jīva

i-daṁ: Everything known as "this", as opposed to "*ahaṁ*" or "I"

ī-śva-ra: The Creator and Controller. As Brahman wielding the power of *Māyā*, Īśvara is the creator of the cosmos; pervading all things and beings of creation Īśvara also controls them. It is the macrocosmic counterpart of *Prājña*.

ja-ga-t: The created world which is experienced. See also *samsār*

jī-va: sentient beings experiencing the created world

jī-va-n-mu-kta: A jīva that is totally detached from the experienced world and fully established in Self; jīva that is Realized while still embodied.

jñā-na yo-ga: The path to Realization through Knowledge of Reality

jñā-ne-ndri-ya: the five sense organs, namely eyes, ears, nose, skin (touch), and tongue (taste)

kā-ma: Desire

kā-ra-ṇa śa-rī-ra: The causal body, the repository of *vāsanas* in the jīva

kai-lā-s or śi-va-lo-k: abode of Lord Śiva, reached on liberation by the jīvas. See also *Vaikuṇṭh, Viṣṇulok*

ka-lpa: One day of Brahma ji equals of 4.32 billion human years; one night is equally long.

kā-mya ka-rma: Actions prompted by selfish desires

ka-rma: Action

ka-rma yo-ga: The path to Realization through selfless service, surrendering fruits of all actions to the Lord, and accepting whatever life offers as a blessing from the Lord

ka-rme-ndri-ya: The five organs of action, namely hands, feet, mouth, genitals, and anus

ka-rta-vya ka-rma: Actions undertaken as one's obligation to community or nation

ka-rtṛ-tvaṁ: The sense of "I am doing"

ku-ṇḍa-li-ni: Spiritual energy that rises up the *suṣumnā nāḍi*

lī-la: sport; in Vedānta the play of the world is considered as a sport of the Creator.

mā-yā: The creative power associated with Brahman using which Īśvara projects the world; it is also the power of illusion which veils the truth from the jīvas

ma-ha-t: The Cosmic Mind on which the creation is projected, similar to a dream that is projected on the individual mind

ma-hā-tmā: A highly evolved jīva

ma-hā-bhū-ta: The five great elements of which both the subtle and gross are made of; these are space, air, fire, water, and earth.

ma-na-nam: Reflection on the teachings of the scriptures

ma-na-s: Mind, the part of subtle body where arise contrary thoughts, doubts, emotions, and feelings

ma-ntra: A verse from Upaniṣads or other scriptures that is particularly suitable for chanting, worship, and reflection

mu-mu-kṣu-tva: the intense desire for liberation

mū-lā-dhā-ra: the lowest of the seven *cakra*s associated with survival instincts nā-ḍi: The pathways through which spiritual energy flows; the spiritual counterpart of the body's nervous system

ni-dhi-dhyā-saṁ: spiritual practice- see also *sādhana*

nir-gu-ṇa bra-hma-n: Brahman in Its "native" state without any attributes. See *saguṇa Brahman*

ni-rvā-ṇa: State of Realization where all desires and vāsanas have been exhausted

niṣ-kā-ma ka-rma: Actions undertaken out of Love, selfless service

nyā-ya śā-stra: Hindu system of logic

pa-ñcī-ka-ra-ṇaṁ: The process by which the five great elements, *mahābhūta*s, are transformed from their subtle state to gross state

pā-pa: Sinful action

prā-jña: The jīva identified with its causal body

pra-la-ya: dissolution of the cosmos back into the unmanifest Prakṛti,

prā-ṇa: the five vital functions of breathing, circulation, elimination, digestion, and reaction.

prā-ṇa-ma-ya-ko-śa: the vital sheath consisting of the five *prāṇas*

prā-ra-bdha: the effect of past karmas which are experienced in the present life.

pra-ja-lpa: prattle of mind.

pra-kṛ-ti: Nature, consisting of inert objects and sentient beings and the vāsanas causing the changes in these

pra-mā-ṇa: the basis, or means, of knowledge

pra-sā-d bu-ddhi*:* Accepting mind which receives gratefully whatever life offers as a blessing from Īśvara

pra-ti-biṁ-ba vā-da*:* The theory that jīva's sentiency results from Consciousness reflecting off the intellect

pū-ja: ritual worship of God.

pu-ṇya: Actions of merit; opposite of *pāpa*

pu-ru-ṣā-rtha: self-effort and free will of the jīva

ra-jas*:* The *guṇa* associated with action, manifesting as desire for fame, power etc

sā-dha-na: Spiritual practice

sā-dha-nā ca-tu-ṣṭa-yaṁ: The four-fold spiritual practice aimed at developing *viveka, vairāgya, samādhi ṣatka saṁpatti, and mumukṣutva*

sā-kṣi: Witness, used in reference to Self

sa-gu-ṇa bra-hma-n: Brahman with attributes; Īśvara with attributes of Knowledge, Virtue, Compassion etc.

sa-mā-dhi ṣa-tka saṁ-pa-tti: The six-fold spiritual wealth of controlled mind, controlled senses, self-withdrawal, forbearance, faith, and tranquility

sa-ma-ṣṭi vā-sa-na: Total vāsanas; aggregated vāsanas of all jīvas

saṁ-sā-ra: The transmigratory life lived by a jīva going from birth to death to rebirth

sa-ñci-ta: The accumulated effect of all past actions which are to be experienced in future births

saṁ-ka-lpa: A thought, a mental resolve

sa-t: Existence, existent or real

sa-ttva: The *guṇa* associated with Knowledge, manifesting as desire for purification of mind, self-reflection etc.

śra-va-ṇaṁ: Listening to and studying scriptures

sthū-la śa-rī-ra: The gross body including the gross sensory and motor organs and brain

sū-kṣma śa-rī-ra: The subtle body, consisting of the *prāṇamaya kośa*, subtle sensory and motor organs, mind, intellect, *ahaṁkāra*, and *citta*

su-ṣuṁ-nā nā-ḍi: The main *nāḍi* along which lies the main *cakras* or energy centers and along which the subtle energy rises; corresponds to the spinal cord of the central nervous system

sva-bhā-va: The own nature of a thing or being

tai-ja-sa: The jīva identified with its subtle body

ta-ma-s: The guṇa associated with inertia and ignorance, manifesting as desire to indulge in sensual pleasures etc.

tri-pu-ṭi: The triad such as the seen- seer- and sight, or the experiencer- experienced- and experiences.

u-pa-ni-ṣa-d: The portion of the *Veda*s dealing with philosophical questions and which provide the framework for Vedānta

vai-ku-ṇṭh, vi-ṣṇu-lok: The abode of Lord Viṣnu which is reached by jīvas on liberation

vai-rā-gya: Dispassion, spiritual detachment

vā-sa-na: The forces of nature affecting inert objects and sentient beings

ve-dān-ta: The philosophy found in Upaniṣads and elaborated in Bhagavad Gītā and Brahma sūtra.

ve-da: The scriptures forming the basis for Vedānta as well as Hinduism

vi-rā-ṭ: The totality of gross manifestation in the cosmos; the macrocosmic counterpart of *Viśva*.

vi-śva: Jīva identified with its gross body

vi-ve-ka: The faculty of discriminating the Real from the unreal and the apparently real.

ya-jña: An action undertaken for the sake of self-purification; a co-operative effort undertaken for the welfare of the community

yo-ga: Transacting with the world without identifying with it, remaining merely a witness to the transaction; any method for achieving this competence. See *Karma Yoga, Bhakti Yoga,* and *Jñāna Yoga*.

yo-gī: One who is in Yoga- opposite of *bhogī*

yu-ga: An epoch in Hindu cosmic calendar. A cycle of four *yuga*s called a *mahāyuga* lasts for 4,320,000 human years and 1000 *mahāyuga*s make one *kalpa*

About the Author

Trained formally in mathematical sciences in his student days, the author found a lasting interest in Vedānta later through his association with the Chinmaya Mission. He was born in the Trichur District of Kerala, India in 1940, and received early education in local schools. He received a B.A.(Hons.) in Mathematics from the University of Madras in 1960, Master's Degree in Statistics from the Indian Statistical Institute, Calcutta in 1962 and doctorate in Operations Research from the Case Western Reserve University in Cleveland, Ohio in 1967.

Dr. Chidambaram's working career spanning more than three decades was mostly spent in Washington, DC in the field of global satellite communications, but he also was at various times engaged in teaching and consulting in the US and India. One of the valuable skills he learnt during this long career was to solve all kinds of problems- engineering, management and financial- by using appropriate mathematical tools.

It is the same skill set that the author found useful in understanding spirituality. In 1978 he had the first opportunity to listen to Swami Chinmayananda at the American University in Washington, DC. The power and logic of Vedānta, as taught by Swamiji, impressed him significantly. Since then both the author and his wife have been students of Vedānta as well as active members of CMWRC, the Chinmaya Mission branch in Washington, DC. The author served as the President of CMWRC during 1991-93 and currently serves in its Board of Trustees. As the Editor of *Smrithi*, a newsletter dedicated to Vedānta, he also published a series of articles on Vedānta during 1987-97 which helped formulate many concepts and thoughts that now find a place in the current work.

After taking early retirement from his career, the author could devote more time to answer a question he was long intrigued with: Are the basic teachings of Vedānta logical and precise enough to be stated mathematically? The first result of that enquiry was a paper published in Dec 2000 titled "*The Vedānta of Decision Making*" in Chinmaya Management Review. Between 2000 and 2007 the research work led progressively to the development of a mathematical theory of spirituality. The results were presented in a series of papers in various WAVES (World Association for Vedic Studies) conferences during 2004-2008, as well as in the 2009 International Vedānta Conference held at Dartmouth, MA.

Currently the author lives in Alexandria, VA with his wife, Shobha, a practicing Neurologist. Of their two daughters, Sharada is pursuing a career in law while Vrinda is in her Ph.D. program in Theoretical Linguistics at the Princeton University. The author's goal in coming years is to actively promote research and education in spiritual science through conferences and publications.

Gurudev Swami Chinmayanandaji with the author's family at the 1991 International Chinmaya Mission Spiritual Retreat at Frostburg, Maryland, USA. Seated are the author's wife Shobha (on the left), Gurudev (center), the author (on the right), and daughters Sharada (standing) and Vrinda (seated foreground).

Readers wishing to share their thoughts on this work,
please visit www.ceasis.com.